Eighteenth-Century Britain

Religion, Politics and Society in Britain
Series editor: Keith Robbins

The Conversion of Britain: Religion, Politics and Society in Britain, c.600–800
Barbara Yorke

The Post-Reformation: Religion, Politics and Society in Britain, 1603–1714
John Spurr

Eighteenth-Century Britain: Religion and Politics, 1714–1815
Nigel Yates

Providence and Empire: Religion, Politics and Society in Britain, 1815–1914
Stewart Brown

Religion and Society in Twentieth-Century Britain
Callum G. Brown

Eighteenth-Century Britain

Religion and Politics, 1714–1815

Nigel Yates

PEARSON
Longman

Harlow, England • London • New York • Boston • San Francisco • Toronto
Sydney • Tokyo • Singapore • Hong Kong • Seoul • Taipei • New Delhi
Cape Town • Madrid • Mexico City • Amsterdam • Munich • Paris • Milan

PEARSON EDUCATION LIMITED

Edinburgh Gate
Harlow CM20 2JE
Tel: +44 (0)1279 623623
Fax: +44 (0)1279 431059
Website: www.pearsoned.co.uk

First published in Great Britain in 2008

ISBN: 978-1-4058-0161-4

British Library Cataloguing-in-Publication Data
A catalogue record for this book is available from the British Library

Library of Congress Cataloging-in-Publication Data
A catalog record for this book is available from the Library of Congress

10 9 8 7 6 5 4 3 2 1
11 10 09 08 07

Typeset in 10/13.5pt Sabon by 35
Printed and bound in Malaysia (CTP - VVP)

The publisher's policy is to use paper manufactured from sustainable forests.

Contents

List of Tables		vii
Series Editor's Preface		viii
Author's Preface		x
Introduction		1

1	Three Kingdoms, Two Establishments	11
	The structure of religion in England and Wales	12
	The structure of religion in Ireland	14
	The structure of religion in Scotland	15
	Jacobites and non-jurors	16
	The dominance of the church Whigs	20
	A Protestant confessional state?	25
	Strengths and weaknesses of the religious establishments	27

2	Dissent from the Religious Establishments	36
	Roman Catholics in England, Scotland and Wales	36
	Roman Catholics in Ireland	46
	Scottish Episcopalians	48
	Irish Presbyterians	50
	Protestant dissenters in England and Wales	52
	Foreign Protestants in Britain and Anglican ecumenism	62

3	The Maintenance of Doctrinal Orthodoxy	70
	Orthodox Anglicans and moderate Presbyterians	70
	Latitudinarians, Arians and Socinians	73
	The Evangelical revival	77
	Evangelicalism in Scotland and Ireland	86
	The rise of Methodism	88
	The role of women in the churches and society	95

4   A Theology of Good Works   104

Morality and social control   *105*
Poverty and social welfare   *109*
Provision for education   *113*
The promotion of culture and learning   *123*

5   The Condition of the Established Churches   130

The clergy: social background and education   *130*
The clergy: incomes and social position   *132*
Diocesan administration   *135*
Religious life in the parishes   *137*
Church building and restoration   *142*
The church in Wales   *144*
The Church of Ireland   *148*
The Church of Scotland   *152*

6   The Beginnings of Ecclesiastical Reform   159

Ecclesiastical reform in Ireland   *159*
Ecclesiastical reform in Wales   *161*
Ecclesiastical reform in England   *165*
Government and parliament   *169*

7   The Threat of Revolution   177

Religious dissent and political radicalism   *177*
Opposition to tithes   *181*
The impact of the French Revolution   *182*
Rebellion in Ireland   *188*
The limits of toleration   *191*

Conclusion   198

Appendices: (1) Chronology of Principal Events   204
             (2) Biographies of Political and
                 Religious Leaders   207
             (3) Churches and Chapels Retaining
                 Substantially Unaltered Interiors   226
Bibliography   232
Index   241

List of Tables

1 Augmentations of poor livings by Queen Anne's Bounty
   1714–1815   30

2 Proportion of Anglicans and dissenters voting for Whig
   candidates in selected borough elections 1734–68   53

3 Numbers of Independent, Baptist, Presbyterian and
   Quaker meeting houses certified as places of worship in
   England 1721–1810   55

4 Total numbers of congregations and adherents of main
   dissenting groups in England and Wales in the 1720s   56

5 Comparison of social structure of Anglican and dissenting
   congregations in selected English towns in the late
   eighteenth century   58

6 Numbers of endowed non-classical schools and charities
   for elementary education established in England and
   Wales 1710–1800   115

7 Social and educational backgrounds of clergy in the diocese
   of Canterbury 1720–1810   132

8 Reasons stated for the non-residence of clergy in England and
   Wales 1804–7   138

9 Frequency of celebrations of Holy Communion in the diocese
   of London 1738–90   140

10 Frequency of Sunday services and celebrations of Holy
   Communion in the diocese of Canterbury 1716–1806   141

Series Editor's Preface

No understanding of British history is possible without grappling with the relationship between religion, politics and society. How that should be done, however, is another matter. Historians of religion, who have frequently thought of themselves as ecclesiastical historians, have had one set of preoccupations. Political historians have had another. They have acknowledged, however, that both religion and politics can only be understood, in any given period, in a social context. This series makes the interplay between religion, politics and society its preoccupation. Even so, it does not assume that what is entailed by religion and politics remains the same throughout, to be considered as a constant in separate volumes merely because of the passage of time.

In its completed form the series will have probed the nature of these links from *c*.600 to the present day and offered a perspective, over such a long period, that has not before been attempted in a systematic fashion. There is, however, no straitjacket that requires individual authors to adhere to a common understanding of what such an undertaking involves. Even if there could be a general agreement about concepts, that is to say about what religion is or how politics can be identified, the social context of such categorisations is not static. The spheres notionally allocated to the one or to the other alter with circumstances. Sometimes it might appear that they cannot be separated. Sometimes it might appear that they sharply conflict. Each period under review will have its defining characteristics in this regard.

It is the Christian religion, in its manifold institutional manifestations, with which authors are overwhelmingly concerned since it is with conversion that the series begins. It ends, however, with a volume in which Christianity exists alongside other world religions but in a society frequently perceived to be secular. Yet, what de-Christianisation is taken to be depends upon what Christianisation has been taken to be. There is, therefore, a relationship between topics that are tackled in the first volume, and those considered in the last, which might at first sight seem unlikely. In between, of course are the 'Christian Centuries' which, despite their label, are no less full of 'boundary disputes', both before and after the Reformation. The perspective of the series, additionally, is broadly pan-insular. The Britain of 600 is plainly not the Britain of the early twenty-first century. However, the current political structures of Britain-Ireland have arguably owed as much to religion as to politics. Christendom has been inherently ambiguous.

It would be surprising if readers, not to mention authors, understood the totality of the picture that is presented in the same way. What is common, however, is a realisation that the narrative of religion, politics and society in Britain is not a simple tale that points in a single direction but rather one of enduring and by no means exhausted complexity.

Keith Robbins, November 2005

Author's Preface

It was a great honour to be invited by Professor Keith Robbins to contribute to this series and to find myself in such excellent company. I owe an enormous debt of gratitude to three people: to my son David, who both word-processed the final text and provided useful comment on it from the perspective of the intelligent general reader; and to my colleague Professor Peter Borsay and to one of my research students, Laura Jarvis, both of whom also read and commented on the text. They have all certainly helped to improve the book, but I must equally absolve all of them from any complicity in any defects or inaccuracies that remain.

I am dedicating this book to two former colleagues in what used to be the Kent Archives Office, and is now the Centre for Kentish Studies, who, sadly, are no longer with us. Kathleen Topping was my deputy and major support during my 12 years as County Archivist and Head of Heritage Services, and she eventually succeeded me in that post. It was an enormous shock to me, and an enormous loss to the cause of historical studies in Kent, when she died, at the obscenely early age of 50, in 2002. Our colleague, Donald Gibson, was somewhat senior to us in age, and he died later that same year though still within a relatively short period from his retirement. He was a genuine eccentric and a true scholar who tried to live the life of an eighteenth-century gentleman. Though his opinions were outrageously, and I suspect determinedly, reactionary in the twenty-first century, there was little doubt that he would have been a low church Whig in the century in which he would have preferred to have lived, whereas moderate liberals such as myself would undoubtedly have been high church Tories.

Nigel Yates
University of Wales, Lampeter
November 2005

Introduction

For those with a general interest in, or understanding of, the broad outline of British history, the period between 1714 and 1815 is usually one that they have least knowledge of. It tends not to form part of the school history syllabus, nor is it particularly popular with history undergraduates at university. Films or television programmes, adapted from the literature of this period or based on the few well-known events during it, such as the 'madness' of George III, tend to portray a society of great formality and rigid social structures which was, nevertheless, capable of a crudity and licentiousness calculated to shock all but the most unshockable. There is currently a major debate among the relatively small number of academic historians looking at this period about the true nature of British society, and the developments within it, between 1714 and 1815. At one end of the spectrum, Jonathan Clark has portrayed the period between 1688 and 1832 in the British Isles as one in which the essential characteristics of an *ancien régime* mostly remained intact and, despite a degree of religious freedom unusual in most parts of Continental Europe before 1789, a confessional religious state existed.[1] Most historians, however, tend to downplay this aspect and prefer, most recently in the work of Jeremy Black and Linda Colley,[2] to emphasise that the period between 1714 and 1815 was one in which the modern British state was being born. In fact these two rather different interpretations are not as polarised as they may superficially appear. In truth Britain between 1714 and 1815 was both an *ancien régime* society and a confessional state, though not to the same degree as pre-revolutionary France, whilst simultaneously witnessing the economic, political and social changes that were to create the very different type of imperial Britain that existed between 1815 and 1914. The period between 1714 and 1815 was essentially one of transition between an early modern and a later modern state, and the tension that this created was to be one of the main features of its economic, political, religious and social history.

Before the beginning of the eighteenth century what eventually became the United Kingdom of Great Britain and Ireland was in fact three separate states. As a result of the Act of Union of 1707 the separate Scottish parliament was abolished and Scottish peers and members of parliament sat at Westminster. Scotland, however, retained its own separate judicial system and its own, Presbyterian rather than Anglican, established church. Ireland retained its own separate political jurisdiction until 1801 when, following a series of political crises and a serious rebellion in 1798, the Irish parliament was abolished and Irish bishops, peers and members of parliament sat at Westminster. Unlike in Scotland the two established churches, both Anglican, were united to form the United Church of England and Ireland, though in practice the four Irish provinces remained self-governing and there was relatively little ecclesiastical interchange in the personnel of the Irish and English churches. Wales was for all practical purposes – administrative, ecclesiastical, judicial and political – a province of England between 1714 and 1815, as it had been for the best part of the two preceding centuries and would remain for the best part of the next two. However, Wales, more strongly than either Ireland or Scotland, retained its native language and, during the course of the late eighteenth and early nineteenth centuries began to develop its own cultural aspirations, which helped to contribute in due course to the creation of a clear nationalist agenda. The British Isles in 1714 was to experience a change of dynasty in the accession of George I, the Lutheran Elector of Hanover. The Act of Settlement of 1701 had ensured that no Roman Catholic could succeed to the British throne so George I, despite his remote relationship to the last Stuart sovereign, Queen Anne, was the Protestant with the best claim to succeed her. It was a succession which proved difficult for many churchmen, some of whom remained loyal to the Stuart cause and *de iure* king, James III, and most of whom were Tories. Both George I and George II formed a political alliance with the leading Whig families which kept the Tories out of both political and ecclesiastical power. This situation was not resolved until the accession of George III in 1760 and the death of James III in 1766. Thereafter churchmen could feel confidence in a Hanoverian monarch who was English by birth and by culture, determined to be politically and ecclesiastically inclusive and keen to recapture a concept of monarchy with which Anglican high churchmen could feel more comfortable. James III's two sons, one wholly dissolute and the other in

Roman Catholic orders, were never the serious pretenders to the British throne that their father had been. Britain after 1760 was more united than it been before 1688, and perhaps more so, as the political divisions of the Civil Wars and Interregnum had not been fully resolved by the late seventeenth century.

The achievements of the early part of George III's reign were, however, thrown into confusion by events outside the British Isles. The attempt to exploit the American colonies commercially and financially, whilst at the same time denying them representation at Westminster, was to lead to increasing conflict by the late 1760s and substantial cost in maintaining a sufficient army presence to ensure that the situation did not get out of hand. Military force, however, was not sufficient to prevent a full-scale rebellion by 1775 and a declaration of independence by representatives of the Thirteen Colonies meeting at Philadelphia in 1776. The subsequent war lasted until 1783, when the British government was forced to concede the independence the separatists had demanded. The humiliation was to create a political crisis at home in which George III seriously considered his abdication. Within six years of the loss of the American Colonies, Europe was to be rocked by the crisis of the French Revolution and the wars that followed, which were to last until 1815. At the outset of the revolution, political radicals in Britain were to express sympathy with the revolutionary agenda, and the overthrow of an absolute and incompetent monarchy, in the belief that the sort of limited monarchy and parliamentary government with which Britain was familiar might be exported to France and other parts of Europe. This belief was shattered by the later phases of the revolution: the execution of the royal family and many of the nobility, the reigns of terror, the attacks on the clergy and the attempts to promote new secular cults. Apart from the military consequences of the revolution and French imperialism, first under the revolutionary government and then under Napoleon Bonaparte, and the disturbing presence of French *émigré* aristocrats and clergy in London and the towns of southern England, what had happened in France was to have a major impact on British politics and religion. The modest reform measures of the 1770s and 1780s were not progressed any further. There was a desperate desire to maintain the political and religious *status quo* and a fear that even the most modest concessions to reformers could lead to political revolution. In this respect the political instability in Ireland in the 1790s greatly enhanced the fear of growing disorder in other parts of the British Isles. The 'French disease', it was thought, might be catching. Whilst repression worked during the two decades of war between 1793 and 1815, it was to create severe problems thereafter, and the major concessions that had to be made in the 1820s and 1830s, in response to widespread disaffection for the political and religious establishments, might have been managed more successfully had it been possible to maintain a programme of more gradual reform through the period between 1790 and 1820.

The political and religious reforms of the middle decades of the nineteenth century were to convince churchmen and politicians of that period that the religious establishment of the period between 1714 and 1815 was hopelessly corrupt, inefficient and lacking in spirituality. These opinions were adopted in the late nineteenth century by historians of the British religious establishment and indeed are still widely held today in church circles, even though they have been undermined by most recent research. The first major attempt to challenge the prevailing view was mounted by Norman Sykes.[3] His views, despite now being more than 70 years old, have taken a long time to be generally accepted. Over the last 40 years a series of both local and national studies have, building on the pioneering work of Sykes, succeeded in painting a very different picture of religion in the British Isles between 1714 and 1815. Whilst recognising that there were undeniable problems in some areas, they demonstrate that corruption, inefficiency and lack of spirituality have all been exaggerated. Coverage, however, has been patchy. Only a few parts of England have been studied in detail and there have been very few revisionist studies of the religious condition of Ireland, Scotland and Wales. Here many of the older views are still deeply entrenched. There has also been a reluctance on the part of several British political and social historians to accept some revisionist interpretations of religious history, believing them to have tilted the balance too far the other way or to be indulging in special pleading. Thus, for example, Paul Langford has written:

Modern scholars have sought a clear idea of the strength of the Church principally by disposing of the obstructive prejudices of their predecessors . . . What weight should be given to this kind of revision is a matter for debate. Not every bishop can plausibly be preserved for accreditation as a representative of a selfless and serious-minded profession.[4]

Clearly religious historians have to be careful not to be so dedicated towards correcting the imbalances of previous interpretations of religious history as to create an imbalance in the other direction, but it is difficult to escape the conclusion that the weight of the evidence points to a generally positive picture of religion in Britain between 1714 and 1815. There is overwhelming evidence of administrative efficiency, spiritual vitality and a commitment to reform in all the mainstream churches. It was, however, a religion which, apart from its Evangelical component, was deliberately low-key and hostile to any forms of religious extravagance. It was precisely because of such attitudes that it was condemned by those in the nineteenth and twentieth centuries for whom a much more exuberant version of Christianity was an essential prerequisite of true spirituality. Indeed much that was written about the alleged corruption, inefficiency and lack of spirituality of the Georgian religious establishment seems to have arisen from the Victorian inability to understand its religious outlook. To comprehend Georgian religion we have to accept it on its own terms and not seek to understand it through the religious prejudices of a different age and, by doing so, find it wanting.

There are five main themes in the religious history of the period between 1714 and 1815 which will be explored in this book. The first is the importance of the relationship between church and state throughout the British Isles. The second is the fact of a degree of religious pluralism in Britain which, unlike most other parts of Europe, tolerated religious minorities and offered them political protection; it was, however, a toleration which was more generous to Protestant dissenters than Roman Catholics or Scottish Episcopalians. The third theme is the theological tensions of the period between high churchmen, Latitudinarians and Evangelicals, especially within the Anglican established churches, but also to some extent within other Protestant religious groups. The fourth theme is the important role of the churches in the provision of education and social welfare at a time when this was not considered the role of national or local government. The fifth and final theme is the reform movement within the churches; this is a topic that has received the most attention from religious historians in recent years and on which a new orthodoxy has been established. Work on the other areas has not been lacking but it has been less extensive and, therefore, less influential in changing the received view of religious history between 1714 and 1815.

In looking at the question of the relationship between church and state we cannot do better than begin with a quotation from John Cannon:

One of the essential features of the old constitution was the identification of Church and State, dovetailed together under aristocratic supervision. Though the term 'Protestant Ascendancy' is usually applied to Ireland, it serves to describe England as well. The basic assumption was that any persons of property – preferably landed property – were fit to be trusted with political power and that they should be in communion with the

Church of England. This assumption also prevailed at local level where in the counties power was exercised by the Lords Lieutenant and the JPs, and in most of the boroughs by self-electing Anglican oligarchies.[5]

Cannon's argument needs no modification for Wales and only a little for Scotland. For Anglicans the strength of this relationship between church and state was observed every year in the three state services annexed to the revised *Book of Common Prayer* in 1662. These celebrated the 'martyrdom' of King Charles I on 30 January, the restoration of King Charles II on 29 May and the preservation of both the monarchy and parliament from the Gunpowder Plot on 5 November. As Andrew Lacey has concluded, the accession of the Hanoverian dynasty in 1714 in no way affected the orthodox Anglican cult of the royal martyr and the opportunities this gave for preaching against rebellion and for emphasising that both monarchy and legitimate government were divinely ordained.[6] Indeed by the 1780s there was a revival in the cult and the defence of the older concept of 'divine right' by Anglican high churchmen such as George Horne and Samuel Horsley, followed by a flurry of pamphlets on the same topic, no doubt provoked by the French Revolution in the 1790s.[7] Whilst Tories and Whigs might have differed in the emphasis they placed on the relationship between church and state, both accepted that the alliance was important. Put rather crudely and simplistically, the Tories believed that the church sanctified and gave moral authority to the state, in much the same way that the papacy viewed its relationship with the catholic sovereigns of Europe; the Whigs, however, tended to see the church as subservient to the state, charged by the government to exercise authority on its behalf in moral and spiritual matters and to set before the people the standards of behaviour that were expected in a Christian nation.

This relationship had to take into account that Britain was not, and to some extent since the Reformation had never been, the sort of country in which only one form of the Christian religion had been permitted despite the official attempts to secure uniformity. In this sense it differed from many other parts of Europe, Catholic and Protestant. In the Lutheran kingdoms of Scandinavia only members of foreign communities were permitted to worship outside the Lutheran state churches. In most of southern Europe, and in France after the revocation of the Edict of Nantes in 1685, only the Roman Catholic church was recognised and Protestants were persecuted. Britain shared with the Netherlands a situation in which, for pragmatic reasons as much as anything else, some toleration had to be granted to those who refused to worship in the established churches.

During the early seventeenth century Britain had been seriously divided religiously between those who had very different concepts of the Protestant establishment they wanted to see. The religious settlement of 1662 had recognised that complete religious uniformity would be impossible to achieve and a grudging, largely unofficial, toleration was granted to those who liked to worship in dissenting congregations. That was formulated more clearly, and more generally, in the Toleration Act of 1689, though divisions between Whigs and Tories over how much toleration should be granted to Protestant dissenters was to remain a political issue for the whole of the eighteenth century and was not finally resolved until the repeal of the Test and Corporation Acts in 1828 and the granting of Catholic Emancipation in 1829.

Although the period between 1714 and 1815 was one of relative religious calm after the religious wars of the seventeenth century, not just in Britain but in Europe as well, it would be incorrect to see the churches as completely united. Two very different movements were to influence all the Protestant churches of northern Europe from the late seventeenth century. One was rationalism, which sought to bring religion more in line with the secular aspirations of society as well as developments in science and intellectual thought. It was to be seen in the Latitudinarian party within the Church of England, represented by bishops like Benjamin Hoadly, which saw the church as the instrument of the state and endeavoured to minimise those aspects of Anglican doctrine which had emphasised the church's divine calling, its independent government and its sacramental piety. However, although the Latitudinarians were to have a major, though not very dominant, role in the established church in the reigns of George I and George II, their influence diminished thereafter and the church was firmly in the hands of high churchmen by the last quarter of the eighteenth century. Rationalism also encouraged the development of unorthodox theologies within many of the Protestant churches of Europe, especially unorthodox views on the doctrine of the Trinity. In England and Wales most Presbyterian, and some Baptist and Independent congregations became Unitarian in belief, denying that Jesus Christ was truly God. These beliefs also caused division within Scottish and Irish Presbyterianism though they never became so fully developed. They even threatened to cause disruption within the Anglican churches, and, though the threat never became a reality, much ink was expended by orthodox Anglican divines in publishing books and pamphlets warning of the dangers of Arianism and Socinianism. Far more impact was to be felt on the Anglican churches from the movement generally termed pietism in Europe, but

Evangelicalism in the British Isles, which endeavoured to revitalise Protestantism by replacing its somewhat dry theology, whether orthodox or unorthodox, by a personal belief in the saving action of Christ, a deep sense of individual unworthiness and a determination to be filled with the Holy Spirit. There was strong opposition to Evangelicalism in all the Protestant churches, from Anglicans, from 'old dissent' and from the 'moderates' in the Presbyterian churches, who viewed such an emotional form of religion as dangerous, not just theologically but politically as well. Evangelicalism began to have an impact on England and Wales, especially the latter, from the 1730s, but its impact in Ireland and Scotland was delayed until the last quarter of the eighteenth century and nowhere, apart from Wales, was it a movement which dominated the religious life of the nation before 1815.

British government in the eighteenth century was essentially small government. There were whole areas of the life of the nation, such as the provision of education, of medical care, of poor relief, in which the government had little or no involvement and which it left largely to private charity. Britain in this sense was different from some of the other countries of Europe in which government was beginning to get more involved in such issues. However, the first attempt at a national system of elementary education did not happen until the 1830s, and then it was confined to Ireland. The rest of the British Isles did not follow until the 1870s. Poor relief remained the responsibility of the parishes in England and Wales until the 1830s and in Scotland until the 1840s. What might have been seen by later generations as a vacuum left by the state was filled by the churches and voluntary societies. Recent research is beginning to show both that much of this charitable effort was substantially effective, and also that there was a stronger element of central direction than has sometimes been thought, the role that the government might otherwise have exercised being taken on by a series of national organisations. The involvement of the churches in charitable work was greatly encouraged by preaching within all the Protestant churches which exhorted individual Christians to undertake good works as a positive illustration of their faith.[8] The response to this preaching was to be found in the large number of schools, almshouses, hospitals and charitable benefactions established, or augmented, throughout the British Isles between 1714 and 1815.

Much traditional historical writing in Britain tended to see religion between 1714 and 1815 as being unexciting and somnolent, and, compared with the religious debates of the nineteenth century, this may have been true. However, the emphasis on the 1830s and 1840s as a period of government-inspired ecclesiastical reform requires some correction and modification,[9] especially as it has overlooked many of the church-inspired ecclesiastical reforms taking place throughout the British Isles from the 1780s. Over the last two decades in particular this reform movement within the churches has received a good deal of attention and it has been shown that many of the reforms not fully completed until the middle years of the nineteenth century, especially those that required government action or parliamentary approval to be effective, had their origins a generation or two earlier. It is also important to recognise that this reform movement was not just confined to England but had its parallels in Ireland, Wales and even in the Isle of Man. It seems to have been less advanced in Scotland, but this may be misleading, as the research on this topic which has been done for most other parts of the British Isles has not been undertaken for Scotland.

Over the last half-century, building on the pioneering work of Norman Sykes, a very clear consensus has emerged on the state of religion, and its relationship with politics and society, in the British Isles between 1714 and 1815. It has been shown that both the established churches, and various dissenting bodies, were more dynamic than had been thought, and that the criticism of the eighteenth century church by Victorian reformers was, on the whole, unfair and unjustified. That is not to say that the churches, and especially the established churches, were not without their faults, but most historians of religion in Britain in the period between 1714 and 1815 are now convinced that they have been grossly exaggerated and, perhaps more importantly, have argued that it is not appropriate to judge earlier societies by the standards of later ones and to find them wanting. In recent years only two religious historians, Donald Spaeth and Peter Virgin,[10] have really stood out against this broad reinterpretation of British religious history between 1714 and 1815, and even they accept substantial sections of the revisionist agenda, whilst emphasising more strongly than others some of the defects of the established church in this period. The pages that follow paint a picture of religion, politics and society in Britain between 1714 and 1815 that reflects these new understandings.

Notes

1 J.C.D. Clark, *English Society 1688–1832*, Cambridge 1985 and *Revolution and Rebellion: State and Society in England in the Seventeenth and Eighteenth Centuries*, Cambridge 1986. See the critical review of these by Joanna Innes,

'Jonathan Clark, social history and England's *ancien régime*', *Past and Present* 114 (1987), pp. 165–200.

2 J. Black, *Eighteenth-Century Britain 1688–1783*, Basingstoke 2001; L. Colley, *Britons: Forging the Nation*, New Haven and London 1992.

3 N. Sykes, *Church and State in England in the Eighteenth Century*, Cambridge 1934.

4 P. Langford, *A Polite and Commercial People: England 1727–1783*, Oxford 1989, p. 259.

5 J. Cannon, 'New lamps for old: the end of Hanoverian England', in J. Cannon (ed.) *The Whig Ascendancy: Colloquies on Hanoverian England*, London 1981, p. 102.

6 A. Lacey, *The Cult of King Charles the Martyr*, Woodbridge 2003, pp. 217–35.

7 H.T. Dickinson, *The Politics of the People in Eighteenth Century Britain*, Basingstoke 1995, p. 261.

8 See the important analysis of this theme in sermon literature by F. Deconinck-Brossard, 'Eighteenth century sermons and the Age', in W.M. Jacob and W.N. Yates, *Crown and Mitre: Religion and Society in Northern Europe from the Reformation*, Woodbridge 1993, pp. 105–21.

9 For a reassessment of this topic see W.N. Yates, 'The administrative reform of established churches in Britain and Ireland during the nineteenth century: the respective roles of church and state', *Jahrbuch für Europäische Verwaltungsgeschichte*, 14 (2002), pp. 171–97.

10 D.A. Spaeth, *The Church in an Age of Danger: Parsons and Parishioners 1660–1740*, Cambridge 2000; P. Virgin, *The Church in an Age of Negligence: Ecclesiastical Structure and Problems of Church Reform, 1700–1840*, Cambridge 1989.

CHAPTER 1

Three Kingdoms, Two Establishments

The British Isles of the eighteenth century comprised three very different areas, in their history and in their administrative arrangements: England and Wales, Ireland, and Scotland; together with the Isle of Man and the Channel Islands these formed the United Kingdom of Great Britain and Ireland. England had been effectively united as one kingdom by the ninth century; from the twelfth century it had absorbed parts of Wales, a conquest finally completed by the end of the thirteenth century, though it was not until 1536 that Wales was divided into shires on the English model and its government fully assimilated with that of England. Attempts had been made to conquer Ireland as well in the twelfth century but here the process of conquest and assimilation was a much longer one. The whole of Ireland was effectively under English rule by the early seventeenth century but it retained its own separate administration and parliament, and the latter, but not the former, was not fully integrated into a British parliament until the Act of Union which became operative from January 1801. Thus for the major part of the period covered by this book Ireland was a quasi-independent country with its own lawmaking powers. Scotland was a completely independent country, despite attempts by successive English rulers to annex it between the late thirteenth and early sixteenth centuries, until 1603 when James VI of Scotland became James I of Great Britain and Ireland. Although it ceased to have its own separate parliament in 1707, it still retained its own judicial system and other independent administrative arrangements which separated it from England and Wales. The Isle of Man did not become a possession of the English crown until 1765 when the British government bought out most of the rights of its then ruler, the Duke of Atholl, in order to prevent the island being a haven for smugglers, but the duke retained some of his rights, including the right to present to the bishopric, for another 60 years. The island, however, retained its own parliament, Tynwald, as it does to this day. The Channel Islands are the sole remaining part of the Duchy of Normandy, otherwise surrendered by the English crown in 1204. Like the Isle of Man they have retained their own judicial and administrative arrangements and never sent representatives to the Westminster parliament.

The ecclesiastical divisions of the British Isles were, between 1714 and 1815, similar, but not identical, to the political ones. In the whole of Britain apart from Scotland, the established churches were Anglican and had an episcopal and diocesan structure. The two provinces of Canterbury and York covered the whole of England, Wales, the Isle of Man and the Channel Islands, the last of which formed part of the diocese of Winchester. All the two provinces' archbishops and bishops, with the exception of the Bishop of Sodor and Man who sat in Tynwald, had the right to a seat and vote in the House of Lords at Westminster. Ireland had four ecclesiastical provinces and its four archbishops and 18 bishops sat in the Irish House of Lords. After the Act of Union the Irish church was represented, on a rota basis, by one of its archbishops and three of its bishops in the House of Lords at Westminster. The Reformation had taken rather a different form in Scotland from that in the other parts of the British Isles and a presbyterian rather than an episcopal Protestant church had been established. With the union of the English and Scottish crowns in 1603 successive Stuart monarchs had endeavoured, so far as they were able, to reintroduce episcopacy into Scotland and to bring the Scottish church more into line with the English one. It was the policy of religious integration which had been a major factor in bringing about the Civil Wars of the 1640s and the temporary abolition of the monarchy in Britain. The attempt at religious integration was eventually abandoned in 1689, when episcopacy in the Church of Scotland was finally abolished and the institution became wholly presbyterian in character. The Scottish church was largely self-governing, its ultimate authority being its General Assembly at which the crown was represented by a royal commissioner, and there was no representation for it in the parliament at Westminster.

The structure of religion in England and Wales

The established church in England and Wales, the Isle of Man and the Channel Islands comprised two provinces and 27 dioceses. The provinces were by no means even in size; that of York comprised only the five northern dioceses of Carlisle, Chester, Durham, Sodor and Man, and

York; all the remaining dioceses, including the four Welsh ones, were in the province of Canterbury. They varied considerably in size from Sodor and Man, with only 17 parishes, and Rochester, which comprised only that part of Kent west of the River Medway, to the enormous diocese of Lincoln which covered the whole of five counties and parts of several others. The dioceses of Canterbury and York also contained peculiars, comprising groups of parishes in other dioceses for which the respective archbishop, and not the diocesan bishop, was responsible. The diocese of Bangor also had two detached groups of parishes entirely surrounded by the diocese of St Asaph but for which the bishop of Bangor was responsible. The diocese of Bristol was in two separate sections comprising a few parishes in and around Bristol and the county of Dorset. Two English dioceses, Chester and Hereford, had some parishes in Wales, and two Welsh dioceses, St Asaph and St Davids, had some parishes in England. Each diocese had a cathedral, over which the bishop had very limited jurisdiction, and which was administered by a chapter headed, in most cases, by a dean. Two cathedrals, those of Llandaff and Sodor and Man, were in ruins by the eighteenth century, though at Llandaff a temporary structure was built in the nave so that services could continue to take place within its walls. Each diocese also had between one and six archdeaconries, administered by an archdeacon who was effectively the bishop's deputy and carried out regular visitations of the churches and clergy within his archdeaconry. There were some exceptions to this arrangement: the royal peculiars of Westminster Abbey, St George's at Windsor and the Chapels Royal; the peculiars which formed part of the dioceses of Canterbury and York; archdeaconries in the dioceses of Bangor and St Asaph which had been combined with the bishopric in order to increase the bishop's income; and the Channel Islands, which formed two deaneries in the diocese of Winchester in which the deans exercised most of the authority of the bishop. Some dioceses, especially in Wales where the archdeacons did not exercise the authority of their counterparts in England, had rural deans who exercised a supervisory role over all the parishes in the deanery, a unit smaller than an archdeaconry, though the duties delegated to them varied from diocese to diocese. The basic unit of ecclesiastical administration was the parish, which varied greatly in size and which might comprise a single settlement with a church, or several settlements with a parish church and, in some cases, one or more chapels-of-ease in which some services took place.

In theory all parishioners were members of the established church, but in practice some were not. There were, throughout England and Wales, small groups of Roman Catholics, Baptists, Independents, Presbyterians and some smaller sects who worshipped in their own chapels, though they were all obliged to pay tithes for the upkeep of the clergy of the established church, rates for the upkeep of its churches, and if they wanted to contract a legal marriage they had to do so by being married in an Anglican church by one of its clergy. Protestant dissenters could license their chapels for worship by applying for permission to do so to the diocesan authorities and licensed chapels had protection in law. However, Roman Catholics did not acquire this right until the last quarter of the eighteenth century, so they, and any group of Protestants who had not licensed their chapels, though they were normally able to worship without molestation, did not enjoy the protection of the law.

The structure of religion in Ireland

In principle the structure of the established church in Ireland was more or less identical to that of the established church in England and Wales. In practice it was rather different. Whereas in England and Wales there were comparatively few Roman Catholics or Protestant dissenters, this was not the case in Ireland. For reasons that are outside the scope of this book,[1] Roman Catholicism had retained the allegiance of the majority of the population of Ireland and the attempts by James VI and I in the early seventeenth century to establish Protestant plantations had succeeded in creating almost as many presbyterian Protestant congregations in Ireland as episcopal ones. The situation of the established Church of Ireland was unique in eighteenth-century Europe, in that a religious body that enjoyed all the privileges of establishment could not command the loyalty of more than a tiny proportion of the population. Throughout the period between 1714 and 1815, and with only the slightest fluctuations, Roman Catholics constituted about four-fifths of the population of Ireland. The remaining fifth, though Protestant, was divided roughly into 60% members of the Church of Ireland (i.e. 12% of the total population of Ireland) and 40% Presbyterians (i.e. 8% of the total population of Ireland). There were many parishes in Ireland in which there were no, or very few, members of the Church of Ireland, and churches fell into ruin through complete disuse. Maintaining the clergy required the creation of, sometimes very large, parochial areas, and the small size of some of the Irish dioceses meant that it was practical to unite them under one bishop. By the eighteenth century the 35 pre-Reformation dioceses were being administered by a total of 22 archbishops and bishops, though even so most were smaller in size than the average diocese in England and Wales. Some dioceses had several cathedrals, others had none because they were in ruins, but most were no more than glorified parish churches, their dignities and prebends filled by local clergy using the modest endowments to boost inadequate parochial incomes. There were archdeacons, though they exercised no powers, and the only diocese to have retained rural deans was Cloyne. Irish bishops did not have the administrative support available to their counterparts in England and Wales though most dioceses appear to have been efficiently administered. Roman Catholics and Presbyterians laboured under the same restrictions as their co-religionists in England and Wales, with the penal laws restricting the freedom of Roman Catholics being enforced rather more stringently, at least during the first half of the eighteenth century.

The structure of religion in Scotland

In Scotland the religious structure was very different from that in the other parts of the British Isles. With the final abolition of episcopacy, and the approval of both the monarch and the Scottish parliament in 1690, a fully presbyterian system of church government was established in Scotland. Under its General Assembly the country was divided into areas covered by provincial synods, each comprising a number of presbyteries, which in turn each comprised a number of kirk sessions, each kirk session comprising the ministers and elders of that parish. At each layer of church government both clergy and laity were represented. These arrangements were not altered by the union treaty of 1707, and the abolition of the separate Scottish parliament, except in one respect. In 1712 the parliament at Westminster, despite the objections of the General Assembly, re-introduced private patronage into the Church of Scotland, restoring to the heritors (landowners) the right to present ministers to vacant charges. Although the presbyterian party in the Church of Scotland had triumphed in 1689–90 no immediate attempt was made to deprive ministers with episcopalian sympathies. What was finally to remove them from the established church was not their doctrinal standpoint but their political one and their continued support for the Jacobite cause. Even then episcopalian clergy were still to be found in parts of the highlands. Episcopal ministers remained in charge of parishes at Contin, Fodderty and Urray until 1721, at Barvas on Lewis until 1722, at Daviot and Dunlichity until 1726, at Glenorchy until 1728 and at Boleskine until 1729.[2] However after the Jacobite rebellion of 1745–6 the small number of surviving episcopalians in Scotland, now fully outside the established church and maintaining their bishops and clergy, found themselves heavily persecuted and labouring under even more restrictions than the small number of Roman Catholics. There were also divisions within the majority Presbyterian community in Scotland, with various groups seceding from the Church of Scotland over issues mostly relating to patronage or the interpretation of the Westminster Confession as the standard of doctrine.[3] None of these groups were very large but they created the same tensions with the established church as Protestant dissenters in England and Wales.

Jacobites and non-jurors

In 1688–9 King James VII and II had been forced into exile. The Act of Settlement of 1701 laid down that, in the event of neither William III nor his sister-in-law Anne having any successors, the throne should pass to the Electress Sophia of Hanover and her heirs. The Act also laid down that every future monarch must be, or become, a member of the Church of England. The succession of William III had caused some problems for Anglican churchmen. Much as they disapproved of James II's Roman Catholicism and his attempts to remove some of the restrictions on his co-religionists, he was still the anointed king and there was some doubt as to whether it was possible to recognise another monarch while he lived. The Archbishop of Canterbury, four English bishops and one Irish one refused to take the oath to William III and were deprived in 1690–1. Although episcopacy had been abolished in Scotland by the General Assembly in 1689, the unanimity with which the Scottish bishops expressed their reluctance to take any but the most circumscribed oath to the new king was a factor in his acquiescence in the Assembly's decision. The lead given by some of these bishops was followed by some of the clergy and a number of non-juring Anglican congregations were estab-lished. Both the English and the Scottish non-juring bishops made provision for an episcopal succession and small groups of non-jurors survived in England until the early nineteenth century.

During the 1690s non-jurors, and many of those who had not become non-jurors but had reluctantly accepted the accession of William III, hoped that their difficulties would be short-lived and that a legitimate succession would be restored after his death. They could maintain this position during the reign of Queen Anne, but her death without an heir and the implementation of the Act of Settlement, resulting in the accession of the Electress Sophia's son, George I, in 1714, created a major crisis for them. They believed that James II's son, 'James VIII and III', should have succeeded Anne, even though he was a Roman Catholic, especially as he had offered to maintain the Protestant established churches in the British Isles. There were two major Jacobite rebellions, in 1715 and 1745, the second of which looked at one point as if it might succeed. Although most Jacobites abandoned the cause after the death of 'James VIII and III' in 1766, some continued to support it during the lifetimes of his two sons, 'Charles III' and 'Henry IX', who died in 1788 and 1807 respectively.

Though all non-jurors were probably Jacobites, not all Jacobites were non-jurors. Many Anglicans who might have outwardly accepted the accession of George I were seen as potential, if not active, Jacobites. Much discomfort was caused to Anglican high churchmen by the refusal of the Hanoverian dynasty to 'touch' their subjects as a cure for scrofula, and some sufferers from the disease resorted to 'touch-pieces' that had been 'touched' by James II or 'James III' until the 1760s.[4] One of the most loyal Jacobite constituencies was the small surviving communities of Roman Catholics in England, Wales and Scotland. The Roman Catholic church in Ireland was also strongly Jacobite in outlook as were the Scottish episcopalians. 'James III' nominated to Irish Roman Catholic bishoprics until shortly before his death in 1766, and the Scottish episcopalians sought the approval of 'Charles III' for the consecration of their bishops until his death in 1788. In Scotland support for the Jacobite cause had been increased by hostility to the Act of Union of 1707, the repeal of which was a main plank in Jacobite propaganda. In the 1715 Jacobite Rebellion there was strong support in Scotland from most of the nobility and lairds throughout the north of the country as well as among the middle classes of Edinburgh and the east coast burghs. By the 1745 rebellion this level of support was confined to the highlands. In England the Jacobite cause was supported by significant groups in London, Bristol and Manchester as well as by northern and West Country squires. Most of the Welsh squirearchy were Jacobites. However, sympathies were not always translated into action, especially by the time of the 1745 rebellion.[5] One of the main reasons for this seems to have been the fear of many theoretical Jacobites who were loyal Anglicans that a Roman Catholic dynasty could not be relied upon to defend the Protestant establishment. They put 'church first, monarchy second'.[6] This was, of course, the argument that had been put forward by the arch-Whig, Benjamin Hoadly,[7] but many Tories agreed with it and the view that they were committed Jacobites has been successfully challenged by recent political historians.[8] As Linda Colley concludes,

*if large numbers of Britons had really wanted to throw in their lot with
the Jacobite cause, it is hard to see . . . how they could have been stopped.
Yet only the poorer Highland class, a handful of Welshmen and some
300 Englishmen rallied to the Young Pretender*[9]

in 1745–6. To some extent the repression meted out to Jacobite supporters
in England, Ireland and Wales after the 1715 rebellion had persuaded
many potential sympathisers not to support that of 1745. In Scotland,
where the strength of Jacobitism had prevented similar measures being
taken after the 1715 rebellion, the much smaller degree of active support for
rebellion in 1745 permitted severe repression of the Jacobite highlanders
after the defeat of Culloden in 1746.[10]

The gradual collapse of Jacobitism, from the 1720s in most parts of
England and Wales, by the 1760s in Ireland and by the 1780s in Scotland,
was mirrored by the slow return of Anglican non-jurors to the established
church in England, Ireland and Wales, and the beginnings of attempts by
Anglican high churchmen outside Scotland to establish more friendly
relations with Scottish episcopalians. Immediately after the 1715 Jacobite
rebellion there were estimated to have been 'more than a dozen Nonjuring
meetings, some of them of considerable size' in London, and significant
congregations in Manchester and Newcastle. Although many of the non-
juring gentry had returned to the established church during the 1720s, the
Newcastle congregation survived until the 1780s. The Manchester
congregation had 70 communicants in 1757 and still had 30 regular
worshippers in 1804. Many high churchmen who had taken the oath to
George I and George II maintained good relations with the non-jurors
and continued to buy their publications. Thomas Deacon's *Complete
Collection of Devotions* published in 1734, sold 1,400 copies, many being
bought by clergy of the established Church of England. The Jacobite
sympathies of some of these clergy were also well established. Bishop
Crewe of Durham remained a secret Jacobite until his death in 1721,
the collegiate church at Manchester was a Jacobite stronghold until
the 1745 rebellion and some Oxford fellows continued to retain Jacobite
sympathies.[11] It was this continued familiarity between Anglican high
churchmen and non-jurors, and continued support for Jacobitism by some
high church clergy, including those in senior positions, which was to cause
a major political crisis in the early part of George I's reign. Bishop Hoadly
had brought upon himself the wrath of high churchmen by his attack on
the non-jurors and then promptly compounded his iniquities in high
church eyes by preaching a sermon before King George I in which he

denied that Christ had left any authority to his church and that all Christians were therefore free to interpret the scriptures according to their consciences. Such views completely undermined the ability of the Church of England to determine and require subscription to a particular doctrinal stance, and gave power to the state to regulate religion as it saw fit. The resulting furore,[12] termed the Bangorian controversy from the fact that Hoadly was Bishop of Bangor, and Hoadly's protection by the government, was to create a situation in which all high churchmen, especially those who were Tories politically, were regarded as suspect and these suspicions were confirmed by the activities of the acknowledged leader of the Tory bishops, Francis Atterbury, Bishop of Rochester and Dean of Westminster.

Atterbury had, in 1713, been a Tory high church appointee, at the opposite extreme from the arch-Whig, Benjamin Hoadly, and it was the government's support of the latter and its decision to marginalise the Tories, who had been in power throughout the latter half of Queen Anne's reign, that determined Atterbury to take up the Jacobite cause as the best way of restoring Tory influence in both church and state. The economic crisis of 1720, when the South Sea Company collapsed bringing financial ruin to its shareholders, who included many individual clergy as well as ecclesiastical charities and corporations, seemed to offer a golden opportunity for a new and successful Jacobite plot for the first time since the failure of the 1715 rebellion. Atterbury acted as the chief adviser in England to the exiled court of 'James III' in Paris and by the end of 1721 plans for an invasion were well-developed. Security, however, was poor and the plot was soon known to both the British and the French governments. The planned invasion was cancelled and Atterbury was exposed, arrested and accused of high treason. Although the evidence against him was far from conclusive, and he defended himself with vigour at his trial before the House of Lords, Atterbury was found guilty and sentenced to deprivation from his bishopric and deanery and perpetual banishment from the British Isles in 1723. This exile was made more comfortable by the decision of the chapter of Westminster that Atterbury, as dean, should receive his share of the fines from leases before the date on which his banishment was to take effect, and many country Tories pledged a regular contribution to Atterbury's expenses in exile. Atterbury was to spend the last nine years of his life in Paris as an adviser to 'James III' but the British government permitted the return of his body to England, and its burial in Westminster Abbey, on 22 May 1732, provided there was no public funeral.[13]

The dominance of the church Whigs

The downfall of Bishop Atterbury marked the end of any continued Tory involvement at the senior levels of church government, and even the marginalisation by the government and its chief minister, Sir Robert Walpole, of any bishop seen as being too defensive of those with Tory sympathies. Thus the moderate Whig Archbishop of Canterbury, William Wake, was replaced as the effective leader of the bishops in the House of Lords and the government's chief ecclesiastical adviser, by the much more reliably Whig Edmund Gibson, translated from the bishopric of Lincoln to that of London in 1723. Gibson was to retain this position until his death in 1748, and the effective 'primacy' of the Bishop of London was to continue under his successor Thomas Sherlock (1748–61). It was only in 1758, when the exceptionally able Thomas Secker was translated from the bishopric of Oxford to the archbishopric of Canterbury, that the authority of the primatial see was restored. With the accession of King George III in 1760, the Tories were once again to be included in government and the dominance of the church Whigs in matters of both church and state came to an end. Whilst there were certainly differences between Tories and Whigs in their attitude to the nature of the church–state relationship one must be careful not to exaggerate them. There was certainly a difference over the nature of monarchy and the role that this played in relation to an established church. Whereas 'most Whigs accepted an established church as an essential feature of the constitution' Tories went a good deal further. They were committed to a highly religious theory of kingship and to the notion that 'resistance to the Lord's Anointed was a damnable sin'. In return for demanding 'reverence for the king, they expected that the . . . royal prerogative would be used to assist the church', since it was 'an essential instrument for the preservation of social order and political stability'. Most of the clergy were Tories and 'could certainly be trusted to preach the doctrine of non-resistance and passive obedience. Even the most moderate clergy were convinced that it was their duty to preach a doctrine of subordination'.[14] The moderate Whigs accepted much of this philosophy though they tended to express it in less theological language. It was only the more radical Whigs who were 'determined critics of the established church'. They wanted its 'special privileges', which moderate Whigs were prepared to support, eliminated, more concessions made to dissenters and the established church placed 'firmly under the control of the civil power'.[15] It was the fear of the Tory clergy that the radical Whigs would eventually convert the more moderate Whigs to their cause that created

their widespread support for 'the church in danger' campaigns of the
1720s and 1730s.

A major issue which divided politicians and churchmen in the reigns of
George I and George II was the future of the Convocations of Canterbury
and York, the representative bodies of the lower clergy and the clerical
counterpart of the House of Commons. Convocation was less important
to the bishops since they could maintain their influence over government
through their right to speak and vote in the House of Lords. Whereas
the government could seek to modify criticism from the episcopate, at least
over a period of time, through their influence over episcopal appointments,
it was impossible to control Convocation which was determined to discuss
'the church in danger' agenda which most concerned the clergy. This
came to a head in 1717 when Convocation insisted on condemning the
erastian views of Bishop Hoadly. Although this was the official reason for
the prorogation of Convocation, to prevent further debate on matters
uncomfortable to the government, it has been seen by recent historians
as an essential plank of Whig ministers in seeking a more effective type
of church–state relationship which culminated in the designation of Bishop
Gibson as their principal ecclesiastical adviser in 1723.[16] The Tory clergy
were furious with the Whigs for their attempts to grant greater toleration
to Protestant dissenters. Whilst most 'Tories agreed with Whigs that
religious persecution was wrong . . . they drew the line at legislative
measures which gave aid and encouragement to non-Anglican sects'.[17]
Some of the bishops hoped that the prorogation of Convocation would
not be permanent, and in 1741–2 brief meetings were held at which
motions were tabled on the reform of the ecclesiastical courts, clandestine
marriages and curates' stipends. However, continued concern by church
leaders that the Tory majority among the lower clergy were determined
to embarrass the government resulted in the brief experiment being abandoned, and no future meetings of the clergy for the purpose of debate were
held until the 1850s. Norman Sykes viewed the silencing of Convocation
as a major brake on ecclesiastical reform. It prevented any further amendment of the church services which became fossilised in their late seventeenth century form. Matters which could have been debated in detail by
Convocation before appropriate measures were submitted for parliamentary approval were simply not discussed, as parliament was unwilling
to spend sufficient time discussing ecclesiastical matters until such time
as these became urgent, very often as a result of pressure from those
outside the church rather than in response to demands from the bishops
or clergy.[18] Whilst the new form of church–state partnership which emerged

after the silencing of Convocation and the banishment of Bishop Atterbury, and for which Bishop Gibson of London deserves most of the credit, worked for the government it did so rather less well for the established church, and led to considerable frustrations among the bishops and clergy in the late eighteenth and early nineteenth centuries.

Nevertheless the new arrangements had their defenders. Chief among them was the future bishop of Gloucester, William Warburton, who first published his *Alliance between Church and State* in 1736. Whereas high church Anglicans, especially those who were Tories in politics, had seen church and state as a unity through which monarchical authority was exercised in both the spiritual and the temporal spheres, Warburton expressed the relationship in a form which was essentially pragmatic, but which also bore a closer resemblance to its reality than the theoretical notions of Anglican high churchmen. He outlined 'the Motives the State had to seek, and the Church to accept an alliance' and concluded that the usefulness of the alliance to the state could be seen in the following ways:

By bestowing additional Reverence and Veneration on the Person of the Civil Magistrate and on the Laws of the State . . .
By lending the state a coactive Power . . .
By conferring on the State the Application of this Efficacy of Religion; and by putting it under the magistrate's Direction . . .
By engaging the Church to apply its utmost endeavours in the Service of the State.[19]

The benefits to the established church were perhaps less obvious but Warburton argued that the principal motives the church had in accepting the alliance were 'to engage the state to propagate the Established Religion by Force: and the other, to bestow Honours, Riches, and Powers upon it'.[20] In the third chapter of the second part of the book Warburton described the 'Terms and Conditions of the Alliance' as 'reciprocal' and he analysed 'what the Church receives from the State' and 'what the church gives to it'. These included:

a public endowment for its ministers . . .
a place for her superior Members in the Court of Legislature; which with us, is the Bishop's Seat in Parliament . . .
a jurisdiction assisted by coactive Power, for Reformation of Manners.[21]

He concluded that the essence of the alliance was 'that the Church should serve the State, and the State protect the Church'.[22] Historians who have argued that Warburton departed from the orthodox understanding of the relationship between church and state previously held by Anglican divines are, of course, correct.

Warburton was atypical, not because he rejected the orthodox theory, but because he did not share a set of widely-held assumptions about Church and State: that the civil magistrate had a duty to support the propagation of the true religion; that religion was necessary for the security of the state, not only on grounds of civil utility, but also because of the nature of God's providential government; in short, that in a Christian commonwealth Church and State, though independent societies, were necessarily incorporated . . . Moreover, the implications of the Alliance *were too erastian for most; contrary to the author's own belief it was the state which appeared to be the main beneficiary.*[23]

Orthodox high churchmen had argued that church and state were effectively one and that 'the office of the civil magistrate extended to the care of souls',[24] in other words the sort of view that Anglican high churchmen had propounded in the seventeenth century. However, Warburton belonged to a new generation of Anglican churchmen, who, whilst theologically orthodox in general terms, were deeply influenced by the rationalism of much contemporary philosophy,[25] and this shift in the position of many within the Church of England from a theoretical to a pragmatic justification of the political, religious and social order was a feature of the eighteenth century which to some extent challenges Jonathan Clark's arguments for the survival of a confessional state throughout this period. Indeed it has been argued that the wide acceptance of Warburton's views by the late eighteenth century 'opened the way for the complete secularization of politics' by the early nineteenth century and that 'not until the days of the Oxford Movement was the search for ecclesiastical independence resumed'.[26]

In England and Wales the alliance between church and state, in the form of the close relationship which was created between Bishop Gibson and Sir Robert Walpole, was consolidated in a series of episcopal appointments in 1723 resulting from the deprivation of Bishop Atterbury and the deaths of Bishops Fleetwood of Ely and Trimnell of Winchester. All Gibson's recommendations for appointments to a total of nine bishoprics were accepted. The more advanced high churchmen, especially those with inadequate Whig credentials, were excluded, but so were the extreme Latitudinarians such as Bishop Hoadly. Gibson prevented his translation from the bishopric of Salisbury to that of Durham in 1730, and himself refused translation from London to Winchester in 1734 in order to prevent

Hoadly from succeeding him. Gibson did not attempt to block Hoadly's translation to Winchester, where he thought he could do less harm. Gibson deliberately sought to improve the standing of the government in the eyes of a still largely hostile, mostly Tory and in some cases Jacobite, clergy. This was particularly the case with the Universities of Oxford and Cambridge who were to benefit from Gibson's scheme for the appointment of Whitehall preachers, choosing one Oxford and one Cambridge college fellow who were appointed preachers for a month at the Royal Chapel in Whitehall at a stipend of £30. This was followed by the endowment of regius professorships in modern history at both universities together with a number of scholarships for men of outstanding academic ability who had already taken a BA degree, though only the professorships were maintained after the first few years of the scheme's operation. Gibson's ability to control episcopal appointments continued through the late 1720s and 1730s,[27] though he was occasionally obliged to compromise with Queen Caroline, the wife of George II, who also had strong views on who ought and who ought not to be bishops. The alliance between Gibson and Walpole survived into the parliamentary session of 1735–6. Then, as a result of pressure from dissenters, a number of measures were introduced which strained the relationship to breaking point. Although Walpole used his influence to secure the defeat of attempts to repeal the Test and Corporation Acts, which limited the political rights of dissenters, he was unable, and to some extent unwilling, to use it to prevent the passing of the Mortmain and Quaker Tithe Bills. The first of these measures placed important restrictions on the making of new ecclesiastical endowments whilst the latter provided relief to members of the Society of Friends from suits to enforce the payment of tithes. Gibson responded by organising petitions against such anti-clerical measures and securing the defeat of the Quaker Tithe Bill in the House of Lords. When Archbishop Wake died in 1737, Gibson, who was the obvious candidate to succeed him at Canterbury, having in effect exercised the power and influence of the primacy for 14 years, was passed over in favour of the nondescript Bishop Potter of Oxford.[28]

Just as Archbishop Wake had been the primary casualty of Bishop Gibson's rise to power in England and Wales, so the early 1720s marked a change in the ecclesiastical leadership of Ireland. Archbishop King of Dublin had prevented major outbreaks of Jacobitism in Ireland in 1715 but, like Wake, was seen to be too close to the Tories and seemed to give proof of this when he opposed the granting of increased toleration to Irish Presbyterians in 1719. He was therefore eventually excluded from the commission of lords justices for Ireland and in 1724 passed over for the primatial see of Armagh in favour of the Bishop of Bristol, Hugh Boulter. This was part of a deliberate Whig policy of appointing more English-born, instead of Irish-born, bishops to Irish bishoprics, which was to continue for the first half of the eighteenth century. Indeed in the case of the primatial see of Armagh no Irish-born candidate was appointed until Lord John George Beresford was translated from Dublin in 1822. The new Archbishop of Armagh, Hugh Boulter, was to become the dominant figure in the Church of Ireland from 1724 to his death in 1742 and was to pursue similar policies in Ireland to those pursued by Bishop Gibson within the Church of England. In particular he pressed for the appointment of more Englishmen, preferably those of Whig opinions, to Irish bishoprics. These bishops in turn used their patronage to promote other Englishmen to benefices in Ireland, though this policy was in reverse by the last quarter of the eighteenth century and many of the leading bishops in the Church of Ireland then had acceptable Irish, or at least Anglo-Irish, pedigrees.[29] Whilst there was no ecclesiastical equivalent to Gibson or Boulter in Scotland, resulting from the different nature of Scottish church establishment, it is notable that there were many similarities between the respective developments of Anglicanism and presbyterianism in the eighteenth century. Neither Anglican nor presbyterian leaders 'had any time for puritanism' and 'both believed that the social order was already organised in a way highly satisfactory to God and both assumed the Lord to be as moderate in His religious views as they were themselves'. By 1750 the moderates were in the ascendant everywhere in Scotland, even in the former puritan strongholds of the south, and the Scottish universities, 'which had traditionally enjoyed close links with the Continent, could not remain always untouched by rational and liberal ideas that were stirring the intelligentsia abroad'.[30]

A Protestant confessional state?

What had largely kept the Whig alliance of church and state in being throughout the 1720s and 1730s was fear of Jacobitism and the belief that the Hanoverian dynasty was not secure. That fear was still alive in the 1740s, despite the collapse of the alliance between Gibson and Walpole, and meant that Tories were still marginalised in the higher reaches of the Church of England. By the 1750s the danger of Jacobitism really had effectively disappeared and it was dealt its final death-knell by the accession of George III in 1760. The third of the Hanoverians was in a very different mould from his grandfather and great-grandfather and was keen to reinvent the monarchy in a different image. Born in England in 1738, he was seen by some Anglican high churchmen as seeking to return to an older model of kingship, with a greater emphasis on the divine nature of monarchy and with a greater attempt to create a broad political alliance which would include Tories as well as Whigs. Linda Colley argues that, despite his later illness, George III had largely succeeded in getting this new, or in a sense revived, view of monarchy accepted by the 1780s and making it a more popular institution. Whereas the deaths of George I in 1727 and George II in 1760 had passed largely unnoticed, that of George III in 1820 was marked by the shops shutting, many people wearing symbols of mourning and a crowd of 30,000 in Windsor on the day of the funeral 'even though it was a strictly private occasion'.[31]

The political transformation that occurred between 1760 and 1780 is in many ways crucial in answering the question as to whether Britain remained a Protestant confessional state for the whole of the period between 1714 and 1815. Certainly that was what George I had inherited in 1714 but its continuation depended on the Tories, who were its principal sponsors, retaining some political influence, whereas in practice this was lost during the reigns of George I and George II. Whilst Whigs were keen to maintain the sort of pragmatic alliance between church and state that Warburton had advocated this fell somewhat short of what could really be considered a confessional state. Britain was in any case not one but three such states, the nature of the ecclesiastical establishment being that bit different in each. In all three states some toleration had been granted to Protestant dissenters and the more radical of the Whigs wanted to broaden the nature of this toleration further. The political situation in Ireland, with such a large Roman Catholic population, meant that, whatever penal laws remained on the statute book, they had to be enforced rather half-heartedly and sporadically, and this toleration in practice had to be extended to the other parts of the British Isles. Had the Tories continued to be marginalised after 1760, as they had been for the previous 40 years, it is likely that a Protestant confessional state would have been further undermined. As it was, the new political landscape after 1760 enhanced its survival and, as Jonathan Clark has noted, the first signs of its revival can be seen in the two decades before this. Viscount Bolingbroke's *Idea of a Patriot King*, written in the late 1730s but not published until 1749, was a sign of things to come, especially as it put forward a continuation of political philosophies designed to appeal to both Whigs and Tories.[32] The rehabilitation of Tories in the political sphere also meant that Tories in the church were not to be blocked from promotion in the way that they had been by Bishop Gibson, and Tory high churchmen still believed, in a modified way, the doctrines of divine right and passive obedience preached by their predecessors before 1714. George Horne, who became Bishop of Norwich in 1790, preached a sermon for the Feast of King Charles the Martyr in 1761 in which the pragmatism of Warburton's views on the alliance of church and state were rejected and the case made for a return to the traditional models of a church–state relationship in which the role of the crown, as the head of both, was crucial. Similar views were propounded by an even more influential figure in the established church, Samuel Horsley, bishop successively of St Davids, Rochester and St Asaph between 1788 and 1806. They were not, however, just espoused by churchmen. Edmund Burke, originally a Whig, was also, partly as a result of his attitude to the French Revolution, converted to similar views on the nature of monarchy and the indivisibility of church and state as the best guardian against tyranny and arbitrary power.[33] The concept of a Protestant confessional state, perhaps rather shaky in the 1750s, seemed to be very much alive and well in the 1790s, and was undoubtedly bolstered by the desire of both churchmen and politicians to protect the British Isles from the political turmoil that had affected France and its immediate neighbours as a result of the 1789 revolution.

Strengths and weaknesses of the religious establishments

Despite pressure from the more radical Whigs and the example of collapsing religious establishments in other parts of Europe, Britain remained, in general terms, a confessional state throughout the period between 1714 and 1815, and indeed for some time thereafter. The Church of Ireland was not disestablished until 1869, the Church of England in Wales not until 1920; the Churches of England and Scotland remain established, though clearly not in the same way that they were in the eighteenth century. Whilst belief in the value of establishment remained strong, it was, however, the case that the established churches were in some respects rather weak and it could be argued that, whilst the churches maintained their side of Warburton's 'alliance', the state was less good at providing the support for established churches that, in theory at least, it should have done. Many of the problems that were to lead to government actions to reform the established churches in the 1820s and 1830s, or to the divisions within the

Church of Scotland in the 1840s, were the result of government inaction, despite the promptings of churchmen, in the century beforehand.

The Anglican church was in political thrall to Whig politicians who had every intent in preserving a decent and respectable church as the first support to their power, but little or no interest in the much-needed structural reform of that church.[34]

Although the Church of Scotland enjoyed a much greater measure of political independence than the established churches in other parts of the British Isles, there were significant areas in which its freedom of action was circumscribed by the political decisions of a non-Scottish parliament. The basic administrative unit of the Church of Scotland was the kirk session; kirk sessions were grouped into presbyteries and presbyteries into synods. The supreme governing body was the General Assembly which in the middle years of the eighteenth century comprised 364 members, 202 of which were ministers and 162 laity. A total of 290 members (201 ministers and 89 elders) were appointed by the presbyteries, 57 lay members by royal burghs, 5 (either ministerial or lay) by the universities and 2 (a minister and an elder) by the Scottish church at Campvere in the Netherlands. The government attempted to influence the deliberations of the General Assembly through some of the lay members, many of whom were lawyers, as in 1749–50 when demands by the ministers for the augmentation of their stipends were suppressed by those members.[35]

The most serious issue, however, as far as many Presbyterians were concerned, was the reintroduction of lay patronage into the Church of Scotland as a result of an act passed by the Westminster parliament in 1712. Under the provisions of this legislation ministers could be nominated by the heritors (landowners) for ordination and induction, and such nominations could only be refused if it could be shown that the nominee's qualifications were inadequate. This arrangement struck at the heart of a jealously guarded Presbyterian demand that a congregation should be free to 'call' its own minister. It had two major effects. The first was that it led to schisms which weakened the established church: the Sandimanians in the 1720s, the Secession Church in the 1730s and the Relief Presbytery in 1750. Although each of these new groups had relatively few members, the frequency of these schisms were seen to be undermining the official Presbyterian church. The second was that because of the tensions between the heritors and the congregations over the appointment of ministers, those appointed came to be seen, and indeed even to see themselves, as the creatures of the heritors to whom they owed their appointment.[36] There were several cases in which congregations endeavoured to frustrate the appointment of ministers they had not chosen, as at Bathgate (West Lothian) in 1717 or in several parishes in the central lowlands, the southeast, Fife and Angus between the 1750s and 1770s, though when the cases went to the church courts the rights of the heritors were generally upheld.[37]

In England and Wales the major ecclesiastical problems were rather different: the inequality in the size of dioceses, pluralism resulting from inadequate endowments and the lack of church provision in the larger urban communities. Bishop Gibson of London put forward, unsuccessfully, a series of proposals for the equalisation of dioceses, including the suppression of the small dioceses of Bristol, Gloucester and Rochester and the creation of new bishoprics and cathedrals at Brecon, Eton and Southwell. The new diocese of Brecon was to take in the counties of Breconshire, Cardiganshire and Radnorshire from that of St Davids. The new diocese of Eton was to take in the counties of Bedfordshire, Buckinghamshire and Huntingdonshire from that of Lincoln and the county of Hertfordshire from that of London; the bishop was to be the provost of Eton College and the fellows were to become the prebendaries of the new cathedral. The new diocese of Southwell was to take in the county of Derbyshire from that of Lichfield and the county of Nottinghamshire from that of York. Some of these proposals were eventually implemented nearly two centuries later. In 1884 a new diocese of Southwell was formed on the boundaries proposed by Gibson. In 1923 a new diocese of Swansea and Brecon was created but parts of Glamorganshire were substituted for Gibson's suggestion that it should include Cardiganshire. Gibson's proposals also included the merging of the diocese of Canterbury and Rochester; the enlargement of Carlisle at the expense of Chester, Ely at the expense of Norwich, Oxford at the expense of Salisbury, and Peterborough at the expense of Lincoln; and the merger of the suppressed dioceses of Bristol and Gloucester within those of Bath and Wells, Salisbury and Worcester. Gibson also proposed alterations in diocesan endowments to make episcopal incomes more equal and thus prevent the necessity of translation between poorer and richer dioceses.[38]

Gibson was also keen to address the more serious effects of pluralism,

to reduce the distance between livings held in plurality to fifteen miles, to require the holders to reside two months in each benefice and to preach thirteen sermons annually . . . In addition no benefice exceeding £200 per year was to be held in plurality.[39]

On the whole, as we shall see, pluralism was caused largely by the poverty of some livings and some of the worst effects of this were to be relieved through the establishment of Queen Anne's Bounty, whereby the income from the payment of first fruits and tenths to the crown was invested and managed by a corporation which made grants to raise the value of poorer livings. From 1717, when Convocation ceased to meet, until 1836 the corporation was 'the church's only functioning representative organ'.[40] The principles under which the corporation acted were that augmentation of poorer livings was to be made by capital grants which were to be invested in land. Livings were divided into two classes: those under £35 per annum for which a private benefaction needed to be offered to secure a Bounty grant; and the very poorest livings which might be augmented even without a benefaction; livings in the second of these groups were chosen by lot. In 1718 the maximum value of livings to be assisted was raised from £35 to £50 per annum. Although the Bounty corporation included both clerical and lay governors, in practice it was the bishops who were the most frequent attenders, with the result that meetings sometimes included the discussion of other episcopal business, such as resisting attempts to repeal the Test and Corporation Acts in 1787.[41] The number of grants made by Queen Anne's Bounty, as shown in Table 1, was considerable. However, the balance of the grants changed.

TABLE 1 *Augmentations of poor livings by Queen Anne's Bounty 1714–1815*

Years	Augmetations to meet benefactions	Augmentations by lot
1714–30	744	151
1731–47	358	611
1748–64	385	754
1765–81	429	1,079
1782–98	194	1,472
1799–1815	259	916

Source: G.F.A. Best, *Temporal Pillars: Queen Anne's Bounty, the Ecclesiastical Commissioners and the Church of England*, Cambridge 1964, pp. 537–8.

In the early years most benefactions were to support benefactions from other sources. By 1739 the number of grants made by lot were almost equal to those made to supplement benefactions and thereafter the majority of grants were those to the poorest livings chosen by lot. The role of landowners was crucial in the process of increasing the value of livings. Many put up the benefactions which helped to assist the augmentation of the benefice income provided by Queen Anne's Bounty. The sixth Earl of

Thanet helped augment several livings in Westmorland and the third Viscount Lonsdale contributed £70 to the augmentation of the rectory of Shap in the 1740s. Landowners also provided sites for new church buildings or undertook the costs of routine maintenance. There was sometimes an element of self-interest in this since landowners who were patrons of benefices could use their patronage to offer employment to their relatives and friends, or appointments to clergy prepared to support their political aspirations at election time. During the eighteenth century landowners, particularly aristocrats, increased their patronage of livings by acquiring new ones. The Dukes of Devonshire increased their patronage from 29½ to 37 advowsons and the Dukes of Rutland from 24 to 29. In the first half of the eighteenth century 49 aristocratic families held eight or more advowsons, but by the end of the century this had increased to 64.[42]

By far the most serious problem for the established churches in the eighteenth century was the antiquated parochial boundaries, which reflected a predominantly agrarian society in an increasingly industrial age. This was allied to a serious shortage of new churches in growing centres of population. Thus Cheshire and Lancashire had only 156 parishes whereas Essex, Norfolk and Suffolk, the rich areas of the late middle ages, had 1,634. In Sheffield only two new churches were built despite an increase in the population from 5,000 to 40,000 during the eighteenth century. Manchester had only one parish church for 20,000 people in 1750, Marylebone only one seating 200 for a population of 40,000 in 1800. Only 12 of the 50 churches projected by the London Churches Act of 1711 were actually built. It was impossible to create new parishes without the consent of bishops, clergy and patrons, some of whom had a vested interest in preserving the status quo, and the promotion of legislation in parliament. Many Anglicans argued, not always very convincingly, that the paucity of churches in large towns encouraged the growth of dissent. In London in 1812 there were 186 Anglican to 256 dissenting places of worship.[43] Some relief could be provided by what were known as proprietary chapels.

Private Chapels sprang up within the established Church as in Dissenting sects. Provided they did not interfere with the authority of an incumbent or encroach on his tithes, they were easy to establish. Financed by pew rents or congregational contributions they were eagerly sought by fashionable preachers, more particularly since they were often filled by election rather than nomination . . . In this sense at least the Church was by no means lacking in creativity.[44]

But proprietary chapels were not the real solution. They catered for middle-class parishioners who could pay the pew rents and not the poorer members of society. The two such chapels in Bath, St Mary's in Queen Square and the Octagon in Milsom Street, were built as places of worship for the wealthy: 'a stranger cannot get a sitting under half a crown a time, or a guinea for the season'.[45] It was not just proprietary chapels that appeared to provide as much of a social as a religious function. Some fashionable churches were used for match-making and it was alleged that at Bath Abbey 'there is more *billet-doux* conveyed to the ladies, than notes to desire the prayers of the congregation'.[46]

Whilst the established churches in the British Isles were certainly not without their weaknesses between 1714 and 1815 they also had their strengths. As we shall see, in the later chapters of this book, they were generally well-administered and socially active. Whatever critics were to allege, both then and later, the confessional state in Britain and Ireland was of benefit to both church and state. The churches provided much of the support for education and social welfare that in some other parts of Europe was beginning to be provided by the state. They were also used by politicians and landowners as agents of social control, with many clergy being actively involved in both the political process and in local administration as justices of the peace. Whilst there may have been occasions when the state failed the churches, particularly in its unwillingness to promote the ecclesiastical reforms requested from time to time, it generally fulfilled its part of the church–state relationship as the protector of the interests of the established churches and in the maintenance of the privileges that establishment involved. It has been argued that:

> the Church of England was possibly the most powerful and certainly the largest and best organised vested interest in the country. It rarely needed to act as an extra-parliamentary pressure group, however, because it was a rich state institution with political influence at every level of society from the royal court to the smallest parish. When its interests and privileges were threatened, it was able to mount major propaganda campaigns and to enlist both influential and popular support on an impressive scale.[47]

The confessional state, despite some modifications in the way that concept was expressed, was as alive and well in 1815 as it had been a century beforehand.

Notes

1 See A. Ford, *The Protestant Reformation in Ireland 1590–1641*, new edition with new introduction, Dublin 1997, for a detailed explanation of the failure

to implement the Reformation in Ireland in the late sixteenth and early seventeenth centuries.

2 D.M. Bertie, *Scottish Episcopal Clergy 1689–2000*, Edinburgh 2000, pp. 539, 542, 616, 618, 625.

3 Useful chart of these secessions incorporated as a separate pull-out section in J.H.S. Burleigh, *A Church History of Scotland*, London 1960.

4 P.K. Monod, *Jacobitism and the English People, 1688–1788*, Cambridge 1989, pp. 129–30.

5 *Ibid.*, pp. 134–8; D. Szechi, *The Jacobites: Britain and Europe 1688–1788*, Manchester 1994, pp. 18–20; G. Holmes and D. Szechi, *The Age of Oligarchy: Pre-Industrial Britain 1722–1783*, London 1993, pp. 92, 97.

6 Szechi, *Jacobites*, p. 22. See also J.S. Chamberlain, 'The Jacobite failure to bridge the Catholic/Protestant divide, 1717–1730', in W. Gibson and R.G. Ingrams (eds), *Religious Identities in Britain, 1660–1832*, Aldershot 2005, pp. 81–95.

7 B. Hoadly, *A Preservative against the Principles and the Practices of the Nonjurors both in Church and State*, London 1716.

8 W.A. Speck, 'Whigs and Tories dim their glories: English political parties under the first two Georges', in J. Cannon (ed.), *The Whig Ascendancy: Colloquies on Hanoverian England*, London 1981, pp. 56–60.

9 L. Colley, *Britons: Forging the Nation 1707–1837*, London 1994, p. 81.

10 A.I. McInnes, 'Scottish Jacobitism: in search of a Movement', in T.M. Devine and J.R. Young (eds), *Eighteenth Century Scotland: New Perspectives*, East Linton 1999, pp. 74–5.

11 Monod, *Jacobitism and the English People*, pp. 141–4, 148–54.

12 See W. Gibson, *Establishment Prelate: Benjamin Hoadly, 1676–1761*, Cambridge 2004, pp. 147–98.

13 G.V. Bennett, *The Tory Crisis in Church and State 1688–1730: The Career of Francis Atterbury, Bishop of Rochester*, Oxford 1975, pp. 205–307.

14 H.T. Dickinson, *Liberty and Property: Political Ideology in Eighteenth-Century Britain*, London 1977, pp. 19, 53, 84.

15 *Ibid.*, pp. 167–8.

16 P. Langford, 'Convocation and the Tory clergy, 1717–61', in E. Cruickshank and J. Black (eds), *The Jacobite Challenge*, Edinburgh 1988, p. 107.

17 F. O'Gorman, *The Long Eighteenth Century: British Political and Social History 1688–1832*, London 1997, p. 147.

18 N. Sykes, *From Sheldon to Secker: Aspects of English Church History, 1660–1768*, Cambridge 1959, pp. 53–7.

19 W. Warburton, *The Alliance between Church and* State, 4th edn, London 1767, pp. 93–7.

20 *Ibid.*, p. 106.

21 *Ibid.*, pp. 115, 123, 170.

22 *Ibid.*, p. 202.

23 S.J.C. Taylor, 'William Warburton and the alliance of church and state', *Journal of Ecclesiastical History*, 43 (1992), pp. 271–86, quotation on last page.

24 *Ibid.*, p. 276.

25 See R.G. Ingram, 'William Warburton, divine action and enlightened christianity', in Gibson and Ingram (eds), *Religious Identities in Britain*, pp. 97–117.

26 J.B. Owen, *The Eighteenth Century 1714–1815*, London 1974, p. 157.

27 N. Sykes, *Edmund Gibson, Bishop of London, 1669–1748: A Study of Politics and Religion in the Eighteenth Century*, Oxford 1926, pp. 83–107, 137–42. Despite its date this is still a valuable study, but see also Sykes's revision of his earlier text in *William Wake, Archbishop of Canterbury, 1657–1737*, 2 vols, Cambridge 1957, ii, pp. 144–7.

28 W. Gibson, *The Church of England 1688–1832: Unity and Accord*, London 2001, pp. 89–91.

29 P. O'Regan, *Archbishop William King of Dublin (1650–1729) and the Constitution of Church and State*, Dublin 2000, pp. 210–332.

30 T.C. Smout, *A History of the Scottish People 1560–1830*, London 1969, pp. 230–2.

31 Colley, *Britons*, pp. 204–7, 229–30.

32 J.C.D. Clark, *English Society 1688–1832*, Cambridge 1985, pp. 179–84.

33 *Ibid.*, pp. 221–2, 230–4, 249–57.

34 O'Gorman, *Long Eighteenth Century*, p. 170.

35 A.C. Chitnis, *The Scottish Enlightenment: A Social History*, London 1976, pp. 49–51.

36 O'Gorman, *Long Eighteenth Century*, p. 296; Smout, *A History of the Scottish People*, p. 233.

37 C.G. Brown, *Religion and Society in Scotland since 1707*, Edinburgh 1997, pp. 18–19, 78.

38 Sykes, *From Sheldon to Secker*, pp. 194–6.

39 Ibid., pp. 198–9. See also S. Taylor, 'Bishop Edmund Gibson's proposals for church reform' in S. Taylor (ed.), *From Cranmer to Davidson: A Miscellany*, Church of England Record Society 7 (1999), pp. 169–202.

40 G.F.A. Best, *Temporal Pillars: Queen Anne's Bounty, the Ecclesiastical Commissioners and the Church of England*, Cambridge 1964, p. 85.

41 *Ibid.*, pp. 87, 93, 124–5.

42 J.V. Beckett, *The Aristocracy in England 1660–1914*, Oxford 1986, pp. 352–3.

43 Holmes and Szechi, *Age of Oligarchy*, p. 113; R. Porter, *English Society in the Eighteenth Century*, Harmondsworth 1982, pp. 190–1.

44 P. Langford, *A Polite and Commercial People: England 1727–1783*, Oxford 1989, p. 264.

45 P. Borsay, *The English Urban Renaissance: Culture and Society in the Provincial Town 1660–1770*, Oxford 1989, p. 242.

46 *Ibid.*, p. 247.

47 H.T. Dickinson, *Politics of the People in Eighteenth Century Britain*, Basingstoke 1995, p. 81.

CHAPTER 2

Dissent from the Religious Establishments

The established churches of the British Isles had, at no point since the Reformation, enjoyed a complete monopoly of religious belief and practice among the people. Small groups of Roman Catholic recusants had survived in England, Scotland and Wales and in Ireland, as previously stated, the majority of the population had remained Roman Catholic. From the early years of the seventeenth century groups of Protestant dissenters had seceded from established churches that they considered insufficiently pure in their Protestantism. In this chapter we will consider the strength of all these dissenting groups and their impact on the religious condition of the British Isles between 1714 and 1815.

Roman Catholics in England, Scotland and Wales

Throughout the seventeenth century the Roman Catholic communities of the British Isles had suffered sporadic persecution and there had been periods of political instability when the penal laws against Roman Catholics had been rigorously enforced. All this changed during the eighteenth century. Despite the complicity of many Roman Catholics in the Jacobite rebellion of 1715 no new measures were taken against them and the oath that they were obliged to take stated that they would 'live peaceably and quietly under his Majesty, King George, and the present government . . . and . . . not make use of any papal dispensation from the said oath'.[1] Although a vast amount of anti-papist legislation from the reigns of Elizabeth I, James I, Charles II and William III remained on the statute books little of it was enforced. Roman Catholics were, however, excluded from political office and practising as lawyers and they had to pay a double land tax. In the aftermath of the Atterbury plot a bill was passed to raise a levy of £100,000 on the Roman Catholic population, though it appears that only about two-thirds of this amount was actually collected.[2] Although Roman Catholics were excluded from political office they could, as landowners, influence elections and, although they were officially disenfranchised, there is some evidence of Roman Catholics having voted, for example in the Durham election of 1729.[3] Generally speaking, however, Roman Catholics accepted this political status, lived 'peaceably and quietly' and cultivated good relations with their Anglican neighbours.[4]

The Roman Catholic church outside Ireland was a missionary church, without a diocesan structure, ruled by bishops known as vicars apostolic. England and Wales had been divided into four vicariates in 1688, though there were periods when some of these were not filled. The London vicariate covered the south-east of England, the Midland vicariate a central section of England from the Welsh border to East Anglia, the Northern vicariate Cheshire, Lancashire, Yorkshire and the counties bordering Scotland and the Western vicariate south-west England and the whole of Wales. Many of the vicars apostolic were members of the aristocratic and gentry families that provided the lay leadership of the Roman Catholic community in England and Wales: Bishop Giffard of the London district (1703–34) was a member of a distinguished landed family in Staffordshire; Bishop Witham of the Midland district (1703–16) and the Northern district (1716–25) was born and died at Cliffe Hall in Yorkshire; his successor in the Midland district, Bishop Stonor (1716–56) was the grandson of the eleventh Earl of Shrewsbury; and Bishop Petre of the London district (1734–58) was a member of a wealthy family in Essex.[5] The most distinguished, however, of the eighteenth-century vicars apostolic was Richard Challoner, consecrated as coadjutor to Bishop Petre in 1741 and succeeding him in the London district in 1758. Unlike Petre, and most of the other vicars apostolic of this period, Challoner was of relatively humble birth, the son of a Sussex wine-cooper. His father was a Protestant dissenter but his mother, who was widowed early, was probably a Roman Catholic who entered the service of the Roman Catholic Gage family at Firle on the death of her husband. In 1704 she became housekeeper to Lady Anastasia Holman who arranged for the young Richard Challoner to be sent to Douai to train for the priesthood. Challoner had established his reputation as a devotional writer with his *Garden of the Soul* published in 1740. This was a detailed commentary on the Mass designed to provide a series of prayers for the laity to accompany the priest's actions at the altar. Challoner was a strong disciplinarian determined to correct what he considered the loose morality

and spiritual laxity of some of the London clergy. He instituted conferences of the clergy to discuss theological matters and issued regulations for
the conduct of their ministries. Since Petre was inactive for most of his
episcopate, Challoner effectively governed the London district for 40 years
until his death in 1781, transforming the effectiveness of the Roman
Catholic missions in the south-east of England.[6]

Although reliable statistics are not available it is likely that the number
of Roman Catholics in England and Wales declined from about 115,000 in
1720 to about 80,000 50 years later. This represents between one and two
per cent of the total population of England and Wales at the time. Some of
the more well-to-do families, frustrated at their inability to participate in
political and public life, converted to the established church.[7] The determination of Roman Catholics to keep a low profile and not to proselytise also
prevented an increase, and rather assisted a decline, in their numbers. The
Anglican incumbent of the parish that included the Essex estate of Lord
Petre stated in 1766 that 'there is no School for Popish Children; neither
hath any Visitation or Confirmation ever been held . . . none have been
converted to popery . . . within twenty years'.[8] The most reliable statistics
of the Roman Catholic population of England and Wales date from 1767
when an official census, authorised by Parliament, was carried out. This
suggested a Roman Catholic population of 69,376 though Bossy has
suggested that this is probably an underestimate and postulated the figure
of 80,000 mentioned earlier. In a series of distribution maps he shows
how the principal strength of landowning in 1715–20 was in Lancashire
where Roman Catholics owned more than 20% of the landed property
by value; this figure was above 10% in Monmouthshire and above 5%
in Sussex and some of the Midland counties. This distribution was
largely replicated in the 1767 census figures. Roman Catholics formed
more than 20% of the population in Durham and Lancashire, more than
10% in Northumberland, Monmouthshire, Staffordshire, Worcestershire
and Yorkshire, but less than 1% of the population in Cambridgeshire,
Cornwall, Devon, Northamptonshire, Westmorland and the whole of
Wales. The vicars apostolic reckoned that there were 392 Roman Catholic
priests in England and Wales in 1773, of which 217 were regulars (121
Jesuits, 44 Benedictines and 52 for other religious orders) and 175
seculars. Of these the largest numbers were in Lancashire (69), London
(42) and Yorkshire (36). There were only three priests in the whole of
Wales. In London the number of priests was swelled by those serving the
chapels of foreign embassies; elsewhere the number of priests was roughly
the same as the number of missions.[9]

The importance of Lancashire as providing the bedrock of Roman Catholic recusancy in eighteenth-century England cannot be over-emphasised. They were concentrated in areas around Blackburn, Lancaster, Liverpool, Manchester and Preston, where 5.6% of Roman Catholics belonged to gentry families compared with 1.6% of the population as a whole. In 1725 the Roman Catholic gentleman, John Shireburne, established six almshouses at Ribchester for a school teacher and Roman Catholic widows or single women. Not all the Roman Catholics in Lancashire were the servants or tenants of Roman Catholic landed families. There were also important groups of Roman Catholic artisans at Brindle, Little Plumpton, Samlesbury and Walton-le-Dale on the rural outskirts of Preston. In Preston itself there were five or six houses where Roman Catholics gathered to hear Mass and a contemporary commentator records that priests serving the adjacent rural missions used to gather there to consult on market days and that the vicar apostolic of the Northern district carried out regular visitations. Altogether he estimated that there were in the region of 700 Roman Catholics within the borough boundaries. The needs of Roman Catholic congregations were met by the publication of much devotional literature. In addition to Challoner's *Garden of the Soul*, John Gother published *Instructions and Devotions for Hearing Mass* which went through nine editions between 1705 and 1767. Another publication by Gother, containing translations of the collects, epistles and gospels read by the priest in Latin, together with devotions for the sick and instructions for confession, communion and confirmation, went through 15 editions between 1702 and 1796.[10]

Although it was not legal for Roman Catholics to build their own chapels until 1791,[11] we need to beware of the notion that Roman Catholic worship in England and Wales was liturgically impoverished or private chapels poorly furnished. Just as the hidden churches of the Netherlands could disguise their lavish Baroque interiors (as survive in Amsterdam, Delft and The Hague) so the Roman Catholic chapels of eighteenth-century England were fitted up to provide for the needs of worship, which was normally decent and occasionally even elaborate. A good example of such a chapel, retaining its original furnishings, survives at Milton House, near Oxford.[12] Between 1770 and 1776, as part of the rebuilding of Wardour Castle, the eighth Lord Arundell included an enormous Baroque chapel opened by Bishop Walmesley; its high altar was designed by the Italian architect Quarenghi and included a tabernacle of silver gilt; the chapel was further enlarged in 1788.[13] Even before free-standing chapels became legal in 1791, Thomas Weld of Lulworth had built one in the grounds of his

Dorset estate in 1786–7. The chapel at Stonor, free-standing but attached to the house, was refitted in 1796–1800. Both these early chapels survive more or less intact.[14] Roman Catholic worship in the eighteenth century was to some extent adapted to meet the needs of the local situation. Various forms of prayer, in English, were grafted on to the Latin Mass and included psalms, the Lord's Prayer, Acts of Faith, Hope, Charity and Contrition, the Litany of the Saints, *Te Deum* and prayers for the departed, the sick and the royal family. By the end of the eighteenth century most missions had a weekly, and some a daily, Mass. Communion was usually preceded by confession and fasting. Baptisms and confirmations were regular. Roman Catholic families were encouraged to observe the practice of household prayers and to keep the church's feast days as ones on which they should hear Mass and do no work.[15]

One significant problem for Roman Catholics from 1753 was Hardwicke's Marriage Act which, with the exception of Jews and Quakers, made all marriages celebrated outside the established church illegal. The legislation had been introduced by Lord Chancellor Hardwicke in order to deal with the growing problem of clandestine marriages and stated that for a marriage to be legal it had to be conducted by a clergyman of the Church of England in the parish church of one of the parties to the marriage, either after the publication of the banns of marriage, or by episcopal licence. The vicars apostolic disagreed on their reaction to the legislation, Bishop Stonor taking a fairly pragmatic view and Bishop Challoner being greatly disturbed by the necessity of Roman Catholics having to participate in a Protestant order of service. What eventually happened was that Roman Catholics had two marriage services, the legal one according to the rite provided in the *Book of Common Prayer* and a Roman Catholic one thereafter.[16]

For most Roman Catholics in the eighteenth century the services they attended would have been fairly simple Low Masses without music or much ceremonial. There were, however, exceptions to this rule, chief among them being some of the embassy chapels in London. The chapel of the Sardinian embassy was rebuilt in 1760 and provided an elaborate Baroque setting for equally elaborate services. On Sundays there were a series of Low Masses, High Mass and Vespers. The last two would have had a sermon – frequently preached by Bishop Challoner – and once a month Vespers would be followed by Benediction of the Blessed Sacrament. The Portuguese embassy chapel had seven Low Masses, High Mass and Vespers on Sundays and the full Holy Week Liturgy in the middle years of the eighteenth century. Many of the London chapels had elaborate musical settings for the main services.[17]

The continued existence of the Roman Catholic community in England and Wales depended on adequate provision for the catechising and religious education of children. The first cheap catechism was produced in the late seventeenth century and an even simpler version, for very young children, produced in the 1720s. In 1770 Bishop Challoner produced a much more extended catechism, containing 250 questions and answers, entitled *Abridgement of Christian Doctrine*. By the 1770s Bishop Walmesley was instructing his clergy to catechise regularly and gentry families to provide catechisms for the benefit of their servants and poor people on their estates. Roman Catholic schools proved harder to establish. A boarding school was established at Sedgley Park in Staffordshire in 1762. Some of the larger towns may have had private schools run by Roman Catholics, but the known presence of such an establishment was likely to lead to complaints from Anglican clergy, so Roman Catholic children were probably educated at Church of England charity schools. Some of the rural clergy endeavoured to provide some education for the Roman Catholic children in their mission districts or a landowner might establish a school for the children of his Roman Catholic tenants.[18]

Despite their growing integration into British society during the eighteenth century, negative feelings about Roman Catholics remained a powerful sentiment among much of the Protestant population. Linda Colley has argued that the emphasis placed by some historians on the differences between Anglicans and Protestant dissenters has tended to 'obscure what was still the most striking feature in the religious landscape, the gulf between Protestant and Catholic'.[19] There was a genuine fear of invasion designed to restore Roman Catholicism and the publication in 1732 of a new edition of Foxe's *Book of Martyrs*, with its graphic and exaggerated descriptions of the atrocities committed by Roman Catholics against Protestants, helped to ignite anti-Catholic feeling. Further editions of Foxe were published in 1761, 1776, 1784 and 1795.[20] Estimates in the press that there were 600,000 Roman Catholics in the country, an almost ten-fold exaggeration of the actual numbers, further inflamed popular anti-Catholicism.[21] It is not surprising that such sentiments occasionally led to violence against Roman Catholics and their property. There were such incidents at Stokesley (Yorks.) in 1745 and Hereford in 1756.[22] Anti-Catholic feelings were also released by press reports from Europe about either atrocities perpetrated against Protestants by Roman Catholic governments, especially Huguenots in France, or cases involving sexual indiscretions by Roman Catholic priests. Anti-Catholicism was also whipped up by some Anglican preaching on the theme of 'a just

Abhorrence of Popery', especially in the years following the 1745 Jacobite rebellion.[23] Between 1765 and 1771 a notorious anti-Catholic, William Payne, visited several Roman Catholic chapels in London in order to collect evidence to bring prosecutions under legislation which had not been removed from the statute book but which had rarely been implemented over the previous half-century. An Irish priest in London, John Baptist Molony, was prosecuted and found guilty of exercising the functions of a priest. Under the provisions of William III's anti-Catholic legislation he had to be sentenced to life imprisonment. The government was horrified and, after a decent interval had elapsed, Molony was granted a royal pardon on condition that he left the country.[24]

Government intervention to protect the Roman Catholic community was the first stage in a recognition that a repeal of anti-Catholic legislation was long overdue. One of the reasons for such legislation was the suspected political disloyalty of Roman Catholics, many of whom had been Jacobites. Jacobitism among Roman Catholics was in terminal decline by the late 1740s; 'once the Roman Catholics proved that they too were not necessarily enemies of the State then the penal laws against them were also gradually relaxed'.[25] In 1778 the first Catholic Relief Act was passed. Its provisions were fairly limited. In return for taking an oath of allegiance designed to be acceptable to Roman Catholics they were allowed to purchase land legally and their priests and schoolmasters were freed from the threat of arrest and imprisonment.[26] It was not extended to Scotland where Roman Catholics were still suspected of harbouring Jacobite sympathies. However, despite its fairly limited provisions, the Act was still too much for some Protestants, and the backlash that it provoked was to delay further measures of Roman Catholic relief in England and Wales until 1791 and in Scotland until 1793.[27] A Protestant Association, which argued that measures of Roman Catholic relief put the established churches of England and Scotland in danger and 'that the whole Protestant constitution was under threat', was set up in Edinburgh but had spread to London by 1779. In the same year there were anti-Catholic riots in Edinburgh and Glasgow and a petition demanding the repeal of the Act – the largest petition ever presented to Parliament during the eighteenth century – was signed by 26,000 people in Glasgow, 7,661 in Newcastle and 120,000 in London. The impact of the opposition to the Act was counter-productive since 'the mindless and alarming violence of the rioters' persuaded Parliament not to give in to the demands for repeal.[28]

The Protestant Association, under the leadership of Lord George Gordon, established branches in several English towns and cities – Bath,

Bridlington, Bristol, Canterbury, Carlisle, Norwich, Plymouth, Portsmouth, Rochester – and many small towns, and even villages, raised petitions for the repeal of the Act and the prevention of any further measures of Roman Catholic relief. The high point of the opposition to the Act was a week's rioting in London which began on 2 June 1780. A crowd of 60,000 marched on Parliament. There were attacks on the Sardinian and Bavarian embassy chapels; the former was burnt to the ground and the latter was ransacked and its contents burnt in the street. There were also attacks on other Roman Catholic chapels, on the houses of known Roman Catholics and those of prominent supporters of the Relief Act. The rioters attacked Newgate gaol, released all the prisoners and set the gaol on fire. Other prisons and business premises were attacked, one being a distillery where the alcohol burst into flames burning several of the employees alive. The military had to be called in to suppress the riots. Altogether 210 were killed during the riots and a further 75 subsequently died of their wounds. Although no other English towns experienced anything on the scale of the riots in London, there were smaller-scale demonstrations and riots in several other places. Roman Catholic chapels were destroyed at Bath and Hull and there were a large number of attacks on Roman Catholic families.[29] Colin Haydon, in opposition to the Marxist interpretation of the Gordon riots put forward by George Rudé,[30] sees the opposition to the Act 'as essentially reactionary and defensive, supportive of the pre-1778 *status quo*', the primary reason for such opposition being a belief that those who advocated relief for Roman Catholics were themselves 'Popishly inclined, since it was held that true Protestants could never entertain such views'. The Act had been, as far as they were concerned, simply 'a Catholic conspiracy'.[31]

It is, however, not without coincidence that the first measure of Catholic relief and its unfortunate aftermath should have come at a time when the Roman Catholic community in England and Wales was, for the first time in 200 years, beginning to increase in size. There were three reasons for this. The first was the non-implementation of statute-book provisions against Roman Catholics coupled with the strengthening of the Roman Catholic community by effective vicars apostolic such as Richard Challoner. A second was the beginning of Roman Catholic immigration from Ireland which had a particular impact on the north-west of England. The Lancashire towns of Liverpool, Manchester, Preston and Wigan had 4000 Roman Catholics in 1767 but 22,000 by 1810.[32] A third was the arrival of Roman Catholic refugees, especially priests and members of religious orders, from France and adjacent parts of Europe as a result of the anti-clericalist programme of the French government following the

Revolution of 1789. In this case the population of England had to decide which was more important to them, fear of Roman Catholicism or horror at events in France and sympathy for its victims, and the latter won. In 1794 Carmelite nuns from Antwerp settled in Cornwall, where in 1799–1800 the first clothing of a nun or building of a convent chapel since the Reformation took place. Several other foreign communities settled in England and new provision was made for Roman Catholic education for the laity, as well as the training of priests, with the establishment of the colleges at Stoneyhurst (Lancs.) and Ushaw, near Durham.[33] The expansion of English Roman Catholicism also led to an important shift in its social composition and the leadership traditionally associated with landed families. In Leeds before 1776 Roman Catholic worship had been provided at Red House, Roundhay, by the Duke of Norfolk. Following his death, responsibility for the provision of a place of worship came to be shared between his kinsman Lord Stourton and a merchant convert to Roman Catholicism, John Wade. In 1786 a new mission was established in Leeds by the cotton spinner Joseph Holdforth. Although in some places, such as Bath and Bristol, Roman Catholic landed families still effectively controlled the missions, there were large swathes of the North and Midlands, as well as London, where the leadership of the Roman Catholic community was passing from the aristocracy and gentry to the bourgeoisie.[34]

Roman Catholicism in Scotland was a very different phenomenon in the eighteenth century from what it was in England and Wales. In addition to the longer association with Jacobitism, the geographical distribution and social composition of the Roman Catholic community was very different, with very few Roman Catholics in the overwhelmingly Presbyterian lowlands and small but significant areas of Roman Catholic strength in the western highlands and islands, which had much more in common with Irish Roman Catholicism than that of England and Wales. This situation was recognised in 1727 when the number of vicariates was increased to two, with a new vicar apostolic for the *Gaidhealtachd*, the first appointee, Hugh Macdonald, being consecrated in 1731.[35] In parts of this new highland district no Presbyterian ministry had ever been established. It was alleged in 1720 that in 'Moydart, Knoydart, Arisaig, Morar, Glengarry, Braes of Lochaber, . . . the Western Isles of Uist, Barra, Benbecula, Canna, Egg . . . nothing is professed but the Roman Catholick religion'.[36] Returns in the late eighteenth century estimated between 1,200 and 1,250 Roman Catholics in Barra, between 2,300 and 2,500 in Uist, between 848 and 894 in Moidart, between 739 and 824 in Arisaig and between 1,340 and 1,400 in North Morar and Knoydart. These were large numbers for sparsely populated areas. There was, however, a serious shortage of clergy, with only about one priest for every 1,250 laity before 1750. From then the numbers of clergy grew from ten in 1750 to 22 by 1810.[37] By contrast there were very few Roman Catholics in the Lowland districts with only five recusants altogether in the counties of Ayrshire, Bute, Dunbartonshire, Lanarkshire, Renfrewshire and Wigtownshire. There were only five Roman Catholics in Glasgow in the 1780s. The main Roman Catholic presence was to be found in parts of north-east Scotland and on the Roman Catholic aristocratic estates of Drummond Castle, Stobhall, Terregles and Traquair. The weakness of Roman Catholicism in Scotland has been blamed on the serious lack of funds to support missions and the refusal of the Congregation of *Propagande Fide* in Rome to provide more financial support, divisions caused by Jansenism (which plagued other parts of the Roman Catholic church in the early eighteenth century), and the support offered by the vicars apostolic and their clergy to the Jacobite cause until well after the 1745 rebellion. Some Roman Catholic priests even apostatised to become Presbyterian ministers; others were guilty of sexual incontinence or alcoholism.

During the second half of the eighteenth century the Roman Catholic church in Scotland began to recover. The Highland vicariate opened a seminary on Lismore in 1768. Towards the end of the century two new churches were built on South Uist and one on Barra.[38] Emigration from the poverty-stricken highlands to the growing cities of the central lowlands resulted in the establishment of new and much more stable Roman Catholic congregations. This was the case at Edinburgh where the first proper chapel was opened in 1786. Glasgow acquired its first resident priest in 1792, the Roman Catholic community having grown substantially as a result of immigration from Ireland, and a subscription list for a new chapel was opened in 1797. The Roman Catholic community in Dundee grew from 14 communicants in 1782 to a congregation of 100 by the end of the decade. One of the most successful Roman Catholic missions was that around Braemar in Upper Deeside and it was largely unaffected by the decline of Roman Catholicism in other parts of rural Scotland. Between 1703 and 1736 776 baptisms were recorded with a total Roman Catholic population of 900 by 1764. By 1800 the parish of Braemar itself had a Roman Catholic majority and in the neighbouring parishes about a third of the population were Roman Catholics. Compared with England and Wales, Roman Catholic worship in Scotland was marked by liturgical poverty and shabbiness. Music was frowned on as it might upset the local Protestants. Low Mass and public recitation of the Rosary was the norm.

When High Mass was celebrated at the opening of a large new chapel for the Huntly mission in 1792 it was claimed to be the first time this had happened in Scotland since the Reformation.[39] The long, low building converted from a house and byre to serve as a chapel at Tynet (Moray) in 1787, the interior of which remains largely intact, is much more typical of the sort of building familiar to Scottish Roman Catholics before the nineteenth century.[40]

Roman Catholics in Ireland

As in other parts of the British Isles, attempts had been made, unsuccessfully, to extirpate Roman Catholicism in Ireland through sporadic persecution. Although Roman Catholicism had survived, the diocesan structure of the church had all but collapsed and many dioceses had no resident bishops for years on end. During the period of 1714 to 1815 between three-quarters and four-fifths of the population of Ireland were Roman Catholics.[41] By the 1720s, although all the penal legislation remained on the statute book, little attempt was made to enforce it and there was a resigned acceptance that the majority of the population would never be converted to Protestantism. However, Roman Catholics were barred from acquiring land, except on short leases, and from pursuing parliamentary, administrative, legal or military careers and some apostatised in order to avoid the restrictions on them. Between 1703 and 1800 there were 5,797 known converts from Roman Catholicism to the Church of Ireland. Despite this, the Roman Catholic communities in the towns gradually improved their economic and social position during the eighteenth century and by the 1760s the principal trade of Cork, Galway, Limerick and Waterford was in the hands of Roman Catholics. In Dublin Roman Catholic merchants were active within both the Committee of Merchants and, after 1783, the Chamber of Commerce. The cessation of active persecu-tion allowed the Roman Catholic church in Ireland to become pastorally effective. By 1731 there were 1,445 secular and 254 regular clergy and 892 mass-houses, though there were still places where Mass was celebrated in the open air. Most Roman Catholic dioceses had been provided with bishops though some were non-resident. In the larger towns new, and much more elaborate, chapels were built and at some there were choral services with a fair amount of ceremonial.

The British government recognised that the non-implementation of the penal legislation was not enough and put pressure on the Irish Parliament to agree to relief measures for Roman Catholics. The first step was the introduction of a new and more acceptable oath of allegiance in 1774. An Act of 1778 permitted Roman Catholics to lease land on much more generous terms than previously. In 1782 Roman Catholics were permitted to own land outright and not just to lease it. In the same year an Act of 1704, which had enforced the registration of priests, was repealed and Roman Catholics were permitted to become schoolteachers provided they only taught Roman Catholic children. In 1792 a very reluctant Irish Parliament was pressured to permit Roman Catholics to practice as lawyers and to marry Protestants. An Act of 1793, also passed under pressure from the British Government, permitted Roman Catholics to vote and gave them further educational rights. Before 1789 most priests serving in Ireland had been educated at seminaries in Catholic Europe but this became impossible after the French Revolution and in 1795 the British government made an initial grant of £8,000 to the Irish Roman Catholic bishops to establish a seminary at Maynooth. When rebellion broke out in Ireland in the 1790s very few Roman Catholic clergy were involved and the bishops were united in their opposition to it. As a result the British government relied heavily on the support of the Roman Catholic bishops to achieve its objective of abolishing the Irish Parliament and creating a United Parliament for Britain and Ireland. The Act of Union came into force on 1 January 1801. One of the considerations that had induced the bishops to support the union was the clear hints given by the British government that union would be speedily followed by full political emancipation for both Roman Catholics and Protestant dissenters. Unfortunately the government was unable to persuade King George III to agree to the necessary legislation and the Roman Catholics of Ireland felt bitterly betrayed by the government's inability to deliver its side of the bargain.

From the last quarter of the eighteenth century a major reform movement took place in the Roman Catholic church in Ireland, spearheaded by bishops such as Francis Moylan of Kerry (1775–87) and Cork (1787–1815) and John Thomas Troy, Bishop of Ossory (1776–86) and Archbishop of Dublin (1786–1823). This included the carrying out of more frequent and more exhaustive visitations and the publication of new diocesan statutes. Those for Ferns in 1771 laid down that the sacraments must not be administered to any apostates or those who had broken the rule of abstinence from meat on fast days; they tightened the regulations governing the hearing of confessions and the saying of Mass; priests or friars were not allowed to beg, or to celebrate in chapels belonging to others without the bishop's permission; and patterns – religious festivals which it was claimed had too often degenerated into drunkenness and debauchery – were strongly discouraged. The Raphoe Statutes of 1782 forbade arranged marriages and ordered the recitation of public prayers at Mass for the royal family and the Lord Lieutenant. Bishops strongly encouraged the proper keeping of parochial registers, preaching and the prevention of mixed marriages between Roman Catholics and Protestants. New devotions imported from Europe were also promoted by reforming bishops and clergy and the first Irish branch of the Confraternity of the Sacred Heart was established in Dublin in 1809. The Christian Brothers were founded, as a teaching order, in 1801 and the Patrician Brothers in 1808. The Ursuline Sisters were established in Cork from 1771 and the first convent of Presentation Sisters, a native Irish order, was founded in 1775.

The poverty of Irish Roman Catholics meant that well into the nineteenth century church buildings, and the services carried out within them, were very modest, even shabby. This was especially the case in the country areas. Most churches were simple, thatched, barn-like structures which often doubled up as schools. Good examples of such churches survive in the former Tullyallan mass house, built in 1768 and now re-erected with a reconstructed interior at the Ulster American Folk Park near Omagh, and at Ardkeen (Co. Down) where the chapel of 1777 has late eighteenth- or early nineteenth-century furnishings. From the last quarter of the eighteenth century a major programme of church building was inaugurated by reforming bishops. Thirty new chapels were erected in the diocese of Clogher between 1786 and 1814, and the church erected at Callan (Co. Kilkenny) cost £4,000. When funding was not available for a complete rebuilding, existing chapels were repaired and often extended, additional accommodation frequently being provided by the erection of galleries. Because churches often had to serve a very large Roman Catholic population they normally contained little seating and this was usually in the form of private pews erected by the more prosperous families at their own cost. In the larger towns more expensive and elaborate chapels were being erected from the middle years of the eighteenth century. These included the handsome cathedral at Waterford, built in 1793–6 at a cost of £20,000, and the more modest cathedral at Cork in the following decade. The foundation stone of an ambitious new pro-cathedral in Dublin was laid in 1815, though the building took a further 20 years to complete.

Scottish Episcopalians

For the first 30 years after the formal abolition of episcopacy in Scotland in 1689, episcopalian clergy continued to minister in parts of the now fully

presbyterian Church of Scotland. What finally drove them out of the established church was their continued support for the Jacobite cause and,
in the wake of the disastrous rising of 1745–6, they suffered under penal
legislation that was even more severe than that to which Roman Catholics
were subjected. Their position was further weakened by the fact that there
were groups of Anglicans worshipping in Scotland in what were known as
'qualified chapels', buildings which had official sanction, where the clergy
took an oath to the crown, and where services were conducted according
to the liturgy of the *Book of Common Prayer*.[42] The surviving bishops
of the pre-1689 Church of Scotland, although initially unwilling to set up
a rival church, did take action in 1705 to maintain the episcopal succession
and invited English non-juring bishops to participate in these consecra-
tions. The links between the Scottish episcopalians and the English
non-jurors were to lead to a good deal of common liturgical thinking
across the two communities, which produced the non-jurors' liturgy of
1734, Thomas Rattray's liturgy of about 1740 and the Scottish
Communion Office of 1764.[43] The last of these came to be the normal
usage of episcopalians operating outside the orbit of the qualified chapels,
though it was celebrated with very little in the way of ceremonial, the
episcopal clergy wearing the black gowns (rather than the surplices
used in the Church of England) also worn by Presbyterian ministers and
designing their buildings so that, even internally, they were largely indis-
tinguishable from those of the established Church of Scotland. Doctrinally,
however, the Scottish episcopalians adhered to a distinctly 'high church'
theology which was at variance with their liturgical practice. On the death
of Prince Charles Edward Stuart, the 'Young Pretender', in 1788, the
Scottish bishops finally abandoned their Jacobitism and resolved to pray
publicly for George III, and in 1792 most of the penal legislation against
episcopalians was repealed, though they were still prevented from holding
benefices, and even celebrating services or preaching, in the Church of
England. By that date episcopalianism was largely confined to the north-
east of Scotland, though with pockets of strength in the western highlands
and islands. There were only seven episcopalian clergy in the south of
Scotland though there were a number of qualified chapels. In 1804 an
accommodation was agreed between the Scottish bishops and the clergy
of the qualified chapels, whereby the Episcopal Church formally accepted
the Thirty-Nine Articles of Religion and the use of the *Book of Common
Prayer* alongside that of the Scottish Communion Office. Over the half-
century following this agreement all but one of the qualified chapels
formally entered the Episcopal Church.

One of the major centres of episcopalianism in Scotland was Aberdeenshire and it was here, under the leadership of Bishop John Skinner, that the surviving episcopalian remnant began to revive and to lay the foundations of the modern Episcopal Church. Parishes with large numbers of episcopalians in the 1790s included Crimond, Cruden, Deer, Forgue, Fyvie, Longside, Lonmay, Rathen and Turriff. There were over 1,000 episcopalians in the town of Peterhead, about a quarter of the total population. In the western highlands and islands, where episcopalianism was still strong in the early years of the eighteenth century, congregations had to struggle against both their restrictions under the penal legislation and the difficulty of recruiting Gaelic-speaking clergy. As a result some episcopalians, as at Duirinish on Skye, attended and communicated in the parish church. By the 1790s the only strong congregations were those of Appin, Daviot and Dunlichity, Killearnan, Kilmale and Urray. There were also significant groups of episcopalians in Perthshire at Blair Atholl, Logierait and Muthill. Shortage of clergy meant that, even where chapels existed, services were only held once or twice a month as the clergy had to serve several chapels at some distance from one another. The survival of episcopalianism, like that of Roman Catholicism, owed much to the rigidity with which some landed families remained true to the episcopalian cause. Where this did not happen, as in Morvern, where Presbyterian landowners ensured that an area was provided with an energetic parish minister, strong areas of episcopalianism had become equally strong areas of Presbyterianism by the end of the eighteenth century. This was compounded by the difficulty of finding Gaelic-speaking clergy to serve Gaelic-speaking congregations at the same time that the Church of Scotland was at last beginning to address the spiritual and social needs of Gaelic-speaking communities.

Irish Presbyterians

Irish Presbyterianism was a legacy of Scottish immigration into Ireland in the seventeenth century. It was strongest in the north-east province of Ulster but there were also groups of Presbyterians in Dublin, the other larger towns in Ireland and some 'plantation' towns of the south-west.[44] Although Irish Presbyterians suffered from the same political restrictions as English and Welsh nonconformists, they were permitted to worship freely and they even enjoyed some financial support from the government in the form of the *regium donum* paid to Presbyterian ministers. Their ministers were largely educated at the Scottish universities with the result that doctrinal divisions in the Church of Scotland tended to be replicated in Ireland. In 1726 there was a schism within the Synod of Ulster which led to the setting up of the separate Presbytery of Antrim, which wanted a more liberal interpretation of the doctrines of the Westminster Confession. By the end of the eighteenth century Irish Presbyterians were divided into four groups: the liberals in the Presbytery of Antrim, the moderate conservatives in the Synod of Ulster and two groups of strict Calvinists, split, as in Scotland, into Burghers and Anti-Burghers. In 1799 there was a total of 266 Presbyterian congregations across the four groups. On the whole Irish Presbyterians tended to espouse the same radical causes as English nonconformists with the result that more Presbyterian ministers than Roman Catholic priests were accused of involvement in the Irish Rebellion of 1798.

Irish Presbyterians and their clergy tended to belong to the same social grouping as Irish Roman Catholics. About a third of the clergy were sons of farmers and many Presbyterian ministers, like Roman Catholic priests, supplemented their incomes by farming. The cost of following a university course in Scotland through to graduation led to the setting up of academies, to provide a pre-university education for ministers, at Belfast and Strabane in 1785. In 1810 the Belfast Academical Institution was established with a government grant of £1,500. Unlike the Church of Ireland or the Roman Catholic Church, Presbyterian laity in Ireland exercised a significant role at every level of church government. The fundamental unit of administration was the kirk session which comprised the minister and elders of each congregation. Children were baptised, catechumens admitted to communion and marriages conducted only by resolution of the kirk session. The session also examined each member prior to a communion service, usually held only once or twice a year, and decided who would receive tokens allowing them to participate. It was also responsible for the administration of poor relief among the congregation and deciding who should and who should not be helped. Decisions about participation in communion and receipt of poor relief tended to be made on the basis of the ministers' and elders' perception of the individual morality and spirituality of each adult member of the congregation. The kirk sessions also maintained the church and its furnishings, appointed a precentor to lead the singing (musical accompaniment not being permitted), regulated the seating arrangements in church, organised missionary societies and Sunday schools, provided Bibles to members of the congregation who could not afford them, set up libraries and, wherever possible, established schools and appointed the teachers. From time to time kirk sessions would hold 'trials' of members of the congregation accused of crimes such as adultery, fornication, assault, drunkenness, theft, fraud, gaming, perjury or witchcraft. Those found guilty had to make a public confession of their sins before the whole congregation and, for the most serious offences, were excommunicated. As was the case for both the Church of Ireland and the Roman Catholic Church, the late eighteenth and early nineteenth centuries were a period of church building and extension for Irish presbyterians. The most ambitious, though it has been altered internally, was the Rosemary Street Chapel in Belfast, a handsome, elliptical building of 1783.

Protestant dissenters in England and Wales

The Toleration Act of 1689 had effectively given Protestant dissenters freedom of worship but had restricted them politically and, to some extent, socially. Under the Act they were exempted from the earlier compulsion to attend parish churches, they could worship in their own chapels provided these had been licensed by either the diocesan authorities or the justices of the peace and provided the doors were unlocked during services, and their ministers were allowed to function provided they took an oath rejecting the doctrine of transubstantiation and subscribing to 35 of the Thirty-Nine Articles of Religion (Baptists being also exempted from the article on infant baptism and Quakers from that on taking oaths).[45] There were attempts in the reign of Queen Anne 'to revive a coercive Church-State . . . when anti-Dissenter legislation sought to stamp out occasional conformity and bring all forms of education under Anglican control', but these were short-lived. Between 1714 and 1815 the principal disabilities of dissenters were having to pay church rates as well as contributing towards the upkeep of their own meeting houses, having to marry in the parish church (a position enforced by Hardwicke's Marriage Act of 1753) and sometimes being refused burial in parochial churchyards by high church Anglican clergy.[46] Politically, the position of dissenters was anomalous and depended on their willingness to communicate at Anglican celebrations of Holy Communion. Provided they could produce a certificate recording their reception of the sacrament, dissenters could attend the universities, enter the civil service and hold political office, a position known as 'occasional conformity'. It was estimated that there were about 40 occasional conforming members of Parliament in the eighteenth century.[47]

The Whig governments of the 1720s and 1730s were generally sympathetic to lifting restrictions on dissenters and reducing the privileges of the Church of England though they were unwilling to go too far in this direction. The provisions of an act passed in 1711 for building 50 new Anglican churches in London was abandoned in 1725 long before the projected programme was completed. Bills to prevent suits for tithes and the translation of bishops were proposed in 1730, and bills to reform the ecclesiastical courts and church rates in 1733. In 1735–6, though attempts to repeal the Test and Corporation Acts were unsuccessful, the Mortmain and Quaker Relief Bills were passed by the House of Commons, though subsequently defeated in the House of Lords.[48] As a result most dissenters were Whigs in politics. Although they were disappointed that Walpole had not supported the repeal of the Test and Corporation Acts in 1736, or subsequently in 1739, they applauded the repeal of the Occasional Conformity and Schism Acts in 1718 and the grant of *regium donum* payments to dissenting ministers, replicating those to Presbyterian clergy in Ireland, in 1723.[49] The strength of dissenting support for Whig candidates can be seen in election voting figures, as shown in Table 2. The political opinions of dissenters were informed by a vibrant nonconformist press not replicated by Anglicans. These included such publications as the *Old Whig* established by the London dissenting minister, Samuel Chandler, in 1735.[50]

TABLE 2 *Proportion of Anglicans and dissenters voting for Whig candidates in selected borough elections 1734–68*

Borough election	Date	Anglicans voting for Whig candidates (%)	Dissenters voting for Whig candidates (%)
Abingdon	1734	53.2	100
Abingdon	1754	32.1	100
Bristol	1754	50.3	82.4
Great Yarmouth	1754	47.5	65.6
Shrewsbury	1734	50.0	100
Shrewsbury	1747	45.2	100

Source: J.E. Bradley, *Religion, Revolution and English Radicalism: Nonconformity in Eighteenth-Century Politics and Society*, Cambridge 1990, p. 109.

One of the pressure groups set up to obtain further political advantages for dissenters, and particularly the repeal of the Test and Corporation Acts which necessitated occasional conformity to secure political or public office, was the Protestant Dissenting Deputies, formed in 1732 by representatives of Presbyterian, Independent and Baptist congregations meeting in and around London.[51] Although they had been set up primarily as a pressure group for specific political purposes, the Deputies frequently got involved in legal disputes about such matters as the registration of meeting houses and the payment of church rates. Between 1740 and 1812 they intervened in 241 such disputes, though they would only do so, and contribute to the costs, if they had been consulted beforehand. Occasionally they paid the fines of people convicted of breaches of the law. They also initiated legal actions where they felt that magistrates had interpreted the law incorrectly, as was the case at Stratton (Wilts.) in 1741 where they had refused to grant warrants against rioters who had broken the windows of a meeting house and insulted the congregation. In 1792 they successfully petitioned the government to offer a reward for the apprehension of those burning down a meeting house at Guilsborough (Northants.). They did not, however, totally ignore the purpose for which they had been established, namely to secure changes in the laws that restricted the activities of dissenters. In 1779 dissenting ministers were released from the obligation to subscribe to most of the Thirty-Nine Articles and could be licensed provided they accepted the Bible as the basis of Christianity.[52] Further attempts, however, to repeal the Test and Corporation Acts in 1787, 1789 and 1790 were unsuccessful; even so it is notable that, even though only six MPs were dissenters on these occasions, between 98 and 105 MPs voted for repeal, possibly, in some cases, in order to placate dissenters in their constituencies.[53] One of the Deputies' major campaigns was to oppose a bill introduced in the House of Lords by Lord Sidmouth in 1810 to prevent the licensing of any person

as a preacher or teacher, unless he had attained the age of twenty-one, was appointed to a congregation, and could produce testimonials of his fitness for his office from some persons of the same religious persuasion.[54]

Sidmouth had alleged that people were being licensed as dissenting ministers in order to claim 'exemption from parish offices and the militia'. The Deputies disputed this claim and secured the eventual defeat of Sidmouth's proposals.

The general picture of the pattern of dissent in the eighteenth century was one of decline in the first half and revival, partly associated with that of Evangelicalism (discussed in the next chapter), in the second half. Indeed membership may have shrunk by about 40% in the years between 1700 and 1740 and has been described as 'moderate, anti-enthusiastic, and moral-minded . . . essentially bourgeois'.[55] It was particularly weak outside the towns, though in most of the larger ones, such as Bristol and Norwich, as many as a third of the population were dissenters.[56]

TABLE 3 *Numbers of Independent, Baptist, Presbyterian and Quaker meeting houses certified as places of worship in England 1721–1810*

Decade	Independents	Baptists	Presbyterians	Quakers
1721–30	38	37	32	33
1731–40	4	58	62	85
1741–50	27	56	74	75
1751–60	56	64	106	32
1761–70	101	86	52	25
1771–80	191	74	56	13
1781–90	221	119	15	12
1791–1800	644	244	16	23
1801–10	603	314	23	32

Source: A.D. Gilbert, *Religion and Society in Industrial England*, London 1976, p. 34.

Presbyterians and Quakers continued to decline throughout the eighteenth century, many of the congregations becoming Unitarian in doctrine. Most of the other groups of dissenters experienced a revival in the second half of the eighteenth century. The Independents increased from 15,000 in 1750 to 26,000 by 1790 and 35,000 by 1800; the Particular Baptists from 10,000 in 1750 to 17,000 by 1790 and 24,000 by 1800.[57] A similar increase is shown in the statistics of congregations shown in Table 3. A very detailed analysis of both the size and distribution of Protestant dissent in England and Wales is provided by the Evans manuscript in Dr Williams's Library. This was a list compiled by Dr John Evans of every Presbyterian, Independent and Baptist Congregation. It can be supplemented by other sources to give an indication of the total number of dissenting congregations and the total number of dissenters in the 1720s as shown in Table 4. It can be seen from these figures that the size of Protestant dissent in England and Wales in the second decade of the eighteenth century was not a serious threat to the Anglican establishment.

An analysis of the distribution of dissent in this period reveals very few counties in which any particular dissenting group accounted for more than one-twentieth of the population. The exceptions were Presbyterians in Bristol, Carmarthenshire, Cheshire, Devon, Dorset, Lancashire, Northumberland and Somerset; Independents in Cardiganshire and Radnorshire; Particular Baptists in Bedfordshire, Monmouthshire and Radnorshire; and Quakers in Bristol. The highest proportion of any

TABLE 4 *Total numbers of congregations and adherents of main dissenting groups in England and Wales in the 1720s*

Dissenting group	Congregations	Adherents	% of population
Presbyterians	662	185,430	3.22
Independents	229	67,580	1.18
Particular Baptists	220	44,570	0.77
General Baptists	122	18,800	0.33
Quakers	696	39,510	0.69
All Dissenters	1,929	355,890	6.19

Source: M. Watts, *The Dissenters from the Reformation to the French Revolution*, Oxford 1978, pp. 269–70.

dissenting group to the population as a whole was in Carmarthenshire where Presbyterians numbered 4,750 (13.8%) out of a total population of 34,430.[58] One of the features of nonconformity in Wales was the rejection of Calvinism and adoption of Arminianism by most of the Presbyterians and some of the Independent congregations. Many of these Arminians later became Arians (believing that the Son was not of the same substance as the Father) and thereafter Socinians or Unitarians. A strong influence on these developments was 'the liberal atmosphere of Carmarthen academy', one of the principal places of education for future ministers. A former Carmarthen student established the Arminian, later Unitarian, meeting at Llwynrhydowen (Cards.) in 1733, and 'half a dozen Arminian congregations in the Teifi valley' by 1770.[59]

Anglican attitudes to dissenters tended to be mixed. Some high church-men, who had supported the measures against dissenters in Queen Anne's reign, deplored the more tolerant attitude of the Whig administrations under George I and George II and a good deal of polemical anti-dissenting literature continued to be produced throughout the eighteenth century. Anglican high churchmen were certainly in the forefront of lobbying groups that pressed successive governments against further measures of toleration, particularly the repeal of the Test and Corporation Acts, and they were critics of the practice of occasional conformity. Other Anglicans, including several bishops, supported it. Dissenters generally, with the exception of the Baptists, tended also to support the practice. Edward Calamy, a Presbyterian divine, 'argued that Dissenters were in fact united to the Anglican church in faith and doctrine and should demonstrate their love for the Church by occasional communion with her'.[60] Many Anglicans also took the view that there was little doctrinally to separate 'orthodox' (i.e. non-Arian or non-Socinian) dissenters from the Church of England and a number of unsuccessful attempts were made to amend the Thirty-Nine Articles and the *Book of Common Prayer* to make them more acceptable to dissenters. Dissenters and 'low church' Anglicans sometimes united politically at election time against 'high church' Anglicans to return Whig candidates and defeat Tories. Thus at St Albans in 1722 dissenters and Anglican low churchmen combined to defeat the Tory candidate favoured by Anglican high churchmen by 287 votes to 226. Of the 287 votes cast for the Whig candidate, 158 came from Anglicans. Political cooperation between dissenters and 'low church' Anglicans also ensured that some municipalities, such as those of Bridport, Coventry and Nottingham, were effectively controlled by 'Dissenting oligarchies'.[61]

The traditional view that there were significant differences between Anglicans and dissenters in terms of their position in the social structure of England and Wales can no longer be sustained. All the evidence, such as that indicated in Table 5, suggests that, on the contrary, there was no significant difference between Anglicans and dissenters in social terms. Bradley concludes that:

The most certain conclusion to be drawn from these occupational data . . . is that Dissenters held about as many professional, wholesale and retail positions as Anglicans . . . and thus Nonconformists, at least in the large urban centres, were clearly not inferior to Anglicans from an occupational standpoint.[62]

There were of course, exceptions to this overall picture. The Presbyterian meeting at Court Yard, Southwark, in 1729–35 had a rather different social mix: no gentlemen or merchants and only 2.6% of the congregation were professionals, compared with 21% tradesmen, 68.4% artisans and 5.3% labourers or servants. The Particular Baptists at Hengoed (Glam.) could number only two gentlemen in a congregation otherwise composed of 85 farmers and 140 labourers.[63] In the sections that follow we will look at the overall fortunes of the four main groups of dissenters – Presbyterians, Independents, Baptists and Quakers – in England and Wales between 1714 and 1815, and more specifically at their development in one part of England, Lincolnshire.

The Presbyterians, as we have seen, began this period as the largest single group of Protestant dissenters but they ended it much weaker than either the Baptists or the Independents. The Presbyterians were the principal successors of that Puritan tradition which had been largely excluded from the Church of England in 1662. More than any of the other dissenting

TABLE 5 *Comparison of social structure of Anglican and dissenting congregations in selected English towns in the late eighteenth century*

Bristol	Anglicans (%)	Dissenters (%)
Gentlemen/professions	2.4	9.9
Merchants	3.0	9.7
Shopkeepers	21.8	30.3
Artisans	44.3	38.4
Labourers	27.6	10.8
Others	0.9	0.7
Hull		
Gentlemen/professions	3.5	5.4
Merchants	2.4	5.1
Shopkeepers	18.3	16.3
Artisans	33.8	34.4
Labourers	41.2	36.6
Others	0.7	2.2
Liverpool		
Gentlemen/professions	4.8	2.9
Merchants	5.4	7.7
Shopkeepers	12.9	14.5
Artisans	46.7	37.6
Labourers	30.0	33.8
Others	0.2	3.5
Newcastle		
Gentlemen/professions	6.8	4.3
Merchants	5.4	7.7
Shopkeepers	12.9	14.5
Artisans	46.7	37.6
Labourers	30.0	33.8
Others	0.2	3.5

Source: J.E. Bradley, *Religion, Revolution and English Radicalism: Nonconformity in Eighteenth-Century Politics and Society*, Cambridge 1990, pp. 63–6.

groups they were pervaded by rationalist influences from Europe during the eighteenth century and moved towards Arianism and Socinianism as the century progressed and away from subscription to the Westminster Confession that they had formulated in the 1640s. At the beginning of the eighteenth century there were 18 Presbyterian congregations in

Lincolnshire including two each in Lincoln and Stamford. By 1800 seven out of ten of their meetings were in the towns of the county. Although most still described themselves as 'Presbyterian' they were in practice 'Independent', and in many cases 'the deed to which they subscribed lacked a formal doctrinal statement', the meeting at Lincoln identifying itself as 'that separate congregation or Church of Christ'. Numbers were generally in decline. There were 253 'hearers' at Boston in 1717, but when a new meeting house was built in 1738 it only provided sittings for 60 people. With ministers not being required to subscribe a formal confession of faith, they had 'the liberty to pursue new theological perspectives'. The meeting at Gainsborough had become Arian by the early eighteenth century and its minister for over 40 years, Jeremiah Gill, was considered by contemporaries to be 'not an orthodox preacher'.[64]

Independents did not exist in early eighteenth-century Lincolnshire, and their growth during the late eighteenth and early nineteenth centuries resulted largely from the collapse of Presbyterianism in the county. Nationally they were the descendents of those Puritans who had rejected both episcopacy and presbytery in the 1640s and 1650s. They believed in the concept of the 'gathered church', each congregation being able to regulate its own doctrine and ministry. Many churches came into being as a result of lay rather than ministerial initiative. They differed from Presbyterians 'in demanding not only a profession of faith from candidates for membership and for admission to Holy Communion, but an account of Christian experience', what in later Evangelical parlance would be described as 'conversion'. The strength of Independency in the eighteenth century was in those counties which had been the earliest centres of Puritanism in the late sixteenth century and the strongest supporters of the parliamentary cause during the English Civil Wars: East Anglia, Hertfordshire, Northamptonshire, Monmouthshire and other parts of South Wales. Whilst generally Calvinist in doctrine until the eighteenth century they were also heavily infected with Arian and Socinian doctrines, though not to such a great extent as the English and Welsh Presbyterians.[65]

By the eighteenth century the Baptists in England and Wales had lost their reputation for extreme religious radicalism that had characterised the Anabaptists during the Reformation. They were divided theologically into Arminian or General Baptists and Calvinist or Particular Baptists. What they agreed on was the necessity for adult baptism after a personal confession of faith and they therefore rejected the practice of infant baptism carried out by Anglicans, Roman Catholics and most other Protestant dissenters. Most ministers were part-time, supporting themselves in another profession or trade, and the administration of the meeting house and of charity towards the poorer members of the congregation was entrusted to deacons. The more limited theological education of Baptist ministers tended to make them, and their congregations, most resistant to the liberal theology that had such an impact on Presbyterians and Independents. They were the first religious group in England and Wales to adopt the singing of hymns in their worship, a practice strongly resisted by both Anglicans and other Protestant dissenters, in some cases until well into the nineteenth century. Baptists developed an enormous seriousness about the two biblical sacraments of baptism and Holy Communion. Few congregations, except in the large towns, had specially constructed baptisteries for total immersion and tended to use local streams or baptise in the sea. Church members were expected to communicate at what was normally a monthly celebration of Holy Communion and disciplinary action was frequently taken against a member who did not 'fill up his place at the Lord's Table'. It was common practice to 'fence' the tables before communion and to have a communal meal, a 'conscious remembrance of the New Testament *agapē*', afterwards. Baptists were, as a result, divided over 'whether they should communicate only with baptized believers, or should open the Table to other than those baptized as adults', with Particular Baptists normally adopting the former, and general Baptists the latter, practice. Discipline in the congregation was strict with members being punished for moral lapses, attending other churches or other 'improper' behaviour.[66]

The Baptists were the strongest of the dissenting groups in Lincolnshire, accounting for about half, possibly slightly more, of the Protestant dissenters in the county. The meetings were grouped into a County Association which laid down stringent conditions for personal behaviour and sought 'to bear witness against vain apparel, mixed marriages, games of chance, and other practices . . . inconsistent with the simplicity and gravity of the Christian character'. At a general meeting of the Boston congregation in 1765 a division was made between 'atrocious crimes' – adultery, theft, fornication, covetousness, extortion and drunkenness – and 'disorderly walking': members who did not work, busybodies and 'division makers'. Isaac Yates, a member of the Coningsby meeting, was condemned in 1723 for swearing, playing cards and attending cock fights. In 1743 Isaac Turner of Boston was excommunicated for 'the great sin of fleshly fornication with his servant girl she being with child by him'. Some Baptist congregations declined during the first half of the eighteenth century – Boston had

73 members in 1738 but only about 40 by 1762 – but generally recovered during the second half, several congregations being described as 'pretty large' in the 1770s.[67]

In the seventeenth century the Quakers, more correctly but less popularly known as the Society of Friends, were one of the more radical religious groups, but by the eighteenth century they had become respectable and one of the dissenting groups most devoted to 'good works'. They were still regarded as 'mildly eccentric' but were generally treated with respect. They were 'either by law or their own convictions' excluded from the universities, the army, the law and parliament, with the result that they channelled their energies into trade and industry and used their new-found wealth to fund charitable institutions such as schools and hospitals. They included among their numbers such major banking families as the Barclays, the Gurneys, the Hoares and the Lloyds, as well as physicians and advocates of penal reform.[68] They were also very skilful lobbyists, succeeding in getting parliamentary changes made to the Affirmation Act of 1696 in 1722 and the Quaker Tithe Bill through the House of Commons in 1736; this was, however, defeated in the House of Lords, as were attempts to pass similar legislation, designed to prevent the prosecution of Quakers for non-payment of tithes, in 1786 and 1796.[69] The Quakers were quite numerous in Lincolnshire, with 16 meeting houses in 1727 catering for a membership of over 1,000, but they suffered a major decline in the 70 years thereafter and only had a membership of 180 across the county in 1799. As with the Baptists, discipline was strict, particularly in relation to marriages. In 1744 the Lincolnshire Quarterly Meeting set its face against the approval of marriage between Quakers and non-Quakers, though this did happen from time to time and indeed could result in the non-Quaker being brought into the Society of Friends. The number of prosecutions for non-payment of tithes appears to have decreased in Lincolnshire during the eighteenth century, partly because some Quakers were clearly paying them. In 1777 the Gainsborough Monthly Meeting recorded that, although most of its members were still refusing to pay tithes, 'yet some others are deficient therein'.[70]

Whereas the Quakers deliberately set themselves apart from other religious bodies and organised their own charities, other Protestant dissenters were more willing to accept that they were 'parishioners', even if they did not worship in the parish church. Presbyterians willingly accepted the poor relief provided by the overseers of the poor elected by the annual parochial vestry meeting. Independents and Baptists accepted parish relief but, unlike Presbyterians, made separate provision for assisting their poorer members. All these bodies were also willing to contribute to appeals for money from parochial sources. The Independents at Wrentham (Suff.) raised 2s 5½d for the victims of fire in Dorchester, 5s 3d for those of storms in Staffordshire and 11s 1d for those of floods in Lancashire.[71] These sums, in response to parochial briefs, were frequently larger than those contributed by Anglicans to such appeals, even though it was the government and parish churches that operated the system of briefs. Baptists and Quakers were generally able to raise more to support their poorer members in need of financial assistance than Presbyterians and Independents as, unlike them, they did not have a paid ministry. Paying the clergy could be a heavy burden on Presbyterian and Independent Congregations. Philip Doddridge at Knibworth (Leics.) had to survive on a salary of not more than £35 a year in 1723; although this was similar to the stipend of a poorer Anglican incumbent, the latter might also be provided with a house, whereas a dissenting minister normally had to find his own and pay for it out of his salary. Unlike his Anglican counterpart, he had no security of tenure and could be removed, almost at will, by the congregation. At Guestwick (Norf.) the congregation decided in 1721 to build a manse for the minister but found themselves with a very unsatisfactory one that they could only get out of the manse by paying him £15 in lieu of salary.[72]

In the first half of the eighteenth century Protestant dissenters, despite theological differences, tended to express their doctrines in the same rather dry and pragmatic way that characterised the established churches. This was almost certainly the reason for their decline in this period. The Evangelical Revival, which will be discussed in the next chapter, had as much impact on Protestant dissent as it had on the established churches. As a result there was a revival in what became known as 'old dissent' brought about by what was then termed 'new dissent', those movements in the established churches, in England and Wales especially, which resulted in new sects of Methodists and dissident Calvinists that eventually separated themselves from the established churches to set up their own denominations. Without the Evangelical Revival it is likely that 'old dissent' would have been in terminal decline by 1815.

Foreign Protestants in Britain and Anglican ecumenism

From the late sixteenth century England, and to a lesser extent other parts of the British Isles, had provided a refuge for foreign Protestants facing persecution in Catholic Europe. The most important of these exiled communities were the French Huguenots, who had established themselves in southern England during the early seventeenth century and whose numbers greatly increased after the Revocation of the Edict of Nantes, which had guaranteed freedom of worship to French Protestants, in 1685. By 1700 there were 14 Huguenot places of worship in London alone. The principal contribution of the Huguenot community to the British economy was in tailoring, wigmaking and the manufacture of gloves, hats and shoes. Huguenot craftsmen were also highly skilled as jewellers, silversmiths and watchmakers. One of these, Francis Perigal, became watchmaker to George III. Other Huguenots became bankers, doctors or merchants, or served in the armed forces, whilst the poorer refugees tended to find work in weaving or the manufacture of silk. The Huguenot communities remained tight ones with their own churches and their own charitable institutions. The French Hospital in Clerkenwell was founded in 1718 and the French Protestant School in Westminster in 1747. William Hogarth painted the Huguenot congregation leaving L'Église des Grecs in Soho in c.1736.

Huguenots who attempted to practise their religion in France could be condemned to serve as slaves on French galleys or to suffer imprisonment, torture and execution. The wide circulation in Britain of the sufferings of the Huguenots led to their exiled communities being not just tolerated, but actively welcomed, by the British people, who were also impressed by their thrift and dedication to hard work. In addition to the French churches in London there were also Huguenot congregations meeting in Bristol and Southampton; in Kent at Canterbury, Dover and Faversham; in Devon at Barnstaple, Bideford, Dartmouth, Exeter and Plymouth; in East Anglia at Colchester, Ipswich, Norwich, Thorney and Thorpe-le-Soken; and at Rye in Sussex. Some of these congregations used a French translation of the Book of Common Prayer and frequently held their services in Anglican churches; others had their own places of worship in which they used the forms of worship they had been familiar with in France. During the first half of the eighteenth century the larger Huguenot communities in Britain tended to keep to themselves, to maintain their own customs, and to retain the use of French within that community. By the last quarter of the eighteenth century the Huguenot communities began to disintegrate, the use of French was abandoned, and their members became much more integrated into British society. Some famous people, generally regarded as wholly British, were in fact the descendants of Huguenot immigrants, examples being the actor David Garrick (1717–79), the distinguished lawyer and politician Sir Samuel Romilly

(1757–1818), the pistol manufacturer Isaac Riviere (1781–1851) and the banker Phillip Cazenove (1798–1880).[73]

The Church of England in the eighteenth century still saw itself as having clear links with the other Protestant churches of Europe, even if they did not have bishops, but some Anglicans were also interested in the possibility of reunion with the Roman Catholic and Eastern Orthodox churches. The leading ecumenist of the early eighteenth century was William Wake, Archbishop of Canterbury from 1716 to 1737. At the outset of his career, in 1682–5, Wake had served as chaplain to the English ambassador in Paris, and he had made contact there with both Huguenot ministers and some of the Roman Catholic clergy. Wake believed that the growing Gallican tendencies of the Roman Catholic church in France, and the desire of the French monarchy to restrict papal influence to a minimum, might offer opportunities for some sort of union between the established churches of England and France, and in 1718–19 he was engaged in a lengthy correspondence with two doctors of the Sorbonne, Ellies du Pin and Piers Girardin, about the possibilities, though in the end nothing was achieved. Wake was also interested in promoting union between the Church of England and Protestants in Europe and saw the link between England and Hanover after 1714 as a means of achieving such a union. However, by 1723 he had to admit that no progress was being made and the discussions with Protestant church leaders and theologians were also abandoned.[74] The ecumenical project which Wake was himself forced to put a stop to was an attempt by the English and Scottish non-jurors to forge links with the Eastern Orthodox churches. On 2 September 1725 he wrote to the Patriarch of Jerusalem, with whom the non-jurors had been negotiating, to inform him that:

certain schismatic priests of our church have written to you under the pretended titles of archbishop and bishops of the Church of England, and sought your communion with them; who having neither place nor church in these realms, have bent their minds to deceive you, who are ignorant of their schism.[75]

Wake, though he asked the patriarch 'to remember me in your prayers and sacrifices at the holy altar of God', did not use this opportunity to open a dialogue with the Eastern Orthodox churches himself.

There was slightly more collaboration between the Church of England and the Lutheran churches of Denmark and Sweden. A Danish church was opened in London in 1696, and a Swedish one in 1710, both churches being closely associated with their respective embassies. As a concession to the strength of anti-Catholicism in England, the Swedish chaplain in London had abandoned the traditional use of eucharistic vestments at the services, but this merely confirmed some of the Swedish bishops in their view that the Church of England was still in reality a Calvinist church. When the then Swedish ambassador, Count Carl Gyllenborg, proposed that the Churches of England and Sweden should establish 'greater intimacy' in 1717–18, the idea found little favour in Sweden and was denounced by Bishop Lund of Växjö. A further attempt at increased ecumenical relations was made by Jacob Serenius, Swedish chaplain in London from 1720. Serenius established a close friendship with Bishop Gibson of London and published a detailed account of the similarities between the English and Swedish churches in 1726. In the 1760s the son of Bishop Wallin of Gothenburg visited England, and there was much interest in Sweden in the Wesleyan Methodist movement, but no form of intercommunion was ever seriously considered by either national church.[76] There was, however, close cooperation between Anglicans and Lutherans in the area of foreign missions. Between 1710 and 1728 the Anglican Society for the Promotion of Christian Knowledge contributed financially to the Danish-Halle Mission in South India. From 1728 the Society and the Mission jointly employed Lutheran missionaries to work in close conjunction with the East India Company. They did so because it was virtually impossible to find English clergy prepared to undertake this work and no question was raised over the validity of holy orders conferred by the Danish bishops. The Lutheran missionaries used the *Book of Common Prayer* for their services and also translated it into Tamil. The Church Missionary Society, established in 1799, also used, in the absence of Anglican volunteers, both Lutheran and Reformed clergy to staff their missions.[77]

Notes

1 M. Mullett, *Catholics in Britain and Ireland, 1558–1829*, Basingstoke 1998, p. 88.

2 C. Haydon, 'Parliament and popery in England, 1700–1780', in J.P. Parry and S. Taylor (eds), *Parliament and the Churches 1529–1960*, Edinburgh 2000, pp. 50–4.

3 R. Porter, *English Society in the Eighteenth Century*, Harmondsworth 1982, p. 187; J.A. Williams, 'Change or decay? The provincial laity 1691–1781', in E. Duffy (ed.), *Challoner and His Church*, London 1981, p. 37.

4 *Ibid.*, pp. 52–3.

5 B. Hemphill, *The Early Vicars Apostolic of England 1685–1750*, London 1954, *passim*.

6 See Mullet, *Catholics in Britain and Ireland*, pp. 152–9; E. Duffy, 'Richard Challoner 1691–1781: a memoir', in Duffy (ed.), *Challoner and his Church*, pp. 1–26.

7 Porter, *English Society*, pp. 194–5.

8 Mullett, *Catholics in Britain and Ireland*, p. 144.

9 J. Bossy, *The English Catholic Community 1570–1850*, London 1975, pp. 184–6, 218–19, 406–11.

10 Mullett, *Catholics in Britain and Ireland*, pp. 88–93.

11 *Ibid.*, p. 139.

12 W.N. Yates, *Buildings, Faith and Worship: The Liturgical Arrangement of Anglican Churches 1600–1900*, new edn, Oxford 2000, p. 205.

13 Mullett, *Catholics in Britain and Ireland*, pp. 142–3; R. O'Donnell, 'The architectural setting of Challoner's episcopate', in Duffy (ed.), *Challoner and His Church*, pp. 60–2.

14 Yates, *Buildings, Faith and Worship*, pp. 197, 205. For other early Roman Catholic chapels, subsequently altered, see B. Little, *Catholic Churches since 1623*, London 1966, pp. 27–54.

15 Mullett, *Catholics in Britain and Ireland*, pp. 159–62.

16 For a discussion of Challoner's and Stonor's attitudes to the legislation see J. Bossy, 'Challoner and the Marriage Act', in Duffy (ed.), *Challoner and His Church*, pp. 126–36.

17 O'Donnell, 'Architectural Setting', pp. 66–9.

18 Bossy, *English Catholic Community*, pp. 272–7.

19 L. Colley, *Britons: Forging the Nation 1707–1837*, London 1994, pp. 18–19.

20 *Ibid.*, pp. 25–6.

21 P. Langford, *A Polite and Commercial People: England 1727–1783*, Oxford 1989, p. 40.

22 Haydon, 'Parliament and Popery', p. 61.

23 C. Haydon, *Anti-Catholicism in Eighteenth-Century England, c.1714–80: A Political and Social Study*, Manchester 1993, pp. 128, 134–40.

24 *Ibid.*, pp. 172–4.

25 H.T. Dickinson, 'Whiggism in the eighteenth century', in J. Cannon (ed.), *The Whig Ascendancy: Colloquies on Hanovarian England*, London 1981, p. 33.

26 For the background to the passing of the Act see N. Abercrombie, 'The First
   Relief Act', in Duffy (ed.), *Challoner and His Church*, pp. 176–93.

27 J. Black, *Eighteenth-Century Britain 1688–1783*, Basingstoke 2001,
   pp. 139–40.

28 H.T. Dickinson, *The Politics of the People in Eighteenth Century Britain*,
   Basingstoke 1995, p. 82.

29 Haydon, *Anti-Catholicism in Eighteenth-Century England*, pp. 204–18.

30 G. Rudé, 'The Gordon Riots: a study of the rioters and their victims',
   Transactions of the Royal Historical Society, 5th Series, vi (1956), pp. 93–114.

31 Haydon, *Anti-Catholicism in Eighteenth-Century England*, pp. 224–5.

32 J. Cannon, 'New lamps for old: the end of Hanovarian England', in Cannon
   (ed.), *The Whig Ascendancy*, p. 105.

33 Mullett, *Catholics in Britain and Ireland*, pp. 151–2.

34 *Ibid.*, pp. 145–8.

35 *Ibid.*, p. 105.

36 *Ibid.*, p. 170.

37 Ibid., pp. 172–4, 176; J.F. McMillan, 'Mission accomplished? The Catholic
   underground', in Devine and Young (eds), *Eighteenth Century Scotland*,
   pp. 94, 102–4.

38 C. Johnson, *Developments in the Roman Catholic Church in Scotland
   1789–1829*, Edinburgh 1983, pp. 41, 153.

39 Mullett, *Catholics in Britain and Ireland*, pp. 106, 108, 116–17, 177–80.

40 Yates, *Buildings, Faith and Worship*, p. 220.

41 This section is based on the much more detailed study of Roman Catholicism
   in Ireland in W.N. Yates, *The Religious Condition of Ireland 1770–1850*,
   Oxford 2006.

42 There is no good detailed study of Scottish episcopalianism in the eighteenth
   century. The following account is based on sections of R. Strong,
   *Episcopalianism in Nineteenth-Century Scotland: Religious Responses to a
   Modernising Society*, Oxford 2002, pp. 13–21, 33–40, 70–93.

43 Commentary and texts in W.J. Grisbrooke, *Anglican Liturgies of the
   Seventeenth and Eighteenth Centuries*, London 1958, pp. 113–59, 297–348.

44 This section is based on the much more detailed study of Irish Presbyterianism
   in Yates, *The Religious Condition of Ireland*.

45 G. Holmes and D. Szechi, *The Age of Oligarchy: Pre-Industrial Britain
   1722–1783*, London 1993, pp. 396–7.

46 W. Prest, *Albion Ascendent: English History 1660–1815*, Oxford 1998, pp. 134, 136.

47 Porter, *English Society*, p. 187.

48 Holmes and Szechi, *Age of Oligarchy*, pp. 397–8.

49 Langford, *A Polite and Commercial People*, pp. 38–9.

50 J. Black, *The English Press in the Eighteenth Century*, London 1987, pp. 248–51.

51 This section is based on the account in B.L. Manning, *The Protestant Dissenting Deputies*, Cambridge 1952. This volume was prepared for publication after the author's death by Ormerod Greenwood.

52 F. O'Gorman, *The Long Eighteenth Century: British Political and Social History 1688–1832*, London 1997, p. 308.

53 Dickinson, *Politics of the People*, pp. 84–6.

54 Manning, *Protestant Dissenting Deputies*, p. 130.

55 Porter, *English Society*, pp. 194–5.

56 *Ibid.*, p. 196; Prest, *Albion Ascendant*, p. 135.

57 O'Gorman, *Long Eighteenth Century*, p. 307.

58 M. Watts, *The Dissenters from the Reformation to the French Revolution*, Oxford 1978, pp. 272–6, 509–10.

59 J. Davies, *A History of Wales*, London 1994, p. 337.

60 J.E. Bradley, *Religion, Revolution and English Radicalism: Nonconformity in Eighteenth Century Politics and Society*, Cambridge 1990, p. 70.

61 Ibid., pp. 113–17; Langford, *A Polite and Commercial People*, pp. 291–6.

62 Bradley, *Religion, Revolution and English Radicalism*, p. 69.

63 Watts, *Dissenters*, pp. 350, 356.

64 E.G. Rupp, *Religion in England 1688–1791*, Oxford 1986, pp. 108–15; R.W. Ambler, *Churches, Chapels and the Parish Communities of Lincolnshire*, Lincoln 2000, pp. 87, 91–2.

65 Rupp, *Religion in England*, pp. 116–27.

66 *Ibid.*, pp. 128–37.

67 Ambler, *Churches, Chapels and Parochial Communities*, pp. 89, 100–7.

68 Rupp, *Religion in England*, pp. 138–51.

69 Dickinson, *Politics of the People*, pp. 83–4.

70 Ambler, *Churches, Chapels and Parochial Communities*, pp. 92–9.

71 Watts, *Dissenters*, pp. 336–8.

72 *Ibid.*, pp. 341–3.

73 Much of the detailed work on the history of the Huguenot communities in the British Isles has appeared in the *Proceedings of the Huguenot Society of London*. The best general survey is T. Murdoch (ed.), *The Quiet Conquest: The Huguenots 1685 to 1985*, London 1985, produced to accompany a major exhibition on the Huguenots at the Museum of London.

74 Sykes, *William Wake*, i, pp. 252–314 and ii, pp. 1–88.

75 *Ibid.*, ii, p. 179.

76 L. Österlin, *Churches of Northern Europe in Profile*, Norwich 1995, pp. 130–7, 143–52.

77 R. Rouse and S.C. Neill (eds), *History of the Ecumenical Movement 1517–1948*, 2nd edn, London 1967, pp. 160–1.

CHAPTER 3

The Maintenance of Doctrinal Orthodoxy

When the Marchioness of Carnarvon died in 1768 she was described, among her many attributes listed in the inscription of her monument in the Hampshire church of Avington, as having been 'religious without enthusiasm'. For the orthodox churchmen of the eighteenth century enthusiasm was a deeply dangerous disease. It evoked memories of the religious struggles of the seventeenth century, and the resulting breakdown in the social and political order, and was to be avoided at all costs. What was to be emulated was a religion of piety and sobriety but one that did not fall into the temptations offered by the scientific discoveries and secular learning of the age that wanted to banish ideas of a God active in the world that he had created. For orthodox churchmen the two evils to be avoided were extreme forms of personal piety, based on a guarantee of salvation recognised in the experience of conversion, or the attractions of a radical form of deism from which all notions of the inexplicable or the miraculous were to be ruthlessly expunged. Yet orthodox churchmen had to face precisely these challenges to their own religious attitudes as the Protestant churches of northern Europe were deeply influenced by both rationalism and Evangelicalism. In this chapter we will look at the religious tensions caused across the British Isles by such influences and the steps taken by orthodox churchmen to protect their churches against them.

Orthodox Anglicans and moderate Presbyterians

In the early eighteenth century both high and low church Anglicans were Arminians. 'The two great objectives which a rationalistic age lodged against Calvinism, in addition to its threat of "enthusiasm", was that it made God the author of evil, and that in denying free will it wrecked moral responsibility'.[1] Whatever the Articles of Religion might say, orthodox Anglicanism was, as will be seen in the next chapter, in practice more a theology of works than faith. Although the majority of the Anglican clergy throughout the period 1714–1815 were probably high churchmen there is no doubt that their political unreliability reduced the impact they had at the higher levels of the established church during the reigns of George I and George II. However, from the 1760s onwards it is clear that high churchmanship was in the ascendant throughout the senior levels of the church and remained so until well after 1815. The most influential of the early eighteenth-century high churchmen was William Law (1686–1761), who floated between the established Church of England and the non-jurors, and was read by both. His two most significant publications were *Christian Perfection* and *A Serious Call to a Devout and Holy Life*, published in 1726 and 1729 respectively, both of which owed much to the long English tradition of sober mysticism.[2] Later in the eighteenth century the leading figures among Anglican high churchmen were William Jones of Nayland, George Horne and Samuel Horsley. Jones was a disciple of John Hutchinson (1674–1737) who believed in 'the centrality of revelation, tradition, and the Church as the repository of both'. Jones's *Catholic Doctrine of a Trinity* went through at least 12 editions between 1756 and 1830. His *Essay on the Church*, published in 1787, stressed the importance of apostolical succession. Horne criticised the Whig arguments of Warburton, discussed in a previous chapter, and resurrected belief in the divine nature of monarchical government. Horsley was a strong defender of the orthodox position on the doctrine of the Trinity as well as sharing Horne's views on the church–state relationship. Their influence on Anglican orthodoxy was heightened by the elevation of both Horne and Horsley to the episcopal bench.[3]

Peter Nockles characterises Anglican high churchmanship in the late eighteenth and early nineteenth centuries in the following terms:

A High Churchman in the Church of England tended to uphold in some form the doctrine of apostolical succession which was the basis of his strong attachment to the Catholicity and apostolicity of the Church of England as a branch of the universal catholic church, within which he did not include those reformed bodies which had wilfully abandoned episcopacy, so that a distinction was made between Nonconformist congregations and continental Protestant churches. He believed in the supremacy of Scripture and set varying degrees of value on the testimony of authoritative tradition, but generally insisted that the Bible needed to be interpreted in the light of such authoritative standards as the Prayer Book, the Catechism and the Creeds. He tended to value the writings of the early Fathers, especially as witnesses to Scriptural truth when a catholic consent of them could be established. He laid emphasis on the doctrine of sacramental grace, both in the eucharist and baptism, while tending to eschew the principle of ex opere operato. *He tended to cultivate a practical spirituality which many emphasised as based on sacramental grace and nourished by acts of self-denial, rather than on any subjective conversion experience or unruly manifestations of the Holy Spirit. He invariably stressed the importance of a religious establishment but insisted on the duty of the state, as a divinely ordered rather than merely secular entity, to protect and promote the interests of the Church.*[4]

It was this sort of outlook that had become the majority view, certainly among the clergy, of the Church of England by the last quarter of the eighteenth century and which was shared by their fellow Anglican clergy in Ireland and Scotland.

Whereas the Church of England had rejected Calvinism well before 1714, the Church of Scotland was officially still a Calvinist church, though it found the means to interpret its Calvinism in a way that was pragmatic and designed to fit more comfortably with the new intellectual climate of the age of enlightenment. By the end of the eighteenth century the Church of Scotland was divided into two sharply distinguished parties, the majority 'moderates' and the minority Evangelicals. 'Seldom has an ecclesiastical party been condemned by posterity quite so mercilessly' as the Moderates though their main concern was to react 'against the rigidity of the Calvinist categories' and to argue 'that all creeds and con-fessions, even that of Westminster [the doctrinal standard of the Church of Scotland], must necessarily be partial and incomplete'.[5] The founders of the Moderate party were two Glasgow professors, Francis Hutchinson and William Leechman, but the real leader from 1752 was William Robertson (1721–93), principal of Edinburgh University from 1762 and moderator of the General Assembly of the Church of Scotland from 1766 until 1780: 'they believed, in common with eighteenth century thinkers, that man was social by nature and that religion was an indispensable sanction for social stability and effective government. The intimate and inseparable connection of church and society ensured social control, and sermons . . . powerfully advocated that view'.[6] Thus, although there were clearly doctrinal differences between the Calvinism of the Church of Scotland and the Arminianism of the Churches of England and Ireland, their respective attitudes on church–state relations or on the government of society were remarkably similar. An illustration of the Moderates' pragmatic approach to such issues was their attitude to attempts by those in the Church of Scotland who wanted to press for the repeal of the Patronage Act. In their view 'an acquiescence in patronage was the price which must be paid for their ideal of a church occupying a central place in the national life' and they disagreed with those who argued 'that the church is a society called out of the world and set over against it'.[7] Robertson took the view that the British government would never agree to repeal and that 'the Kirk would be in a stronger position to assert control over its own affairs if it accepted and enforced the patronage system'.[8]

Scottish historians differ to some extent over how dominant the Moderate party was in the Church of Scotland during the late eighteenth and early nineteenth centuries. Chitnis points out that, between 1752 and 1805, 39 out of 54 moderators of the General Assembly were Moderates and that 24 out of 41 appointments to offices, such as deaneries or royal chaplaincies, went to Moderates. Clark, however, argues that the Moderates secured their position of strength more by 'their superior tactics, and their ability to "manage" elections in lethargic or indifferent presbyteries' than numerical domination. Even though the presbytery of Ayr was considered a bastion of the Moderates, Clark estimates that only 12 of the 29 clergy in 1780 could be described as 'active and consistent' Moderates. Moderate strength lay almost exclusively in two areas of Scotland, the east coast parishes from Aberdeen to Fife and the southern lowland parishes of Lothian, Tweeddale and Galloway.[9] In the long run the Moderates became discredited by their conservatism and complacency.

Whereas the early Moderates had been reformers, and mostly Whigs in politics, their successors shared the reactionary Toryism of many Anglican clergy. Whereas Robertson had defended patronage 'on grounds of expediency', Principal George Hill of St Andrews did so on the grounds that it 'was the law of the land'. By the early nineteenth century 'the Moderates had become the establishment conservatives . . . opposing, for example, the repeal of the Test Acts on the grounds that then was not the most appropriate time to consider such a move.'[10]

Latitudinarians, Arians and Socinians

No part of the British Isles could be immune from the strong rationalist influences developing in the theological faculties of the Protestant universities of Europe in the eighteenth century. The Scottish universities, 'which had traditionally enjoyed close links with the continent',[11] experienced such stirrings, and the Protestant dissenting academies in England and Wales became major centres of such teaching, having in due course a dramatic impact on the theological outlook of many ministers and congregations.[12] Among Anglicans the marginalisation of high churchmen, for political reasons, in the early eighteenth century resulted in the temporary influence of the latitudinarian party at the higher levels of the established church and the early beginnings of Anglican liberal theology. The key figures around whom much of this debate was centred were Benjamin Hoadly and Samuel Clarke. Hoadly's theology devolved from his politics. He was the ultimate erastian, rejecting any idea of a visible church and arguing that 'if there was no visible human authority left by Christ on earth, the state could reasonably claim to be a representative of providential design, and therefore could reasonably act for the Church in matters of clerical discipline and Church government'.[13] In 1735 Hoadly, then Bishop of Winchester, published *A Plain Account of the Nature and End of the Sacrifice of the Lord's Supper* in which he set forth a wholly memorialist interpretation of the sacrament stripped of even the most minimalist definition of the real presence in the Eucharist. Hoadly's views were criticised by many fellow Anglicans, and not just high churchmen. The principal refutation was Daniel Waterland's *Review of the Doctrine of the Eucharist as laid down in Scripture and Antiquity* published in 1737. Whereas Hoadly had argued that the celebrant at Holy Communion merely 'blessed' the bread and wine, Waterland 'held that the priest's consecration of the bread and wine sanctified them and made them holy so that they could convey spiritual benefits' and claimed that his doctrine was the true doctrine of the Church of England.[14] Most Anglicans agreed with him and Waterland's work was still being republished well into the nineteenth century, by which time Hoadly's work was largely forgotten.

Hoadly regarded himself in many ways as a disciple of Samuel Clarke. Clarke had been born in 1675 and became incumbent of the London church of St Benet's, Paul's Wharf, in 1706, succeeding to the rectory of St James, Piccadilly in 1709, holding this until his death in 1729. In 1712 he published his most influential work, *The Scripture Doctrine of the Trinity*, in which he concluded 'that the Athanasian Creed of three co-equal and co-eternal Persons in the Trinity was unscriptural. Scripture, he concluded, showed a supremacy in the Father which, when rightly considered, implied that he alone fulfilled all that was contained in the very conception of the godhead, and that he alone could properly be called God'.[15] Clarke's work was seen as a denial of both the Articles of Religion and the doctrines of the *Book of Common Prayer*. Indeed at his death Clarke left a copy of the prayer book interleaved with blank pages containing his own proposals for its revision along more scriptural lines, rewording some of the collects and other passages to emphasise the supremacy of God the Father and to remove sentences that implied that the three persons of the Trinity were co-equal and co-eternal. The Athanasian Creed was never to be used and the Nicene Creed in the communion service was to be replaced with a psalm. Major revisions were also to be made to the *Gloria in Excelsis*. A printed version of Clarke's revised prayer book was eventually published in 1774.[16] Clarke's views were shared by a number of his contemporaries. William Whiston (1667–1752) was a self-proclaimed Arian.[17] Others challenged various aspects of Christian orthodoxy. Thomas Woolston published his *Six Discourses on Miracles* in 1727–30 and Matthew Tindal *Christianity as Old as the Creation* in 1730. Tindal argued 'that the Religion of Nature is an absolutely perfect Religion; and that external Revelation can neither add to, nor take from its Perfection; and that True Religion, whether internally or externally revealed, must be the same'.[18]

The impact of all this on orthodox churchmen has been well summed up by John Redwood:

The full-bodied attack on miracles, and the immediate and prolonged response to it from senior churchmen, shows something of the danger and strength of the deist cause. Woolston was arguing a position that was to become more and more popular as particular parts of the Bible were brought into doubt by advances in natural sciences and in historical understanding, but it was a position senior churchmen were quick and content to perceive as fundamental to the whole notion of Christianity as they knew it. Miracles were needed as testimonies of Christ's divinity; without them the Unitarians had a chance of swaying opinion. Miracles were needed to attest essential doctrines; without their proof the whole fabric of New Testament Christianity seemed unstable.[19]

Action was therefore being taken by the 1720s to block the promotion of clergy expressing unorthodox, especially anti-Trinitarian, views and to remove them from their positions in the universities. Archbishop Wake's draft bill against blasphemy in 1721 was largely motivated by his concern about writers who denied the divinity of Christ. Norman Sykes suggested that the Georgian church 'stood upon the very threshold of the doctrine of development and the rise of Biblical criticism' but stepped

back. One of the consequences of the debates engendered by the publications of Clarke, Hoadly, Tindal, Whiston, Woolston and others was
to dampen the enthusiasm for theological discussion and speculation in
the Church of England and to encourage what Sykes termed the 'doctrine
of Divine Benevolence', on which all could agree, promoting an emphasis
in both preaching and theological publications on the pursuit of good
works and living as the ideal of a Christian Society.[20]

Whereas Anglicans stepped back from the debates about doctrine
resulting from the publications of their latitudinarian and deist theologians, many branches of Protestant dissent became immersed in them
and both ministers and congregations embraced either Arian or Socinian
opinions.

*Arianism maintained that the Son of God was not eternal but created by
the Father from nothing as an instrument for the creation of the world;
and that therefore He was not God by nature, but a changeable creature,
his dignity as Son of God having been bestowed on Him by the Father
on account of his foreseen abiding righteousness.*[21]

Socinianism or Unitarianism pushed this belief even further, totally
rejecting any expression of Trinitarian doctrine and the divinity of Christ
in favour of the unipersonality of God. Technically those expressing
outright Unitarian positions were in some difficulty. They could be prosecuted under the Blasphemy Act of 1697, and in Scotland this could result
in the death penalty being imposed on anyone convicted of denying the
doctrine of the Trinity. This position remained until a special act was
passed to grant toleration to Unitarians in 1813.[22] Forty years earlier
the growth in the number of Protestant dissenting ministers and congregations adopting Unitarian statements of belief had resulted in the Feathers
Tavern Petition of 1772, requesting 'that subscription be required only to
a formula recognising the authority of the Bible as a repository of divine
truth without any definition of the sense in which it was to be interpreted.'[23] The steady move of most Presbyterian congregations in England
and Wales, as well as some Baptist and Independent ones, into the
adoption of Unitarianism, sent deep shock waves through the Church
of England and the sermon literature of the late eighteenth and early
nineteenth centuries is full of attacks on Unitarianism and the defence
of Trinitarian orthodoxy. However, unlike in France or some other parts
of continental Europe, there was no significant group of intellectuals in
the British Isles before 1815 expressing outright atheist views or promoting anti-clerical and anti-Christian propaganda. This point cannot be

emphasised too strongly as it marks the essential difference between the impact of the 'Enlightenment' in Britain and Ireland and its impact on most parts of continental Europe, especially France where it was to lead to a wholesale programme of anti-Christianisation by the 1790s.

The Evangelical revival

Whilst the unorthodox views of some theologians might have troubled the leadership of the Church of England and divided Protestant dissenters, their impact was minimal compared with the challenge to establishment religion from a very different direction. From the late seventeenth century all the Protestant churches of Europe and North America experienced a movement, variously termed pietism or Evangelicalism, aimed at achieving a spiritual revival in religious bodies exhausted by the religious conflicts of the post-Reformation period.[24] It is important to emphasise the international context of this movement and the comparisons that can be made between its impact in different countries on the Protestant churches there. It did not really have an impact on the Roman Catholic church, largely because of the difference between Protestant and Roman Catholic attitudes towards the supremacy of scripture, though some parallels can be found between Protestant 'enthusiasm' and popular Roman Catholic devotions of the late eighteenth and early nineteenth centuries such as the new cult of the Sacred Heart. Within the British Isles Evangelicalism was to influence, to a greater or lesser extent, all the mainstream Protestant churches, though the chronologies of this influence varied considerably: early in England and Wales, somewhat later in Ireland, Scotland and the offshore islands. There has been a tendency in some of the literature, particularly that on Wales, to emphasise the local factors involved in the Evangelical revival, sometimes to the virtual exclusion of the international ones. Whilst local factors must not be disregarded, it is important to establish which ones were genuine local and individual and those which appear to be responses to much broader spiritual concerns and which have their counterparts in other parts of the world.

The critical link between European and British revivalism was the *Unitas Fratrum* or Moravian Church. They were descendents of a former Hussite sect in Bohemia and Moravia which established a community at Herrnhut on the estates of Count von Zinzendorf in 1722. This community experienced a corporate conversion experience in 1727 as a result of which its members felt impelled to send 'messengers' out to convey the good news of what had happened. Three such 'messengers' visited England in 1728 but their efforts to spread their message were not very successful. However, in 1734–5 the Moravians collaborated with Thomas Bray and others to establish a settlement in Georgia. In 1737 Zinzendorf himself visited England and it was as a result of this visit that cordial relations were established between the Moravians and members of the Church of England, including some of the leading figures in the British Evangelical revival such as Charles and John Wesley, George Whitefield and Howell Harris, though later these relations were to break down.[25] The Moravians also found supporters among some Anglican high churchmen, including Archbishop Potter of Canterbury and Bishop Wilson of Sodor and Man; as a result the bishops promoted a parliamentary bill in 1749 which recognised the *Unitas Fratum* as 'an antient Protestant Episcopal Church'.[26] The sort of conversion experience which the Moravian community had experienced at Herrnhut in 1727 became the standard by which all Evangelical communities in Britain came to be judged. It was the conversion experience which provided the common bond between Evangelicals since, in many other respects, they were frequently divided, initially between Arminians like the Wesleys and Calvinists like Whitefield and Harris, and later on between those who were content, and those who were not content, to remain in their churches of origin. Evangelicalism began as a movement within the existing Protestant churches but, by the early nineteenth century, it had resulted in schism and the creation of 'new dissent'. In this chapter we will make the distinction between the eventual schismatics and those who remained within their existing churches by treating the growth of Methodism separately from that of core Evangelicalism.

Evangelical groups had been established in England and Wales by the 1730s. Whitefield and Harris underwent their respective conversion experiences in 1735 and shortly afterwards the curate of Llangeitho (Cards.), Daniel Rowland, was also converted. Harris and Rowland travelled around South Wales preaching the message of salvation. Whitefield conducted similar missions in Bristol and London. In 1738 John Wesley had his own conversion experience and began preaching in 1739 at the New Room in Bristol. Whitefield visited Scotland in 1741 and a spontaneous revival of the spirit took place in 1742 at Cambuslang, near Glasgow.[27] The major impact of the Evangelical revival in the British Isles was felt on its established churches but some of the Protestant dissenting churches were also affected. In 1770 a new 'connexion' of General Baptists, Arminians 'motivated by conversionist zeal', was formed.[28] In Wales many of the established nonconformist groups welcomed the Evangelical revival and its liturgical innovations, especially hymn-singing, the first collection of Independent hymns being published by Dafydd Jones of Caeo in 1753.[29] Within the Church of England one of the chief features of the Evangelical revival was the difference it made to the attitudes of clergy caught up in it:

Evangelical clergymen were actually conscious of their separateness as an order. They had recaptured . . . that sense of the clergyman's essential difference from the layman . . . Of course this difference did not consist in the sacerdotal prerogatives of priesthood. No set of Anglicans have ever more clearly and forcibly stated the authentic Protestant case against sacerdotalism. But Evangelical clergymen seem generally to have felt a peculiar kind of responsibility for the salvation of the souls of their flock and to have gone about achieving it by more exclusively spiritual means.[30]

It was an attitude that later came to be satirised in quite a few Victorian novels.

Although the early Evangelicals proclaimed loyalty to the churches of which they were members, there is no doubt that one of the attractions of Evangelicalism was that it seemed to address some of the failings in contemporary religious establishments such as 'alleged political subservience . . . to an increasingly secularised state', allegations of pastoral neglect and the 'promotion of morality at the expense of the need for repentance, justification and salvation from sin'.[31] In England the Evangelical revival began with a series of clerical conversions: George Thomson, James Hervey, Vincent Perronet, William Romaine, Henry Venn. There were also a number of conversions of aristocratic laity, notably that of Selina, Countess of Huntingdon (1701–91), who subsequently used her wealth to support the preaching of Whitefield and to establish Calvinist chapels in London, Bath, Brighton and Tunbridge Wells.[32] In Wales an early initiative was the establishment of religious 'societies', or groups of Evangelical believers, by Howell Harris, who had established 30 such societies by 1739, and whose initiative was later copied by Charles and John Wesley.[33] Harris and Daniel Rowland first met in 1737 and initially collaborated in developing a programme of missions throughout South Wales. They were, however, eventually drawn apart by Harris's close association with Whitefield, including long absences in London, and divisions in their theological opinions.[34] In Scotland the earlier Evangelical stirrings were to be found in the establishment of the Associate Presbytery by Ebenezer and Ralph Erskine, over the patronage question, in 1733, and the revivals at Cambuslang and Kilsyth in the 1740s,[35] but Evangelicals did not become a significant force within the established Church of Scotland until the later years of the eighteenth century. In Ireland, despite Moravian and Wesleyan missions from the 1750s, there were few Evangelicals in either the Church of Ireland or the Presbyterian Synod of Ulster before 1800.

In trying to assess the character of mainstream Evangelicals, particularly those that remained within the Church of England, it is instructive to look at four representative figures: Samuel Walker, John Venn, Charles Simeon and Hannah More. Walker, born in 1714, was curate of Truro from 1746 until his early death in 1761. His conversion occurred during 1747, the year in which he was offered, and received a licence of non-residence from the bishop to accept, the vicarage of Talland. Plagued by scruples he resigned Talland and refused any further offers of livings. In 1754 he formed a religious society in Truro for his converted parishioners, all of whom had to be regular communicants and attend weekday services devised by Walker. At about the same time he also formed a clerical club for like-minded clergy in Cornwall. They included Thomas Mitchell of Veryan and John Penrose of St Gluvias. The others have not been definitely identified but may have included James Vowler of St Agnes, Henry Phillips of Gwennap, Mydhope Wallis of St Endellion and Thomas Vivian of Cornwood. Walker, like many of the Evangelical clergy, was sympathetic to Methodism. He gave particular attention to catechising, dividing his younger parishioners into three classes: those under 12, those between 12 and 15 and those between 15 and 20. Catechising took place every Sunday between February and April and again between August and October.[36]

John Venn, born in 1759, was the son of Henry Venn, the Evangelical incumbent of Huddersfield and the founder of a clerical society similar to that established by Walker at Truro. After serving briefly as curate to his father, then at Yelling in Huntingdonshire, he was presented to the rectory of Little Dunham (Norf.) in 1783. Here he introduced two Sunday services and a monthly communion service, even though the population of the parish was only 172. A clerical society was established for sympathetic neighbouring clergy in 1792 shortly before Venn's move to be rector of Clapham in the following year. Venn's predecessor at Clapham had not been an Evangelical so he moved cautiously. The first innovation was a Friday lecture but this was quickly replaced by a third Sunday service, in the evening, in addition to those in the morning and afternoon. A monthly communion service was also established. What was important about Venn's ministry at Clapham, until his early death in 1813, was that the parish became the nucleus of a group of influential Evangelical laity: Henry Thornton, William Wilberforce, Hannah More, James Stephen, Lord Teignmouth, Zachary Macaulay – the so-called Clapham Sect. Venn's most important contribution to the Church of England outside his parish was his establishment of the Church Missionary Society in 1799.[37]

One of John Venn's close friends and exact contemporary was Charles Simeon (1759–1836), incumbent of Holy Trinity, Cambridge from 1783. His appointment was not without controversy and he had to share the ministry of the church with his predecessor's curate, who had been elected by the parishioners to the Sunday afternoon lectureship. When Simeon attempted to introduce a Sunday evening service the churchwardens locked the church to prevent his entry. He responded by hiring a room for the service until the churchwardens relented. Like Walker he established religious societies for his parishioners despite the disapproval of Bishop Dampier of Ely. He was an early supporter of the new Church Missionary Society, but he scandalised some Anglican high churchmen by his friendliness with dissenters in England and his willingness, when on holiday, to preach and even receive communion in the Church of Scotland.[38]

Hannah More was one of the few Evangelicals who had a broad network of friends that included high churchmen as well as fellow Evangelicals. Born in Bristol in 1745 and living until 1833, she had a successful early career as a poet and playwright. Although born into a high church family, More became increasingly attracted by Evangelicalism during the 1770s and was fully converted by the 1780s. During the 1790s she and her sister devoted themselves to establishing a series of schools in northern Somerset which at the height of their success were attended by about 1,000 children, though some were forced to close as a result of opposition from the clergy. More was also active in the wider Sunday school movement of the late eighteenth and early nineteenth centuries in which Evangelicals and high churchmen made common cause. In 1795 she established More's Cheap Repository Tracts, a 'plan to promote good morals among the Poor' and the first in a series of similar publications that were to be one of the hallmarks of Evangelicalism during the nineteenth century.[39]

Hannah More, William Wilberforce and other members of the Clapham Sect were the leading figures in the moral and social reform programme of the late eighteenth century. One of their major initiatives was the establishment of the London Abolition Society, to campaign for the abolition of the slave trade, in 1787. Local committees of the society were established in most of the large British towns. In 1788 a total of 102 petitions in favour of abolition were presented to Parliament and in 1792 a total of 519. Evangelicals set up the first non-slave colony in Sierra Leone in 1791, the year in which the first abolition bill was defeated in

Parliament. Subsequent bills were also unsuccessful until 1807 when abolition was eventually carried. Although there is no doubt that the motives of those who led the anti-slavery campaign, such as Wilberforce and the former slave-trader turned Evangelical clergyman and hymn-writer, John Newton, were primarily religious and ethical, some historians have queried whether the final victory of the campaign was wholly the result of these considerations. It has been suggested that the defence of the slave trade weakened because it was no longer advantageous to the British economy and that for some political supporters of abolition their standpoint 'was merely self-interest masquerading as morality'. More recently that view has been challenged by Boyd Hilton and others, who have pointed out that Britain in the late eighteenth and early nineteenth centuries was still heavily dependent on the colonial sugar plantations operated by slave labour, and that there was still a powerful lobby of those who continued to benefit from the profits of their investment in these plantations.[40] Although the anti-slavery campaign is the initiative for which Evangelicals are best remembered today, that campaign was just part of a much broader campaign to reform society as a whole and to make the nation a truly spiritual one.

All violations of the Sabbath – newspapers, travel and the transacting of any business, but especially amusements such as cards, balls, assemblies or Sunday music, even walks in the country – seemed shockingly unchristian to the Evangelicals. On any day, the theatre, opera and masquerade, village fairs and rural sports, country dances, fiddlers and mountebanks, horse races, boat races, prize fights, 'low' gambling, the fives court and the public house, bear-baiting and bull-baiting, jolly songs, immodest feminine dress, jewellery and other adornment, French fashions (or anything French), improper literature (Shakespeare, Cervantes, Byron) and proper but unreligious literature (Walter Scott) . . . were abhorrent to the truly religious character.[41]

It was this general condemnation of all pleasure that brought Evangelicals into disrepute with many of their contemporaries and has tended, for subsequent historians, to obscure their more positive contributions to education and social reform, though even in these areas the improvement of provision was linked very strongly to the themes of conversion and repentance. Evangelical initiatives included the Society to Effect the Enforcement of His Majesty's Proclamation against Vice and Immorality (1788), the Society for Bettering the Condition and Increasing the Comforts of the Poor (1796) and the Philanthropic Society (1788), which aimed at 'reforming criminal poor children' and putting boys into apprenticeships and girls into domestic service. One of the common features of all these societies was the impressive array of aristocrats, politicians, bankers and industrialists who signed up as patrons or members.[42] Evangelicals may have been a small group numerically but they included some significant figures and powerful supporters, including the future prime minister, Spencer Percival, assassinated by a commercial agent ruined in the Napoleonic wars in 1812.

Older generations of religious historians tended to be critical of the leadership of the Church of England in the eighteenth century for its lack of support for, and frequently outright hostility to, the Evangelical revival. However, the position of those who criticised the Evangelicals is now beginning to be recognised as one of genuine concern rather than narrow prejudice. Above everything else 'they were convinced that fanaticism in religion had done more harm than good, especially in the previous century when puritanism and catholicism had threatened to destroy the very fabric of society'.[43] There was specific condemnation, even by some Evangelicals, of practices such as field preaching, itinerancy and the erection of private chapels for Evangelical services.[44] Opposition, especially to the Methodists, was not just confined to clergy and landowners. Attacks on popular pleasures aroused opposition among ordinary people and resulted in demonstrations. At Congleton opponents of the new Methodist chapel

tried a variety of tactics short of actual physical assault. These included kicking a football, playing a hurdy-gurdy, and beating drums outside the chapel during divine service, letting dogs loose among the congregation, and hurling dirt and rotten eggs at its members.[45]

Some bishops refused to ordain candidates with Evangelical views. There was strong opposition to Evangelicals within the universities, especially Oxford, and some undergraduates holding such opinions were expelled. Attempts by the established church to exercise control over private chapels, notably those financed by the Countess of Huntingdon, forced Evangelicals to licence their chapels as dissenting meeting houses in order to secure legal protection for their buildings.[46] Whilst Evangelical leaders, including the early Methodists, were keen to demonstrate their loyalty to the established church, some of their followers were less so. The early chapel at Groeswen (Glam.) became an Independent one in 1745. There were similar concerns about the theological orthodoxy of some Evangelicals. It was Howell Harris's adoption, under Moravian influence, of 'Patripassionism, the belief that God the Father had died on the cross', that brought about his estrangement from the Calvinistic Methodist leadership in Wales.[47] There was particular suspicion among Anglican high churchmen that Evangelicals were betraying their church by their willingness to collaborate with Protestant dissenters in campaigns for social reform or in missionary endeavours. One such collaboration was in the establishment of the British and Foreign Bible Society in 1804. Christopher Wordsworth, chaplain to Archbishop Manners-Sutton of Canterbury, published in 1810 *Reasons for Declining to Become a Subscriber to the British and Foreign Bible Society*, partly because he felt it was undermining the work of the Society for the Promotion of Christian Knowledge, but much more so because it was not a wholly Anglican society.[48]

Whilst most Evangelicals were figures of absolute respectability in both religious and social terms, there were some whose Evangelical beliefs led them down strange theological paths. A minority strand within the Evangelical revival was the development of millenarianism, a belief in the imminence of the second coming of Christ, in the last decade of the eighteenth century and the emergence of 'prophets' such as Richard Brothers and Joanna Southcott.[49] There had been a number of local 'prophets' throughout the eighteenth century, such as the Wardleys in Bolton in the 1740s, their disciple Ann Lee, before her emigration to America in 1774, Mary Evans in Anglesey in the 1780s and the Buchanites, disciples of Elspeth Buchan, in southern Scotland between 1774 and her death in 1791. In 1792 a former naval officer, Richard Brothers, had a religious experience which convinced him that 'he was descended from King David through James, one of the brothers of Jesus' and that he was both 'the Prince of the Hebrews and nephew of the Almighty'. He attempted to heal the blind and in 1794 published his visions and prophecies in *A Revealed Knowledge of the Prophecies and Times*. His teachings were further popularised in the anonymous publication of 20 pamphlets on prophecy, entitled *The World's Doom*, in 1795. Brothers fixed the date of the millennium, when Christ would come again and rule the earth for 1,000 years, as 19 November 1795. His special task, to take place in 1798, was to lead the return of his disciples, who he believed were the descendents of the ten lost tribes of Israel, to the Holy Land to undertake the rebuilding of Jerusalem. Brothers attracted a number of wealthy supporters and his publications were regarded with some dismay by the government as they contained passages which could be regarded as potentially seditious:

The Lord God commands me to say to you, George the Third, King of England that immediately on my being revealed . . . to the Hebrews as

their Prince . . . your crown must be delivered to me, that all your power
and authority may instantly cease.[50]

He also condemned the government for its treatment of its radical
opponents and for the war against France. In 1795 he was arrested and
examined by the Privy Council with a view to his prosecution for high
treason. It was decided that such a charge could not be proved, but
Brothers was declared insane and committed to a lunatic asylum, where
he remained until his death in 1824.

With Brothers now safely incarcerated, attention turned to another
visionary, Joanna Southcott, the barely literate daughter of a relatively
poor Devon farmer. Though she was apparently very attractive to men she
turned down all her suitors and by the 1780s was working in domestic
service and as an upholsterer in order to maintain herself and her elderly
father. In 1792, after attending Methodist services for some years, she had,
at the age of 42, a series of visions in which she was commanded to write
down what had been revealed to her about forthcoming events. She
correctly foretold the war with France, the naval mutiny of 1797, a series
of bad harvests and the death of the Bishop of Exeter, though she incorrectly forecast that the Irish Rebellion of 1798 would occur in 1795. The
local Methodists and Protestant dissenting clergy repudiated her visions,
which they thought were from the devil, but she attracted the support
of some of the Evangelical clergy in the diocese of Exeter, including Joseph
Pomeroy, vicar of St Kew in Cornwall. She also attracted support from
some of those, including a few clergy, who had championed Richard
Brothers before his confinement. Between 1792 and her death in 1814
Southcott published 65 pamphlets and also produced an equivalent
amount of material which was not published. In 1801 she and her supporters invited the Bishop and Archdeacon of Exeter, together with three
local clergy and seven others, who had been disciples of Richard Brothers,
to examine her writings. All five of the Devon clergy declined but the
others declared that she was a genuine prophetess, and in 1802 she moved
to London where she was maintained by her supporters. Under instructions delivered to her in her visions she began to 'seal' her writings and
then to 'seal' her disciples. In order to be sealed the person had 'to sign a
petition calling for the overthrow of Satan and the establishment of
Christ's Kingdom on earth'. Between 1802 and 1804 a total of 8,144
believers received their seals; the number had risen to 14,000 by 1807.
After concern that some of her supporters were paying for the seals, the
qualifications for 'sealing' were raised, and only a further 6,400 were

'sealed' between then and her death in 1814. Early in that year Southcott announced that she was to give birth to Shiloh, a second virgin birth, and developed what appeared to be clear signs of pregnancy. Seventeen out of 21 doctors who examined her confirmed the pregnancy but, when the expected birth did not materialise, she went into a severe depression and died. Her body was wrapped up and kept warm with hot water bottles in the hope that she would come to life as Jesus had done. When this failed to materialise an autopsy was carried out on the putrefying body and it was declared that no evidence could be found of either pregnancy or any disease that might have caused her death. During her lifetime Joanna Southcott attracted a large number of disciples, mostly in London, Devon, Lancashire, Yorkshire and the Midlands, who were mostly artisans, small tradesmen and women. Although Southcott encouraged her followers to remain faithful to the Church of England, three Southcottian chapels were established in London and there were also chapels in Ashton-under-Lyne, Bath, Bristol, Exeter, Leeds and Stockport. Services in them were conducted from the *Book of Common Prayer* supplemented by Philip Pullen's *Hymns, or Spiritual Songs, composed from the Prophetic Writings of Joanna Southcott.*

These millenarianist sects, which expanded during the nineteenth century, were far from mainstream Evangelicalism, whether it was the church Evangelicalism of Samuel Walker, John Venn or Charles Simeon, the Methodism of the Wesleys, or the Calvinism of the Countess of Huntingdon's Connexion, though some parallels could be found in some dissenting sects, such as the groups of strict Calvinists established in Kent and Sussex by William Huntington (1745–1813), who appended the letters S.S. for Sinner Saved after his name. Two of Huntington's chapels, still preserving their original furnishings, survive at Chichester and Lewes.[51] Visionaries like Brothers and Southcott were as anathema to most mainstream Evangelicals as they were to orthodox Anglicans but their existence undoubtedly helped to substantiate the allegations of some bishops and clergy that Evangelicalism was an extremely dangerous theological position which could easily descend into unsavoury forms of religion and, worse still, political radicalism.

Evangelicalism in Scotland and Ireland

Whereas Evangelicalism was well-established in both England and Wales by the 1750s, this was not really the case in either Scotland or Ireland. The early revivals in Scotland had been limited and short-lived. A much more sustained series of Evangelical missions within the Church of Scotland took place from the 1760s and were concentrated in the parishes of the highlands and islands, where both episcopalianism and Roman Catholicism remained entrenched in some areas and where the Moderate clergy were generally unwilling to accept charges. It was Evangelicals within the Church of Scotland who responded to the challenge of the General Assembly to provide ministers, catechists and schoolteachers for these predominantly Gaelic-speaking areas. As a result there were Evangelical revivals in such highland parishes as Croy from 1766, Tongue from 1773, Ardclach from 1776, Kilbrandon and Kilchattan from 1786 and Moulin from 1797, and revivals in the isles of Arran from 1804 and Skye from 1805. There were also Evangelical missions from non-Presbyterian churches such as the Baptists and Independents, responsible for revivals in Arran and Bute from 1800 and Skye from 1805. By that year there were Baptist churches in the Argyll parishes of Lochgilphead and Strachur, the Caithness parishes of Keiss and Thurso, and the Ross parish of Fortrose. There were also Independent congregations at Thurso and Wick in Caithness, at Fortrose and at three places in Argyll, and eight in Perthshire.[52] The Evangelical revival in Scotland encouraged both much stricter conditions being placed on admission to Holy Communion and the maintenance of traditional discipline within the established church. Lachlan Mackenzie, the Evangelical minister of Lochcarron in Wester Ross was, in 1792, instrumental in revealing that the major landowner in Gairloch, Sir Hector Mackenzie, 'had lived in adultery with his maid Jean Urquhart for four years and had fathered three bastard children'. The minister of Gairloch, who had been bribed by 'the donation of a mortcloth and cash in return for baptising the children and keeping quiet about the laird's domestic arrangements', was ordered by the presbytery to fine Mackenzie £60. Lesser transgressors could be ordered by the kirk session to stand before the congregation for up to three Sundays, sometimes wearing sackcloth, and publicly acknowledge their sins before 'being subjected to a "rant" from the minister'.[53]

The earliest Evangelical initiatives in Ireland came from Moravians and Wesleyan Methodists but their impact was limited and there were fewer than 20,000 Methodists in the whole of Ireland by the end of the eighteenth century.[54] Methodists, who worked within the Church of Ireland and the Presbyterian churches, made no attempt to set up a separate denomination until 1816. They did, however, act as a catalyst for the establishment of Evangelical ministries, separate from Methodism, within those churches. By the end of the eighteenth century such ministries had been established within the Church of Ireland by Peter Roe at Kilkenny, Thomas Tighe at Drumgooland (Co. Down), John Quarry at Shandon (Co. Cork), Robert Shaw at Fiddown (Co. Kilkenny) and Joseph Stopford at Letterkenny (Co. Donegal). In 1786 a number of wealthy Evangelicals in Dublin established the Bethesda proprietary chapel. When John Wesley visited Dublin in 1787 he noted that the chapel attracted between seven and eight hundred communicants on Easter Sunday. At about the same time a similar movement was occurring within Irish Presbyterianism. Partly this took the form of increased support for reformed congregations, which more than doubled from 12 in 1792 to 27 by 1800, and which by 1811 had been formed into a synod with four dependent presbyteries. A number of congregations within the Synod of Ulster also acquired Evangelical ministers, such as Benjamin McDowell at Mary's Abbey in Dublin, Samuel Hanna at Rosemary Street in Belfast and Samuel Dill at Donaghmore (Co. Donegal), a strong opponent of both drinking and gambling. Evangelicals in the different Protestant churches in Ireland collaborated with each other to establish the General Evangelical Society in Dublin (1787), the Ulster Evangelical Society (1798), the Hibernian Bible Society (1806) and the Hibernian Missionary Society (1814). Church of Ireland Evangelicals established the Association for the Discountenancing of Vice and Practice of Virtue and Religion in 1792 and the Ossory Clerical Association in 1800. The leadership of both the Church of Ireland and the Synod of Ulster was almost uniformly hostile to the Evangelicals within their ranks. In 1805 Walter Stephens was dismissed from his post as assistant chaplain of the Magdalen Asylum in Dublin for holding Evangelical views. The Presbyterian minister, John Lowry, was censured for his membership of the Ulster Evangelical Association and condemned for publishing a pamphlet advocating the use of hymns, much favoured by Evangelicals, in worship.

The rise of Methodism

In the early days of the Evangelical revival there had been general coopera-tion between Evangelicals, whether Arminian or Calvinist, Methodist or non-Methodist, but the divisions among Evangelicals on both theological and organisational matters were to cause severe strains by the middle years of the eighteenth century. Within the Methodist ranks a serious division occurred between the Wesleys and their followers, who were Arminians, and the Calvinist groups, who placed enormous emphasis on the doctrines of predestination and election to the total exclusion of the doctrine of free will espoused by the Arminians. These Calvinist groups were led in England by George Whitefield and in Wales by Howell Harris and Daniel Rowland. The limited impact of Methodism in Ireland has already been noted. The impact of Methodism in Scotland was equally limited, largely because the sort of people who were attracted by Methodism in England and Wales were catered for in Scotland by various groups of seceders from the Church of Scotland. The secession that had created the Erskine's Associate Presbytery led to the eventual creation of four different secessionist churches: Old Licht Burghers and Anti-Burghers as well as New Licht Burghers and Anti-Burghers. They were divided on taking oaths to civil authorities and on 'whether the historic covenants were literally binding'. Other new churches included the Glasites and the Relief Church established by Thomas Gillespie of Dunfermline in 1752, though the last of these was liberal in its theology and much influenced by like-minded English dissenters. The strictest Presbyterian group was the Cameronians, formed in 1690, and reorganised during the eighteenth century as the Reformed Presbyterian Church. As well as greatly weakening the appeal of Methodism to Evangelicals in Scotland, especially after the setting up of Independent Evangelical churches by the followers of Robert Haldane, a retired sea-captain, in 1797, these Evangelical Presbyterian bodies also weakened the impact of Evangelicalism on the Church of Scotland, and it did not become a major force within the established church until the conversion of Thomas Chalmers in 1811.[55]

As we have already noted, the two strands of Methodism, Arminian and Calvinist, originated in the 1730s. Both owed a very strong debt to the Moravians especially in their adoption of the conversion experience, the love feast and hymn-singing as essential characteristics of their spirituality. John Wesley, however, broke with the Moravians because of what he regarded as their contempt for prayer, Bible reading and good works; 'they adopted a completely passive attitude towards religion, waiting for inspiration from the Holy Spirit'.[56] What was distinctive about Wesleyan Methodism was the 'methodical' organisation and structure which gave the sect its name and which had evolved by the late 1740s. The basic unit was the 'society' but each society formed part of a 'circuit' to which one or more preachers were appointed for specified periods. Each preacher would visit every society in the circuit as provided for in the 'circuit plan'. The shape of circuits was designed to cover an area that preachers could travel to and from easily in a single day. Each circuit held a 'quarterly meeting' of its officials and the whole 'connexion' was governed by an annual 'conference' which determined doctrine and discipline. Until his death in 1791 John Wesley was the automatic president of the conference but thereafter the conference elected a president and secretary each year. Circuits were then grouped into 'districts' and a district meeting was held twice each year between the annual conferences. Each Wesleyan Methodist society was divided into 'classes' of about a dozen members under a 'class leader' and membership of the connexion was defined by being a member of a class.[57] No doctrinal tests were imposed; potential members merely had to establish their desire to 'flee from the wrath to come, to be saved from their sins'.[58] In the early days of Methodism the principal method of recruitment was through open-air itinerant preaching, but as societies were formed they began to erect their own places of worship and ancillary buildings in which to house preachers, class meetings and, eventually, Sunday Schools. Services in the chapels were organised so that they were additional to, and did not compete with, services in the Anglican parish church, which Methodists were expected to attend. Methodist services comprised preaching, short prayers and hymns. Three times a year societies would celebrate a 'love feast', a service borrowed from the Moravians, which were not eucharists but *agapés*, using cake and water. They also introduced 'watchnight services' on New Year's Eve, both these and the love feasts tending to be very emotional experiences. Methodist leaders who, like John Wesley, were ordained Anglican clergymen, also officiated at celebrations of Holy Communion conducted according to the rite of the *Book of Common Prayer* in Methodist chapels.[59]

It is important to emphasise that it was never Wesley's intention to set up a separate denomination. The Methodists were intended to be a group within the established church which observed certain devotional practices and put a major emphasis on conversion and personal salvation. Nevertheless whatever Wesley might have said about his intentions, there is no doubt that many of his actions, such as his development of an organisational structure, the use of lay preachers and his 'disregard for parish boundaries' suggested that he was dissatisfied with the established church as he found it.[60] However, it was only towards the end of his life that Wesley took the action that would eventually turn Methodism into a separate denomination outside the Church of England, and that was his decision to ordain ministers for the former American Colonies, now part of the United States, in 1784, and for Scotland in 1785. Despite refusing to do so for many years he eventually ordained a small number of English preachers in 1788–9.[61] Such actions were in clear breach of Anglican canon law which insisted on episcopal ordination. They also formed the prelude for the schism that occurred within relatively few years of

Wesley's death. In 1793 the Methodist Conference voted that in those societies in which all the members wished to receive Holy Communion from a local preacher they might do so.[62] However, most Methodists still wished to remain within the established church and the leader of the anti-church party, Alexander Kilham, was formally expelled by the Conference in 1796, taking three preachers and about 5,000 members with him to form the Methodist New Connexion.[63] What eventually pushed the Wesleyan Methodists into formal schism from the Church of England was the increasingly hostile attitude of most bishops and clergy of the established church, who saw Methodists as both political and religious radicals, and local magistrates influenced by them who started refusing to grant licences for Methodist places of worship. In 1811 there was a prosecution under the Conventicle Act for holding a meeting for worship in a private house.[64] The schism between Methodism and the Church of England was not, however, a clear-cut one but a gradual parting of the ways carried out over a number of years. Indeed there were several places throughout the British Isles, especially in Ireland and the Isle of Man, where Methodists attended both Anglican parish churches and their own chapels until well into the second half of the nineteenth century.

It is important not to exaggerate the success of Wesleyan Methodism in England. There were only 24,000 Methodists in 1767 and only 77,000 in 1796.[65] However, Methodism undoubtedly had an appeal in many industrial communities. In 1767 one-fifth of the total membership of the Methodist societies was in Yorkshire, 'mostly in the manufacturing districts of the West Riding'. In Cornwall Methodism was strong among the tin-mining and fishing communities but not among the agricultural ones.[66] Once Methodism had begun to separate itself from the established church it greatly strengthened Protestant dissent, to the extent that a return made by the bishops of the Church of England in 1811 reckoned that dissenting places of worship outnumbered Anglican ones by a ratio of seven to five.[67] Useful comparisons can be made of the impact of Methodism at the local level in recent studies of religion in Kent and Lincolnshire. In Kent Methodism had been supported by two Anglican incumbents, Henry Piers of Bexley (1739–69) and Vincent Perronet of Shoreham (1728–85). Most of the main towns had Methodist chapels by the end of the eighteenth century, and a county circuit was established in 1766, but there were few Methodists in the rural parishes.[68] Methodism was much stronger in Lincolnshire, where a separate county circuit was established in 1753. This had been divided into two circuits by 1766, six by 1801 and ten by 1811. Even so the distribution of Methodism throughout the county was far from even and nearly two-thirds of the Anglican incumbents reported that their parishes had no Methodists in their replies to visitation queries between 1788 and 1792. Methodism appears to have appealed particularly to women, farmers, tradesmen and craftsmen.[69]

Whereas Arminian Methodism as preached by Wesley made a significant impact on England, Calvinistic Methodism as promoted by Whitefield was less popular. There were 31 Whitefieldian societies and 27 preaching stations in 1747. Whitefield's most important convert was the Countess of Huntingdon who seceded from the Church of England in 1782, taking with her the seven Calvinistic Methodist chapels which were her own personal property. Many of the other Whitefieldian chapels, including the Moorfields Tabernacle and the Tottenham Court Chapel in London, were later registered as Independent meeting houses. The Countess of Huntingdon's Connexion survived her death in 1791, but as a relatively small denomination with a clientele of somewhat higher social standing than the Wesleyan Methodists.[70] In Wales the situation was very different. Despite Wesley's frequent visits to Wales, very few Wesleyan societies had been founded there before 1800, and even in 1810 there were only about 100 Wesleyan Methodist congregations in Wales.[71] The Calvinistic Methodists were, by contrast, very much more successful.[72] Their membership appears to have been drawn largely from the families of farmers, craftsmen and tradesmen with a sprinkling of gentry families. Howell Harris was strongly supported by the Countess of Huntingdon who financed a Calvinistic training college at Trefeca. Other early Welsh Evangelicals included the Phillippses of Picton Castle, Lady Charlotte Edwin, the Thomases of Wenvoe and Robert Jones of Fenmon Castle. Calvinistic Methodism in Wales was carried on largely, but by no means exclusively, through the medium of the Welsh language and fostered a strong tradition of hymnology in Welsh, of which the chief exponent was William Williams Pantycelyn. In 1762 there was a major outburst of the spirit in the parishes surrounding Llangeitho (Cards.), where the curate, Daniel Rowland, had had his licence revoked by the Bishop of St Davids. As in England many bishops were strongly critical of Methodism though a few, such as Richard Watson at Llandaff (1782–1816) and Thomas Burgess at St Davids (1803–25), were more tolerant. As was the case with both Calvinistic and Wesleyan Methodism in England, the chief means of spreading the cause was itinerant preaching, with Howell Harris and Daniel Rowland covering much of South Wales between them, supported by a number of clergy sympathetic to Methodism, such as David Jones of Llangan, Edward Davies of Coychurch and Thomas Davies of

Coity, all in the Vale of Glamorgan. Whereas in England the strength of Methodism appeared to lie in industrial communities or the urban areas, in Wales its strength was in the rural areas and especially the Welsh-speaking ones in the Western counties of Cardiganshire and Carmarthenshire.

Before the 1770s Calvinistic Methodism was largely confined to South Wales, but it spread to the north thereafter and, again, was especially successful in the western Welsh-speaking counties of Anglesey, Caernarfonshire and Merioneth. When Daniel Rowland died in 1790, his role as the chief spokesman of Calvinistic Methodism was taken over by Thomas Charles of Bala, another Anglican clergyman. Although the Calvinistic Methodists had erected separate chapels for their supporters from the 1740s, they had, as John Wesley had done, encouraged their supporters to attend their parish churches and had relied on Evangelical Anglican clergy to celebrate Holy Communion in their chapels. The hostile attitude of many of the non-Evangelical clergy and most of the bishops was making many Calvinistic Methodists unwilling to attend Anglican services or receive Holy Communion from clergy that they regarded as 'unconverted' and pressure was put on Charles and the other Methodist leaders to ordain some of the local preachers. The organisation and structure of Calvinistic Methodism in Wales was somewhat looser than that of Wesleyan Methodism. The core was still the society and there were annual gatherings of what was termed the 'association' in both North and South Wales. At the association meetings at Bala (Merion.) and Llandeilo (Carms.) in 1811 Charles eventually agreed to ordain nine preachers for North Wales and 13 preachers for South Wales to supplement the ministry provided by sympathetic Anglican clergy. Thus a formal schism took place and the new church adopted a Presbyterian system of government. Although the Calvinistic Methodist schism greatly weakened the established church in Wales it did help to revive some of the branches of older dissent, especially the Baptists and Independents, as a good deal of transference took place between one sect and another. Many Anglican clergy complained that their laity seemed to have so little understanding of theological differences between the various groups of Christians in Wales that they were prepared to attend any church or chapel where both the preaching and the singing met their expectations. In both respects what particularly captivated the Welsh laity was worship of an extremely emotional type which most orthodox Anglican clergy were unwilling to provide since they regarded it as doctrinally unsound.

We conclude this chapter by returning to the topic with which we began, the maintenance of doctrinal orthodoxy. The Protestant churches of the British Isles were under pressure throughout most of the period between 1714 and 1815 from two movements of a very different character. One was trying to make the churches respond to the results of intellectual advance and scientific discovery. The other aimed at making the churches more responsive to the Holy Spirit working through individual Christians to develop a different type of personal piety. Both attacked what they perceived to be the rather dry orthodoxy of traditional Protestantism. How did the churches respond? Despite the concerns of the Anglican leadership throughout the whole of this period, there is very little evidence to suggest that rationalism made any serious inroads into Anglican orthodoxy. The flurry of deist and rationalist publications in the early years of the eighteenth century had largely dried up by the end of the century. The theological liberalism which was to cause great conflict within the Victorian church had effectively been countered and there was probably more theological agreement in the Church of England between the 1760s and the 1820s than there has been at any point before or since. Whilst the Presbyterians, and other groups of Protestant dissenters, in England and Wales were seriously affected by such liberal tendencies, with many ministers and congregations becoming Arian or Socinian in their theology, there was little damage of this sort done to Presbyterianism in either Ireland or Scotland. The Unitarian tradition which had been established in parts of the British Isles by 1800 was influential, because of the intellectual calibre and wealth of some of those who supported it, but it was never strong numerically.

The impact of Evangelicalism was very different but even here we need to be careful. The relationship between Evangelicals and the churches of which they were a part remained fluid until the last decade of the eighteenth century everywhere, and for a great deal longer in many places. The first schisms of Calvinist Evangelicals from the established church were small and, in the long term certainly, fairly insignificant. The major departures, of Wesleyan Methodists in England and Calvinistic Methodists in Wales, were delayed until the first quarter of the nineteenth century. For Evangelicals who remained within the established churches their day did not come until after 1815. It was in that year, after 80 years of Evangelicalism within the Church of England, that the first Evangelical, Henry Ryder, became a bishop, and then only of Gloucester, one of the less significant sees. In the following year the Irish Bishop Trench of Elphin was converted to Evangelicalism by his own archdeacon. It was to be another 20 years before Evangelicals had to be taken seriously as one of the major groupings in the Anglican church. In the Church of Scotland the

Moderates, who largely controlled the General Assembly and many of the lowland presbyteries, managed to keep Evangelicals out of power until the third decade of the nineteenth century and it was the same in Ireland, where Henry Cooke did not gain control of the Synod of Ulster until the 1820s. Nevertheless Evangelicalism did eventually make an impact far greater than rationalism and can rightly be seen as one of the major religious legacies of the eighteenth century.

There is no doubt that the established churches, throughout the British Isles, responded vigorously to the challenges of the Evangelical revival even if they did not always do so with one voice. Some felt that Evangelicals could be accommodated within the existing structures, others that their presence threatened them and that they had to be resisted. There has been much debate since about who was right and who was wrong. It was perhaps unfortunate that the major programmes of ecclesiastical reform in the nineteenth century, about which churchmen of different theological standpoints tended largely to agree, led them into some misinterpretation of their predecessors' motives. Evangelicalism did not just challenge the way in which the established churches conducted themselves in terms of their administration, their worship, or their spirituality. It also challenged certain core theological beliefs, especially as far as orthodox Anglicans were concerned. The maintenance of doctrinal orthodoxy meant the rejection of beliefs and practices that threatened to undermine essential elements of a church's theology. In the case of rationalism the churches largely succeeded in excluding it from mainstream religious belief in Britain and Ireland for the best part of another two centuries. In the case of Evangelicalism they were very much less successful. By the middle years of the nineteenth century Evangelicalism was to be a major force in the established Protestant churches throughout the British Isles.

The role of women in the churches and society

One of the by-products of the Evangelical Revival was the more significant role it offered women in the life of both the churches and, more generally, society. We have already noted the roles played by Hannah More and Selina, Countess of Huntingdon. Another woman prominent in the campaign for Sunday schools and popular education was Sarah Trimmer, who published *The Servants' Friend* in 1787 and edited the *Family Magazine*. She also ran a school at Brentford, publicised in her *Oeconomy of Charity*.[73] Generally women were prominent in the Evangelical revival, not just as members of the Methodist societies but also as leaders of 'prayer and praise, counsel and exhortation'. In 1803 the Wesleyan Methodists, concerned about the propriety of women preaching at a time when they were trying to disassociate themselves from charges of political radicalism, officially prohibited the practice, though it was later taken up by both the Primitive Methodists and the Bible Christians.[74] Women were also prominent in the Evangelical Revival, and in the promotion of popular education, in Wales. Madam Sydney Griffiths accompanied and supported Howell Harris on his preaching tours, which became the cause of some scandal, and Madam Bridget Bevan took over the management of the Welsh Circulating Schools after the death of Griffith Jones of Llanddowror.

Although it is Evangelical women who have generally received the most publicity from historians of religion, it is important to emphasise that women played an important role in all Christian communities. They were, on the whole, more pious and more regular churchgoers than men, and they were often the leaders of pressure groups that brought charges against clergy for inappropriate behaviour. At Charlton (Wilts.) local women protested against their incumbent's alleged drunkenness. They accused him of 'acrying and belching as though he would vomit and the like at the Administration of the Sacrament thereby making himself ridiculous' with the result that he gave 'great offense and discouragement to the congregation in soe much that . . . divers . . . cannot frequent the said church in time of divine service and participate of the sacraments with any comfort'. It was also women parishioners that complained in 1747 that the incumbent of Wells-next-the-Sea (Norf.) 'was "too often and too much with Strong Liquors" . . . that he omitted the Prayer for Parliament, and failed to conduct baptisms and funerals, to read prayers after announcing them for Wednesday in Holy Week, and to administer the Sacrament on Easter Day'.[75] Women frequently exercised a leading role in the religious societies that existed in many parishes in the early eighteenth century. At the society established at Old Romney (Kent) in 1734 the members 'were to pray daily morning and evening, to fast, to visit and pray with the sick, to "read the Scriptures with attention, reflection, and application", to attend the public services of the Church, to "make diligent improvement of the Sermons heard and delight in the Conversation of devout persons", to be constant and well-prepared in attending "the most Holy Sacrament at all Publick opportunity", and to keep the Sabbath strictly'.[76]

Women's piety was not just restricted to the public worship of the church. Susan White notes that 'many ordinary women regularly used the church's official service book in the liturgical formation of their children'.[77] This approach was part of a rather different attitude towards the rearing of children in the eighteenth century compared with that of the periods both before and after, when there was far more emphasis on the benefits of strict discipline. Whipping as a punishment for children tended to be used only for the most serious misdemeanours and there were several instances, widely reported in contemporary newspapers in terms of the profoundest disapproval, in which parents were taken to court, and sometimes imprisoned, for deliberate acts of cruelty to their children.[78] Linda Pollock attributes this to the much greater emphasis placed in the eighteenth century, largely as a result of religious attitudes, to ensuring that children

absorbed the correct values and beliefs and . . . grew into a model citizen. Both mothers and fathers approached parenthood with apprehension and trepidation, wondering whether or not their modes of child care were correct and whether they were sufficiently competent to rear their children . . . During the early part of the nineteenth century, there was a distinct intensification of adult demands for obedience and conformity, . . . for the children involved it could at times amount to definite cruelty.[79]

It would be appropriate to consider how much this change of attitude was linked to the fears of anarchy and disorder associated with popular reactions to the French Revolution.

Women in the more affluent households in the eighteenth century 'generally organized the working days of their staff in order to accommodate daily prayers'. Lady Elizabeth Hastings had services for her family and servants four times each day. Servants were also prepared, through the reading of devotional works, for Holy Communion. 'Women who could write used their private diaries and journals as mechanisms for reflecting on and deepening their own liturgical piety . . . in order to trace the course of their relationship with God'.[80] Some published these writings. Elizabeth Burnet's *Method of Prayer*, first published in 1709, was read throughout the eighteenth century. Susannah Hopton's *Devotions in the Ancient Way of Offices*, which went through eight editions between 1700 and 1765,

aimed at encouraging women to restore the monastic pattern of daily prayer in their households . . . as book production costs continued to fall, the audience for these kinds of books widened to include women of nearly all social and economic circumstances, even very poor women as they became the objects of various philanthropic efforts.[81]

One aspect of these efforts was undoubtedly the belief that they would assist in the promotion of moral purity. Whereas upper- and middle-class families generally expected that brides would be virgins on their wedding day, this was not the case lower down the social scale. It has been estimated that in the early eighteenth century roughly 40% of brides were pregnant before marriage and that pre-marital unchastity was not merely tolerated but actively encouraged. In some rural communities trial marriage, known as 'bundling', was the norm. Pregnancy was regarded as a sign that the man and the woman were right for one another. Girls and their parents would frequently encourage pre-marital sex as the best means of securing a marriage partner. If she did not get pregnant she was encouraged to discontinue the relationship and try with somebody else. However, if she got pregnant the man was expected to marry her and, if he was unwilling, pressure would be put on him by the respective families and the local community to honour his obligations.[82]

Some clergy wives and daughters saw it as part of their duty to assist their husbands and fathers in the pastoral aspects of their ministry. A good example was Susannah Wesley (1669–1742), who held prayer meetings in the kitchen of her husband's rectory at Epworth. The influence of these meetings on her sons, John and Charles, was to provide one of the inspirations for the class meetings that were to become such a feature of Wesleyan Methodism. Women also made a significant contribution to eighteenth-century hymnology. The sisters Ann Taylor Gilbert (1782–1866) and Jane Taylor (1783–1824), who came from a family of devout Independents, published hymns for the use of children: *Hymns for Infant Minds* (1808) and *Original Hymns for Sunday Schools* (1812). Another female writer of hymns was the Baptist Anne Steele (1717–78). She was the daughter of a minister who, when her future husband was drowned on the day before their wedding, remained at home to look after her father. She published two volumes of hymns, entitled *Poems on Subjects Chiefly Devotional*, in 1760.[83] In a society in which political and social leadership was the preserve of men, religion gave women an opportunity for limited forms of leadership which they were otherwise denied.

Notes

1 R.N. Stromberg, *Religious Liberalism in Eighteenth Century England*, Oxford 1954, p. 114.

2 E.G. Rupp, *Religion in England* 1688–1791, Oxford 1986, pp. 218–42.

3 J.C.D. Clark, *English Society 1688–1832*, Cambridge 1985, pp. 218–26, 230–4.

4 P. Nockles, 'Church parties in the pre-Tractarian Church of England', in J. Walsh, C. Haydon and S. Taylor (eds), *The Church of England c.1689–c.1833: From Toleration to Tractarianism*, Cambridge 1993, pp. 335–6.

5 I.D.L. Clark, 'From protest to reaction: the moderate regime in the Church of Scotland', in N.T. Phillipson and R. Mitchison (eds), *Scotland in the Age of Improvement: Essays in Scottish History in the Eighteenth Century*, Edinburgh 1970, pp. 200, 204.

6 A.C. Chitnis, *The Scottish Enlightenment: A Social History*, London 1976, pp. 43, 59.

7 Clark, 'From protest to reaction', p. 207.

8 Chitnis, *Scottish Enlightenment*, p. 62.

9 *Ibid.*, p. 66; Clark, 'From protest to reaction', pp. 213–14.

10 Chitnis, *Scottish Enlightenment*, pp. 241–2.

11 T.C. Smout, *A History of the Scottish People 1560–1830*, London 1969, p. 232.

12 R. Porter, *English Society in the Eighteenth Century*, Harmondsworth 1982, p. 179; J. Davies, *A History of Wales*, London 1994, p. 295.

13 W. Gibson, *Enlightenment Prelate: Benjamin Hoadly, 1676–1761*, Cambridge 2004, pp. 150–1.

14 *Ibid.*, pp. 236–42.

15 J.P. Ferguson, *An Eighteenth Century Heretic: Dr Samuel Clarke*, Kineton 1976, p. 55.

16 *Ibid.*, pp. 162–5.

17 Rupp, *Religion in England*, pp. 249–50.

18 P. Langford, *A Polite and Commercial People: England 1727–1783*, Oxford 1989, p. 238. Quotation from the facsimile edition of Tindal's work, ed. G. Gawlick, Stuttgart 1967, p. 58.

19 J. Redwood, *Reason, Ridicule and Religion: The Age of Enlightenment in England*, London 1976, p. 149.

20 *Ibid.*, pp. 168–9; N. Sykes, *From Sheldon to Secker: Aspects of English Church History, 1660–1768*, Cambridge 1959, pp. 176–8. For a useful selection of edited writings of eighteenth-century theologians see J.M. Creed and J.S.B. Smith, *Religious Thought in the Eighteenth Century*, Cambridge 1934.

21 F.L. Cross (ed.), *Oxford Dictionary of the Christian Church*, 4th edn, Oxford 1963, p. 80.

22 J. Black, *Eighteenth-Century Britain 1688–1783*, Basingstoke 2001, pp. 127–8.

23 Sykes, *From Sheldon to Secker*, p. 167.

24 There is a substantial literature on this topic of which the following can be especially recommended: W.R. Ward, *The Protestant Evangelical Awakening*, Cambridge 1992, for the international framework; D. Bebbington, *Evangelicalism in Modern Britain*, London 1989 and G.M. Ditchfield, *The Evangelical Revival*, London 1998, for the British context. For the international context of the Evangelical Revival in Wales see D.C. Jones, *'A Glorious Work in the World': Welsh Methodism and the International Evangelical Revival, 1735–1750*, Cardiff 2004.

25 C. Podmore, *The Moravian Church in England, 1728–1760*, Oxford 1998, pp. 5–71.

26 *Ibid.*, pp. 205–65.

27 Bebbington, *Evangelicalism*, pp. 20–1.

28 Black, *Eighteenth-Century Britain*, p. 138.

29 J. Davies, *A History of Wales*, London 1994, p. 311.

30 G.F.A. Best, *Temporal Pillars: Queen Anne's Bounty, the Ecclesiastical Commissioners and the Church of England*, Cambridge 1964, p. 76.

31 Ditchfield, *Evangelical Revival*, pp. 40–5.

32 *Ibid.*, pp. 47–9.

33 Jones, *'A Glorious Work in the World'*, p. 58.

34 *Ibid.*, pp. 105–238. See also the excellent biography by G. Tudur, *Howell Harris: From Conversion to Separation*, Cardiff 2000, and the more limited one by E. Evans, *Daniel Rowland and the Great Evangelical Awakening in Wales*, Edinburgh 1985.

35 Ward, *Protestant Evangelical Awakening*, pp. 329–39.

36 G.C.B. Davies, *The Early Cornish Evangelicals 1735–60*, London 1951, pp. 53–87, 130–47.

37 M. Hennell, *John Venn and the Clapham Sect*, London 1958, pp. 60–213.

38 C. Smyth, *Simeon and Church Order: A Study of the Origins of the Evangelical Revival in Cambridge in the Eighteenth Century*, Cambridge 1940, pp. 284–302.

39 See the excellent biography by A. Stott, *Hannah More: The First Victorian*, Oxford 2003, especially pp. 103–25, 169–90, 232–57.

40 J.B. Owen, *The Eighteenth Century 1714–1815*, London 1974, pp. 325–6; H.T. Dickinson, *The Politics of the People in Eighteenth Century Britain*, Basingstoke 1995, pp. 89–91; B. Hilton, *A Mad, Bad and Dangerous People? England 1783–1846*, Oxford 2006, pp. 184–8.

41 F.K. Brown, *Fathers of the Victorians: The Age of Wilberforce*, Cambridge 1961, p. 15.

42 *Ibid.*, pp. 83–91.

43 Speck, *Stability and Strife*, p. 105.

44 *Ibid.*, p. 119; G. Holmes and D. Szechi, *The Age of Oligarchy: Pre-Industrial Britain 1722–1783*, London 1993, pp. 123–4.

45 Langford, *A Polite and Commercial People*, p. 265.

46 *Ibid.*, pp. 268–70.

47 Davies, *History of Wales*, p. 312.

48 R. Hole, *Pulpits, Politics and Public Order in England 1760–1832*, Cambridge 1989, pp. 187, 190.

49 The section that follows is based on the excellent account in J.F.C. Harrison, *The Second Coming: Popular Millenarianism 1780–1850*, London 1979, especially pp. 28–38, 57–134.

50 *Ibid.*, p. 77, quoting *The World's Doom*, London 1795, i, p. 353.

51 N. Yates, R. Hume and P. Hastings, *Religion and Society in Kent, 1640–1914*, Woodbridge 1994, p. 42.

52 A.L. Drummond and J. Bulloch, *The Scottish Church 1688–1843: The Age of the Moderates*, Edinburgh 1973, pp. 136–7; J. MacInnes, *The Evangelical Movement in the Highlands of Scotland 1688 to 1800*, Aberdeen 1951, pp. 161–6; D.E. Meek, 'Evangelical missionaries in the early nineteenth century Highlands', *Scottish Studies*, 28 (1987), pp. 1–34.

53 C.G. Brown, *Religion and Society in Scotland since 1707*, Edinburgh 1997, p. 72.

54 This section is based on the more detailed account in N. Yates, *The Religious Condition of Ireland 1770–1850*, Oxford 2006, pp. 260–70.

55 Smout, *History of the Scottish People*, pp. 234–6.

56 Speck, *Stability and Strife*, p. 109. There is a substantial literature on Wesleyan Methodism, see especially H.D. Rack, *Reasonable Enthusiast: John Wesley and the Rise of Methodism*, London 1989; D. Hempton, *Methodism and Politics in British Society 1750–1850*, London 1984; R. Davies and G. Rupp (eds), *History of the Methodist Church in Great Britain*, vol. 1, London 1965; F. Baker, *John Wesley and the Church of England*, London 1970; B. Semmel, *The Methodist Revolution*, London

1974; A. Armstrong, *The Church of England, the Methodists and Society 1700–1850*, London 1973.

57 Rack, *Reasonable Enthusiast*, pp. 238–9.

58 Armstrong, *Church of England*, p. 65.

59 *Ibid.*, pp. 72–80; Rack, *Reasonable Enthusiast*, pp. 409–20.

60 For an excellent discussion of these issues see J. Gregory, 'In the Church I will live and die: John Wesley, the Church of England and Methodism', in Gibson and Ingram (eds), *Religious Identities*, pp. 147–78.

61 Rack, *Reasonable Enthusiast*, pp. 508–21.

62 W.R. Ward, *Religion and Society in England 1790–1850*, London 1972, p. 30.

63 J. Walsh, 'Methodism at the End of the Eighteenth Century', in Davies and Rupp (eds), *History of the Methodist Church*, pp. 284–9.

64 Ward, *Religion and Society*, pp. 54–62.

65 Porter, *English Society*, p. 193.

66 Speck, *Stability and Strife*, p. 113.

67 O'Gorman, *Long Eighteenth Century*, p. 297.

68 Yates, Hume and Hastings, *Religion and Society in Kent*, pp. 42–4.

69 Ambler, *Churches, Chapels and Parish Communities*, pp. 131–46.

70 Bebbington, *Evangelicalism*, pp. 29–30; Rack, *Reasonable Enthusiast*, pp. 282–6.

71 Davies, *History of Wales*, p. 343.

72 The section that follows is based on the accounts of Welsh Calvinistic Methodism in W.M. Jacob, 'Methodism in Wales' and W.N. Yates, 'Calvinistic Methodism: growth and schism', in Williams, Jacob, Yates and Knight, *Welsh Church*, forthcoming.

73 Stott, *Hannah More*, pp. 105, 170–1.

74 Bebbington, *Evangelicalism*, pp. 25–6.

75 Quoted in S. J. White, *A History of Women in Christian Worship*, London 2003, p. 296.

76 *Ibid.*, p. 123.

77 *Ibid.*, p. 218.

78 L.A. Pollock, *Forgotten Children: Parent–Child Relations from 1500 to 1900*, Cambridge 1983, pp. 93, 172–3.

79 *Ibid.*, p. 269.

80 White, *Women in Christian Worship*, pp. 126–7, 213–14.

81 *Ibid.*, p. 133.

82 B. Hill, *Women, Work and Sexual Politics in Eighteenth-Century England*, Oxford 1989, pp. 180–4.

83 White, *Women in Christian Worship*, pp. 225, 253–5.

CHAPTER 4

A Theology of
Good Works

At a time when the governments of some European countries were beginning to accept that it was the duty of the state to make provision for education and social welfare, the British government was still committed to the principle of voluntaryism; indeed it was to remain so until the 1830s. There were some areas, such as the relief of the poor, where parishes had an obligation to levy a rate for the purpose, but this was greatly supplemented by private charity, and religious teaching between 1714 and 1815 laid enormous emphasis on the duty of Christians who were well provided for to use their comparative wealth in a compassionate way by contributing either financially or in kind to the needs of their poorer neighbours. The visual record of all this charitable giving can still be seen in the inscriptions on monuments, or on boards recording charitable bequests, in many churches. In this chapter we will examine the various elements of this programme of charitable giving and the impact that it had on improving the lot of the poor in this period. We should, however, at the outset deal with a fundamental debate between historians on the nature of eighteenth-century philanthropy. How much of it was genuine philanthropy and how much of it was an attempt to exercise social control over the poor? Certainly a number of educational and social historians have in the past taken the position that the exercise of social control was the real *raison d'étre* of most eighteenth-century philanthropy, but that view is gradually being rejected, or at least modified. Religious historians have generally taken a similar position and, in particular, endeavoured to establish a clear link between the prevailing theology of the age and its practical implications. Norman Sykes has noted that most eighteenth-century preachers emphasised in their sermons the doctrine of divine benevolence and the need for devout Christians to relate 'their daily occupations to the teachings of religion'. Philanthropy was the natural outcome: 'measured by the standard of the Epistle of St James, the age could challenge comparison with almost any epoch of Christian history. Its faith was abundantly fruitful in good works'.[1]

Morality and social control

Nevertheless there was undoubtedly an element of social control in the philanthropic programmes of the churches in the eighteenth century and this is to be seen nowhere more powerfully than in the two campaigns, at the beginning and the end of the century respectively, for what was initially termed 'the reformation of manners'. Another aspect of the religious element in social control was the significant role of Anglican clergy as magistrates. In 1731 1,038 out of approximately 9,000 magistrates in England were Anglican clergy. In Oxfordshire in 1775 clergy formed 31% of the magistracy, dipping slightly to 28.3% in 1797, but increasing again to 36.8% by 1816. Clerical magistrates tended to be more active than lay ones. In Oxfordshire in 1780 clerical magistrates signed four out of five quarter sessions convictions. They also frequently served as members of urban corporations, as at Banbury and Woodstock, where successive incumbents served as aldermen and mayors of these boroughs.[2] In some ways the period between 1714 and 1815 saw an increase in moral responsibility. The serious concerns about witchcraft, which had been a feature of seventeenth-century society, had died down by the eighteenth century and the laws against it were repealed in 1737. At the same time suicide came to be regarded as the result of mental illness rather than sheer wickedness. There was a decline in support for some previously popular sports and customs. Cock-fighting was banned in Worcester in 1745, in Bewdley and Kidderminster in 1750 and in Liverpool by the late 1770s. An extremely serious-minded incumbent of Haworth (Yorks.) stopped his parishioners from playing football or attending horse races. Even the historic flitch ceremony was abandoned at Dunmow (Essex).[3]

However, in other respects society was seen to be getting worse, particularly in relation to sexual licence, in which by the end of the eighteenth century women could be as involved as men. Sodomy between men, though illegal, was frequently overlooked in cases where the participants were of high social rank, and also in cases where older men had sexual relations with men who 'were young (and thus not fully developed)' as well as with women. There was, however, much criticism of men who dressed in women's clothes or adopted feminine mannerisms. There was a greater tolerance

of cross-dressing among women, partly because it was difficult to pro-
secute women for sexual deviance, since most lawyers took the view
that lesbianism could not be interpreted as a breach of the laws against
sodomy. There was also a rather ambivalent attitude towards prostitution.
Robert Shoemaker suggests that 'many legal and social commentators
viewed prostitution as a necessary evil, in that it served a useful function
in satisfying men's lusts while keeping respectable women pure'. Most
prostitutes, as opposed to mistresses, were of relatively low social standing
and got involved in the trade for largely, sometimes entirely, financial reasons. Prostitution was only illegal if it caused a 'public nuisance', in which
case those convicted might be sent to a house of correction for a short
period of hard labour and whipping. Action against prostitution tended
to take the form of establishing reformatories, such as the Magdalen
Hospital established in London in 1758, in which 'penitent' fallen women
might be resced from a life of sin. There was a deep concern about the
growing circulation of pornographic literature, designed for consumption
by both men and women, during the eighteenth century. These included
factual publications such as *Harris' Lists of Covent Garden Ladies*, which
included detailed descriptions of prostitutes and the prices they charged,
and novels such as John Cleland's *Memoirs of a Woman of Pleasure*,
narrated by a notorious fictional libertine, Fanny Hill.[4] These concerns
were not new. They had been a staple ingredient of Puritan attitudes since
at least the sixteenth century. Whereas many of the religious attitudes
of Puritanism were rejected by eighteenth-century society, some of the
moral attitudes seem to have become more deeply imbedded and no longer
regarded as essentially Puritan.

It was in the context of concerns about growing sexual licence that
the first attempts had been made to bring about improvements in moral
standards during the latter part of the seventeenth century. Though the
various Societies for the Reformation of Manners founded then remained
powerful agents for upholding a strict moral code during the first three
decades of the eighteenth century support for them began to decline in the
1730s. Altogether the societies ensured a total of 101,683 convictions,
mostly 'for lewd and disorderly practices, much of it street soliciting,
indecent exposure and intercourse in the open'. Arrests in 1730 included
those of 'a whore and client fornicating on one of London's new shop
windows, and a group of women . . . exposing their nakedness in the open
street to all passengers and using most abominable and filthy expressions'.
Whereas there had been an annual average of 1,400 society prosecutions
in the early 1720s these had declined to only 170 by the 1730s.[5] The

decline can be seen in more detail by analysing the statistics for the London Society for the Reformation of Manners. It initiated 7,251 prosecutions in 1722 but only 410 in 1734. Before 1727 there were never fewer than 1,000 prosecutions each year, but always fewer than 1,000 each year after 1730. It appeared that 'the pious Puritanism of the reformers may have fallen victim to the prevailing scepticism'.[6] William Jacob, however, suggests some more likely reasons in the decline of prosecutions:

The promoters of Societies for the Reformation of Manners were regarded with suspicion by the majority of their fellow citizens who may have feared an attempt to return to the moral rigours imposed during the Civil Wars . . . Most moderate people seem to have regarded them with unease . . . Whilst the average church person and citizen agreed with the ends of the societies, they had reservations about the means used. Informing was much disliked. After the first flush of enthusiasm it was as difficult to recruit informers as to persuade churchwardens to present their neighbours, and constables to secure warrants against their fellow citizens.[7]

Some successful defendants even brought suits against those who had prosecuted them.

In a sense the Societies were unnecessary. The machinery for the control of private and public morals already existed in the ecclesiastical courts. An older generation of historians assumed that, with the possible exception of the Isle of Man, where the ecclesiastical courts were given a new lease of life following the successful campaign of Bishop Wilson against the island's governor to maintain ecclesiastical jurisdiction as it had existed in the past, such courts had become moribund after the seventeenth century. However, such a view can no longer be sustained. The evidence for dioceses where the court records have survived in quantity show that they were as active between 1714 and 1815 as they had ever been. The courts in the diocese of Norwich handled more business in the mid-eighteenth century than they had before the Reformation. A good deal of the business related to probate matters but they also dealt with disputes between parishioners, clandestine marriages, sexual misdemeanours, defamation, non-attendance at church and profaning the Sabbath. Other cases included disputes over tithes or matters concerning the fabric and furnishings of churches, as well as the maintenance of churchyards. One of the reasons for the continued activity of the ecclesiastical courts was that they were more efficient than the secular courts, with cases being heard more quickly and at less cost. Instead of the fines and corporal punishments inflicted by the secular courts, the ecclesiastical courts tended to impose public penance (sometimes commuted to a payment to a specified charity) or, in severe cases, excommunication.[8] In a judgement given on 7 December 1764 'Mary Cutting of Pyworthy in the County of Devon' was ordered to appear in her parish church

bare-headed with a white sheet about her shoulders, bare-footed and bare-legged, with a white rod in her hand, and shall stand before the Minister's seat or pew until the end of the Nicene Creed, and shall openly confess and acknowledge that she had been delivered of a male child unlawfully begotten on her body, and shall show her hearty sorrow and repentance and shall desire God to forgive her, and the Minister and the People to pray for the amendment of her for the future.[9]

Arthur Warne has shown that, although the ecclesiastical courts in the diocese of Exeter remained active throughout the eighteenth century, the nature of the business began to change. In 1759 there were 26 cases involving bastardy, 9 involving antenuptial fornication, 9 relating to tithes and 47 to probate matters. By 1792 there were no cases of bastardy or fornication, 1 case of incest, 78 relating to tithes and 76 relating to church buildings or churchyards. However, as late as 1807 there was a presentment for non-attendance at church in the archdeacon of Barnstaple's court, a conviction for bastardy in Cornwall in 1802 and the delivery of a sentence of excommunication in a probate case in 1812.[10]

One of the consequences of the Evangelical Revival discussed in the last chapter was the revival of campaigns for public decency and higher moral standards. The Society for the Promotion of Christian Knowledge and a new Society for Distributing Religious Tracts, established in 1782, published popular literature giving advice on moral issues. There were attacks on sexual promiscuity, including nude bathing at the new seaside resorts, and efforts made by Thomas Bowdler and others to remove offensive passages from the plays of Shakespeare and other dramatists. In 1802 a new Society for the Suppression of Vice was established and it immediately attempted to get all fairs banned.[11] Between 1788 and 1790 there were four prosecutions of allegedly obscene publications, including the *School of Venus* and *Fanny Hill*. These new anti-vice meetings were supported, not just by Evangelicals such as William Wilberforce and Hannah More, but also by Bishop Porteous of London.[12] Wilberforce and others established the Proclamation Society in 1787; this 'advocated the moral regeneration of the ruling elite and the restoration of its sense of responsibility'. They strongly supported Sabbath-day observance and the Evangelical prime minister, Spencer Percival, 'refused to call parliamentary sittings on a Monday so that MPs from distant constituencies would not have to travel on the Sabbath'. One of the pieces of evidence that they used to bolster their campaign was the belief 'that the French Revolution had occurred because of the atheism and immorality which had penetrated French society in the last decade of the life of the *ancien régime*'.[13]

The effectiveness of the ecclesiastical courts in England and Wales was replicated in Scotland by the judicial role of the kirk sessions, with some parish ministers also acting, like many Anglican clergymen, as justices of the peace. The power of the kirk sessions in Scotland was in a sense greater than that of the Anglican ecclesiastical courts since they effectively acted as the courts of first instance for both civil and religious offences. They thus dealt not just with matters such as adultery, fornication, drunkenness, sorcery and profaning the Sabbath, but also with cases of theft, assault, wife-beating and suspicious death. The most frequently heard cases were sexual ones, usually the result of one of the elders reporting the pregnancy of an unmarried woman. Callum Brown has revealed that women tended to get a rather rough deal in the male-dominated kirk sessions. Women who claimed that their pregnancy had been the result of rape tended not to be believed and those who denied they had secretly given birth, or had an abortion, or committed infanticide, were likely to be made to have their breasts milked to prove whether or not they were lying. Pregnant women who refused to name the father of their child were frequently interrogated on this point during the pains of childbirth. Women found guilty of adultery or fornication were generally punished more severely than men, a reverse of the situation in England and Wales. Public penance, fines or excommunication were the normal punishments for most crimes not submitted to a higher secular court, the first of these surviving even longer than in other parts of the British Isles. In urban congregations public penance was beginning to be abandoned by about 1800, but in the rural parishes it continued to be enforced for the best part of the succeeding century.[14]

Poverty and social welfare

The statutory provision for the relief of the poor between 1714 and 1815 was the Acts of 1597 and 1601 which had 'provided for the levy of a poor rate and the selection of overseers to care for the "settled" impotent poor of each parish while the able bodied poor were to be set to work'. As Paul Hastings has shown in the case of Kent, the way in which the poor law was administered varied greatly from one parish to another. The poor might receive outdoor relief in cash or in kind (housing, fuel, clothing, food). Some parishes also paid for doctors, nurses and midwives to treat the sick poor. Knatchbull's Act of 1722 permitted parishes or groups of parishes to establish workhouses and by 1776 there were 132 workhouses in Kent with accommodation for 5,819 inmates. Only 29 out of 391 parishes in the county did not use workhouses. The workhouses varied in size from 350 inmates at Greenwich, 250 at Canterbury and Chatham, and 150 at Maidstone to many which held fewer than 30 people and were little more than cottages. Gilbert's Act of 1782 further encouraged the smaller parishes, with uneconomic workhouses, to combine into unions to maintain a central workhouse and 12 such unions were formed in Kent. By 1813, of the 22,263 adult paupers in the county, 14,186 were housed in workhouses and 8,077 were still receiving outdoor relief. All other counties, with the exception of Middlesex, had a high proportion of their poor in workhouses and a lower proportion receiving outdoor relief, which was considered to be more expensive. The most common form of workhouse administration was to enter into a three-year contract with an entrepreneur, who would take on its management for an annual lump sum or a per capita payment in return for profiting from the work of the inmates. This could lead to abuses and the arrangements were abandoned for more direct control and regular inspections in some parishes. It was generally agreed that most workhouses were 'characterised more by slackness and squalor than by deliberate cruelty'. Maidstone workhouse had only one privy for all 150 inmates. As parishes were only obliged to maintain their 'settled' poor, attempts were made wherever possible to remove paupers who had moved from one parish to another and removal orders were commonplace, sometimes resulting in great physical hardship to those removed, especially if they were pregnant women. Pauper children were found appropriate work; when they were old enough boys were normally apprenticed to local tradesmen and girls placed in service.[15]

Churchmen were divided in their attitude to the poor. Bishop Horsley took the view 'that the divine origin of inequality also entailed a divine responsibility for the relief of the poor'. Bishop Thomas Burgess stated in a sermon preached in 1803 that the Christian should 'not be too scrupulous about the objects of his benevolence. Charity shrinks from a cold scrutiny of minute enquiry'. Nevertheless the bishops generally advocated that the poor law should be more efficiently administered. Others, especially Evangelicals, tended to take a harder line, seeing poverty as a consequence of irreligion. The Evangelical Society for Bettering the Condition of the

Poor, established in 1797, 'made it clear, that it had no intention of distributing relief merely because of need'. John Venn of Clapham stated in 1799 that 'before any relief is granted, information should be particularly sought concerning the moral character of the applicant, particularly if he is accustomed to attend public worship; whether he sends his children to school, and trains them in the habit of industry'. Those who could not fulfil these criteria were to be denied relief.[16] Others saw the poor as a social threat, with unemployment leading to crime. Spurred on by Henry Fielding's *Enquiry into the Causes of the Late Increase of Robbers*, published in 1751, they urged a major contraction, and in some cases total abolition, of the poor law. They attacked the ability of the poor to spend sensibly what little they earned and advocated a reduction in wages so that the poor would be unable to waste their money on luxuries.[17] Thus the concept of the 'deserving' and the 'undeserving' poor was popularised, though it had had its origins in the drafting of the original poor law legislation in the late sixteenth century. Nevertheless, though their aims might have been rather restricted, a number of societies were formed during the eighteenth century with the object of dealing with the problems of poverty and 'the aim of encouraging in the labouring poor the petty bourgeois ethic of dedication to industry, thrift, sobriety and self-help'.[18]

By far the greatest contribution to the relief of poverty, over and above that provided by statute, came not from societies but individuals. A monument of *c.*1747 in All Saints, Northampton, records that Mrs Dorothy Beckett and Mrs Anne Sargent had 'jointly settled an Estate in Trust for cloathing and teaching Thirty poor Girls of this Parish'. The monument 'is surmounted by the relief of a girl charity scholar holding a scroll' bearing the inscription 'Go and do thou likewise'. The charity boards in many churches listing 'annual payments in money, bread or warm clothes for the poor, for the education of poor children, for almshouses for the elderly . . . served as an insurance against loss or misappropriation, as a reminder to the poor of their rights, and a reminder to others to emulate their examples'.[19] Sometimes charitable bequests were advertised even more crudely, with the recipients being obliged to wear special clothes and occupy special seats in church. At Leeds parish church there was a pew for 'the master and mistress of the charity school, with 40 poor boys and girls decently clad in blue'. At Bath Abbey, in 1742, the children of the charity schools sat on opposite sides of the aisle, 'the boys on one side, the girls on the other, forming a lane for the congregation to pass through. They were all new clothed, in blue, with white stockings'.[20] Not all charity was in the form of specific endowments. Many aristocratic and gentry families provided regular charity to their poorer tenants. William Bulkeley, in the Anglesey parish of Llanfechell, frequently made gifts to the poor in both cash and kind or employed them in industries on his estates such as spinning, carding and winding wool to make lengths of cloth and blankets.[21]

The effectiveness of parochial charities depended on the proper implementation of the bequest. At South Molton 40 penny loaves were distributed to poor parishioners every Sunday morning, and a further 60 on sacrament days, but in other Devon parishes there was evidence that charities were being maladministered. At Crediton a benefaction of 1,000 pounds to support 'poor widows and orphans, had been lying untouched for two years' and in 1780 it was ordered that the original sum and 'accumulated interest of £221 11s 11d be invested in 3 per cent consoles'. At Cotleigh charity land of ten acres was 'being let to a tenant for the ridiculously small rent of £1 a year', subsequently 'raised to the more realistic sum of £14 10s'. Charitable funds were sometimes lost through poor investment. On the other hand many were well administered. At Heavitree, Prebendary George Moore kept meticulous accounts of the management of the parochial charities. These charities were designed to supplement the system of poor relief exercised at parochial level under the poor law legislation, and in many cases, where such charities did not exist, parishes made every effort to be as generous to the poor as the legislation allowed. Arthur Warne has uncovered excellent examples of the relief of poverty by overseers of the poor in Devon. At Cadleigh the husband of Thomasin Brooks, a poor widow, died in 1763. Each month Thomasin received an allowance of ten shillings for food for her family. Her two boys, Robert and John, were also supplied with clothing, which cost the parish £2 18s 8½d in 1767, and the family was housed rent-free. Thomasin survived both her children. By 1814 her monthly allowance had increased to 16 shillings and when she died in 1817 the parish met the £1 17s cost of the funeral. Similar generosity was shown to the Bassett family at Bradford, the parish paying for all their needs, including clothing and medical care. It later paid for the children to be apprenticed and, when one of the daughters gave birth to an illegitimate child, the parish paid for both the delivery and the baptism. Further illegitimate children were also maintained by the parish.[22]

A very important aspect of eighteenth-century philanthropy was the establishment of hospitals. This began in London with the Westminster Hospital of 1719, Guy's Hospital of 1734, the London Hospital of 1740, the Middlesex Hospital of 1745, the Lock Hospital of 1746, Queen Charlotte's Hospital of 1752, the Royal Hospital of 1757 and the Westminster Lying-in Hospital of 1765. Many of these were well-endowed.

The London Hospital had an average annual income of £4,300 between 1743 and 1754. In 1741 Captain Thomas Coram established the Foundling Hospital in London. New provincial hospitals included Addenbrooke's at Cambridge and the Radcliffe at Oxford. In 1736 Dr Alured Clarke, Prebendary of Winchester, founded a hospital in that city. In 1741 he became Dean of Exeter and immediately set about establishing a hospital there, with accommodation for 160 patients and at a cost of more than £3,000. Many of the hospitals provided not just for the medical care of the patients, but for their spiritual welfare as well. At Bristol Infirmary, established in 1737, religious tracts were given to patients, who were forbidden to swear or gamble, and there were daily prayers. Many hospitals were provided with chapels. That of the Rotunda Lying-in Hospital in Dublin was built in 1751, refurbished in 1757–62, 'and, as a triumph of rococo design, must have been a very expensive item in the cost of the whole building'. The chapel of the London Foundling Hospital cost £4,195 17s 4d, raised by public subscription, and had an organ presented by Handel. Both these chapels were used as venues for fundraising concerts, the chapel at Dublin witnessing the first public performance of Handel's *Messiah*.[23]

Provision for education

The greatest impact of eighteenth-century philanthropy was, however, to be seen in the provision made for education. In some parts of Europe, notably much of Germany and Austria, and in France after 1789, the principle of voluntaryism was being abandoned, and national systems of education being introduced.[24] Frederick William I of Prussia issued an edict requiring compulsory elementary education as early as 1716–17, but it was never fully implemented, and had to be re-issued by Frederick II in 1763. This new edict required six hours of school attendance each day by children aged between 5 and 14. Although every parish in Prussia had an elementary school by the end of the eighteenth century their standards varied considerably. Not all had separate buildings or ones in good repair. There was a shortage of colleges for the training of teachers and many schools were forced to employ anybody willing to do the job. Many schools were poorly equipped with books. In Austria a special board was set up to supervise elementary education in 1760 but here too it was impossible to ensure that provision was of an acceptable standard. There were, however, significant improvements in elementary education in the German states from the last quarter of the eighteenth century as a result of the reforms advocated by J.B. Basendow (1723–90) and F.E. von Rochow (1734–1805).

In France a national system of education was introduced in the wake of the revolution, though it was closely associated with the programme of de-Christianisation taking place at the same time, and would therefore have been discredited in British eyes. Its purpose was to ensure that children were taught not just reading, writing and arithmetic, but the 'principles of republicanism', overseen by the newly established Committee of Public Instruction. The original plan proposed in 1793 was for the establishment of 20,000 public boarding schools. All children between the ages of 5 and 12 would have been separated from their parents and sent to one of these schools. The plan would have been extremely expensive and was therefore never implemented. A much modified scheme permitted any person to open a school provided it was supervised by the municipal authorities and used the text books commissioned or approved by the Committee of Public Instruction. The primers that had been produced by the Roman Catholic church for use in schools before 1789 were replaced by republican ones in both primary and secondary schools. Although this national programme of education was short-lived it provided the model for what eventually became the 'secular public school' in France.

Any such national system of education was entirely foreign to the British way of thinking, except to a limited extent in Scotland, where attempts had been made to establish schools in every parish, though without any system of national oversight, during the seventeenth century. It was not until the 1830s that a national system was introduced in Ireland, and it was a good deal later before similar systems were introduced in England and Wales. Absolutely fundamental to the British position was the establishment of schools through charitable benefactions, though these were supplemented by earlier endowed, especially grammar, schools, by commercially run private schools, and later on by the Sunday schools and schools established by the national societies. An early initiative in the establishment of charity schools was taken by the Society for the Promotion of Christian Knowledge founded in 1698. As Table 6 shows the number of charity schools established in the following century was considerable, though it was clear that the momentum for setting up new schools was in decline from the 1730s. Of the 150 charity schools in London in 1750 only nine had been founded since 1727.[25] Whereas schools before the eighteenth century had mostly been established and endowed by individuals, many charity schools were founded by public subscription. The SPCK also encouraged charity schools to hold annual

TABLE 6 *Numbers of endowed non-classical schools and charities for elementary education established in England and Wales 1710–1800*

Decade	Non-classical schools	Educational charities
1710–20	235	160
1720–30	197	208
1730–40	115	113
1740–50	60	61
1750–60	67	67
1760–70	93	85
1770–80	55	75
1780–90	72	93
1790–1800	73	96
Undated	245	402

Source: M.G. Jones, *The Charity School Movement: A Study of Eighteenth Century Puritanism in Action*, Cambridge 1938, pp. 351–2.

services in their local churches, with a sermon by a well-known preacher, both to publicise their activities and as a means of fund-raising. Many schools provided clothing for the children who attended and the curriculum was based on learning to read and to know the Bible and the catechism. Schools educated both boys and girls, who were normally taught together and it was estimated that by the late 1720s approximately 5,000 children were being taught in London alone and a further 30,000 across the rest of the country. By 1743 about 60% of the parishes in the diocese of York had a school of some sort, whether a charity or a commercially run private school.[26]

The charity school movement did not, however, have unanimous support.

Those who opposed popular education did so on the grounds that it would eventually destroy a society which was based upon rigid social distinctions: thus the only way to preserve it was to deny education to the poor. The motive of the reformers was a charitable one: to modify the ignorance of the poor so that they might read the Scriptures and earn a useful though humble living, grateful to their superiors and always conscious of a duty to them. In this way, it was thought, the continuance of existing social patterns would be ensured.[27]

This is perhaps a rather negative way of expressing contemporary motivation, and tends to ignore the religious factor behind the establishment of schools, but it does contain more than a grain of truth. Some scholars claim that the impact of charity schools has been exaggerated. John Rule suggests that the numbers of new schools 'seems only to have helped stop a poor level [of education] becoming worse', pointing out that many children still had no access to schooling since many parishes had no schools.[28] Nevertheless the statistics for some areas were still quite impressive. Whereas only 39 parishes in Kent had schools in 1662, 172 had them by 1807, though there were still parts of the county, notably the areas to the south and west of Canterbury, where many parishes still had no educational provision.[29] By 1724 a total of 25 towns and villages in Devon had a school; by the end of the eighteenth century this number had risen to 39, only one school, at Topsham, having closed in the intervening period.[30] By 1814 approximately a third of 128 parishes in Lincolnshire had a charity or day school.[31]

The role of lay people in the establishment of schools was particularly important. William Jacob has emphasised that 'the promotion of Christian knowledge was seen as a prime means of building up a nation of Anglican Christians in the face of competition from dissent, popery and infidelity', and that 'in a Protestant society literacy was vital to salvation'. John Leeds, a Bawdeswell weaver, bequeathed land in 1728 to provide an endowment for the appointment of a schoolmaster to teach 12 poor children from Bawdeswell and 8 from the neighbouring Norfolk parish of Foxley, to read and write.[32] In addition to lay involvement in the establishment of Sunday schools, other lay people, especially dissenters, set up private schools run on a non-denominational basis.[33] Some clergy also set up private classical schools which competed with the endowed grammar schools to provide a more advanced level of education for those who could afford the fees.

The masters of these schools can be divided into two groups. The first usually good scholars and professional teachers; they took holy orders because tradition demanded it, and as a rule they were absentees from their parishes and devoted their whole time to teaching. The second group were resident rectors and vicars, who started a boarding school, sometimes to educate their own sons and sometimes to add to their limited incomes. The dividing line was not very definitive; often a professional teacher would resign from his school and towards the end of his life become a resident clergyman. On the other hand some local vicar, who started his school more by chance than design, would be so successful as to become a professional teacher.[34]

Whilst clearly the provision for education varied considerably from one part of England to another, and often between different parts of the same

county, it was very much better at the end of the eighteenth century than it
had been at the beginning, and much, though by no means all, of the credit
for this must be attributed to the efforts of the Society for the Promotion of
Christian Knowledge and its local agents.

The situation in Wales basically replicated that in England but with the
addition of an extra ingredient in the shape of the circulating schools
established by Griffith Jones of Llanddowror (Carms.).[35] Jones's patron
was his brother-in-law, Sir John Phillips of Picton Castle (Pembs.), who
between 1707 and 1727 founded no fewer than 18 charity schools in
south-west Wales. Some of them he co-founded with other people, but
in most cases he appears to have paid the full costs himself, including the
masters' salaries, books and clothing, and food for the poorest children.
Phillips was emulated by other benefactors and by 1737 there were 157
charity schools in Wales with more than 20 each in the counties of
Carmarthenshire, Denbighshire and Pembrokeshire. Griffith Jones became
a member of and local agent for the SPCK in 1713 and assisted Phillips
in the work of establishing charity schools in south-west Wales. However,
by the 1730s it had become clear to him that there was insufficient wealth
in Wales to make the sort of educational provision that could be achieved
in many parts of England and that a cheaper method of education had to
be found. Influenced by his limited knowledge of the ambulatory schools
in Scotland, discussed below, he established a system of circulating charity
schools. These were established on the basis of training and employing a
teacher who would be sent into an area for three months, usually during
the winter when children could best be spared from helping out on the
farms. Jones stripped the curriculum of everything except reading and
learning the catechism; he made no attempt to feed, clothe or house the
children; schools were held in churches, barns or private houses; on this
basis Jones estimated in 1743 that between eight and ten people, either
children or adults, could be educated for a pound. Once the three months
were over the school would move to another area. The schools were taught
in whatever language was spoken in the locality, English or Welsh, and
in both languages if there were linguistic divisions in that locality. At
Eglwyswrw (Pembs.) the master taught 15 scholars in Welsh and 16 in
English. A particular feature of the Welsh circulating schools, later
adopted in the Sunday schools, was that they were not just restricted to the
teaching of children. Adults also were taught to read in the evenings and
at weekends when they were not at work. Jones recorded the progress of
his circulating schools in annual reports, entitled *Welch Piety*: Mary Jones
has calculated that between 1738 and Jones's death in 1761 there were

a total of 1,604 locations at which these schools operated in Wales, though these figures need to be treated with some caution as some schools were entered more than once in the reports. The largest number of schools were in the southern counties of Carmarthenshire and Glamorganshire, with comparatively few in the northern counties. The schools survived Jones's death and there were 279 in operation in 1763 educating a total of 11,770 pupils.[36] His work was carried on by his niece by marriage, Bridget Bevan, until she died in 1779. Although she left her considerable fortune to maintain the circulating schools, her will was contested by her relatives and the ensuing chancery case was not resolved for nearly 30 years. By that time the value of the bequest had been significantly reduced by the legal charges on the estate and when the charity was re-established in the early nineteenth century it was on a very much smaller scale.

In Ireland educational provision was slightly different again. As in England and Wales the earliest provision was through charity schools, of which a total of 173 were established between 1716 and 1730, the largest groups, 27 each, being in Counties Cork and Dublin. After 1730 a series of schools, known as charter schools, were established by the Incorporated Society, formed in Dublin by letters patent in 1733, for the promotion of English Protestant schools in Ireland. The first school was established at Kildare in 1734. From 1738 until 1794 the Society was assisted by an annual government grant of 1,000 pounds, the first direct involvement of the state in the provision of education. The schools had a deliberate policy of converting the children of Roman Catholic parents to the Church of Ireland and were able to persuade such parents to let their children attend as they provided them with food, clothing and shelter. However, in order to prevent children maintaining contact with their families and reconverting to Roman Catholicism, the Incorporated Society introduced a policy of transporting the children to distant parts of the country, far away from their homes. In order to reduce the cost of the schools it was decided that children should, in return for their education and upkeep, undertake manual labour, either in workshops or on farms attached to the schools. Poor management by the society's central committee in Dublin resulted in a whole series of abuses, with children being overworked, underfed and severely punished for minor misdemeanours. As early as 1788 the English prison reformer, John Howard, gave evidence to the Irish House of Commons on the mismanagement of the charter schools. The scandals surrounding the schools made the places in them difficult to fill. In 1791 there were 45 charter schools with a total of 1,455 pupils, but places for 1,775; a further six schools had been discontinued as they had insufficient pupils to cover their costs. The original appeal to potential subscribers to provide funding 'to rescue the souls of thousands of Popish children from the dangers of superstition and idolatry and their bodies from the miseries of idleness and begging' was beginning to fall on deaf ears.[37]

The part of the British Isles with the best educational provision was Scotland. A statute of 1696 had 'decreed that a school should be erected in every parish . . . and the salary of its teacher met by a tax on the local heritors or tenants'. In practice, however, some schools were set up as cheaply as possible to reduce the potential tax burden. Although most lowland parishes had a school by 1760, the geographical size of some parishes meant that it was not accessible to everybody. The growth of population also meant that many went unschooled as the schoolmaster could not teach more than 50 or 60 children. The inadequacy of the parochial school system meant that both private and charity schools were needed to supplement it. Some landowners and the Scottish Society for the Promotion of Christian Knowledge (SSPCK), founded in 1709, a Presbyterian organisation but one which enjoyed good relations with the Anglican SPCK, funded new schools or additional teachers in some existing schools. As in the Anglican parts of the British Isles, religious instruction was considered important in Scotland, and kirk sessions or heritors 'examined the children in their catechism'. Parochial schools were allowed to charge fees. In Aberdeenshire in the 1790s the rates were 1s 6d a quarter for reading and writing and two shillings for Latin and arithmetic. Fees rose after 1803 when an Act of Parliament adjusted the salaries of schoolmasters. However, in some parishes the kirk sessions would pay the fees of children whose parents could not afford to do so. It was customary for children to only go to school for part of the year so that they could help with the harvest and other agricultural needs.[38] Most Scottish parents thought that boys and girls should be educated differently. Boys were to be taught proper academic subjects, but girls were only to be taught 'practical skills which would prepare them for their approved role in society', such as sewing.[39]

The most intractable problems for educational campaigners in Scotland were in the western highlands and islands. Here illiteracy levels were exceptionally high, even as late as the early nineteenth century, ranging from 30% in Argyll to 70% in the 'Outer Hebrides and the inaccessible parishes of the western seaboard'.[40] The SSPCK supported the establishment of ambulatory schools, similar to the circulating schools later established by Griffith Jones in Wales. Some 606 of these existed at various dates between 1711 and 1800, with over 100 each in the highland counties of

Argyll and Inverness.[41] However, whereas Griffith Jones was prepared to teach in Welsh, the SSPCK set their face against teaching in Gaelic, viewing it as 'one of the roots of superstition and barbarity they were pledged to fight'. Even if they had taken a more tolerant view they would have faced problems. Although a Gaelic translation of the psalms had been published in 1690, there were hardly any other publications available in Gaelic. The size of some highland parishes was immense, and most had no proper villages, so finding suitable locations for schools capable of serving a reasonable number of children was very difficult.[42] In 1758 as many as 175 highland parishes were without a school. Even where schools existed, the SSPCK's opposition to Gaelic was helping to maintain levels of illiteracy. Highland children were being taught to read English but had no understanding of what they were reading since it bore no relation to the Gaelic they spoke.[43] Recogition of this farcical situation eventually persuaded the SSPCK to drop its ban on teaching in Gaelic in 1766. In 1739 it had published the first Gaelic–English vocabulary to help children understand English, and in 1758 one of its schoolmasters had published *The Mother's Catechism* in Gaelic. In 1767 the society decided to print 10,000 copies of the New Testament in Gaelic and in 1782 the society and the General Assembly of the Church of Scotland appealed for £1,300 to enable a complete Gaelic translation of the whole Bible to be made. This was eventually published in 1807. In 1755 the SSPCK decided, following the model of the charter schools in Ireland, to establish the first industrial school at Lochcarron, followed by a second at Glenmoriston. They were not a success and were abandoned. However, by the 1780s more success was achieved in setting up spinning schools. There were 36 of these schools in 1787, increasing to 94 by 1797. Unlike the Irish charter schools, they were well-regulated and did not lead to the ruthless exploitation of child labour.[44]

It was primarily as a result of the Evangelical revival that more effective schooling programmes were brought to the western highlands and islands and most parishes had established schools by the end of the eighteenth century, though some neighbouring parishes combined to support a single school as was the case in the three parishes of Harris, North Uist and South Uist, and in Skye the north-eastern parishes of Kilmuir, Portree and Snizort, and the north-western ones of Bracadale and Duirinish.[45] By 1803 only two island parishes, Barra and Lochs on Lewis, still had no school. Roman Catholic children in these highland and island parishes attended the Protestant parish schools. Despite the lifting of the ban on Gaelic by the SSPCK, some Evangelical schoolmasters still insisted on teaching in

English and Daniel Kerr of Glenurquhart 'zealously whipped all pupils found talking Gaelic'. Evangelicals were, however, instrumental in setting up the Gaelic School Society in 1811.[46]

Whereas rural schools were the responsibility of the heritors and the kirk sessions, in the towns schools were generally under the control of the burgh councils. Though the small burghs tended to make good educational provision for their inhabitants, often teaching subjects like geography, Greek and French, the larger burghs were frequently unwilling to make the investment needed to serve growing populations. In 1758 there were only two charity schools, and 22 private ones, in Edinburgh, offering education to only 800 of the 3,000 children in the city 'fit to go to school'. The SSPCK agreed to establish three new schools teaching reading, writing, arithmetic, spinning and knitting, if the corporation would also establish four. However, the corporation insisted on charging high fees and the SSPCK closed all its schools within ten years. Even in the early nineteenth century Edinburgh was still largely reliant on charity and Sunday schools. There were similar problems in Glasgow, Greenock and Paisley. Scottish Presbyterians were greatly influenced by the example of English dissenters to establish academies with strong academic reputations. The first of these new academies was established at Perth in the 1760s, followed by ones at Dundee in 1786, Inverness in 1787, Elgin and Fortrose in 1791, Ayr in 1794, Annan in 1801, Dumfries in 1802 and Tain in 1810. Perth Academy was erected and managed by the corporation but the others were erected by public subscription and managed by trustees including representatives from the respective corporations. The Andersonian Institute at Glasgow was founded in 1796. The Scottish universities also expanded during the eighteenth century to teach other subjects in addition to theology, classical languages, philosophy and mathematics. Professorships of law, medicine, rhetoric, chemistry, natural history, astronomy and agriculture were established at Edinburgh. The number of students also increased. The largest university was Edinburgh with about 1,300 students at the end of the eighteenth century.[47]

The two major educational initiatives of the late eighteenth and early nineteenth centuries were Sunday schools and the two national education societies, the theoretically non-denominational but in practice noncon-formist Royal British or Lancastrian Association, informally in existence from 1808 but formally established in 1810, and the Anglican National Society for the Education of the Poor, founded in 1811 with an initial endowment of £20,000 in gifts and £1,500 in promises of annual subscrip-tions. Ninety-five Lancastrian schools had been established by 1812. The

National Society both set up new schools and also absorbed some existing charity schools. It had 230 schools educating 40,484 pupils by 1813.[48] Support for the National Society came from Anglican high churchmen, like Charles Daubeny and Herbert Marsh, who believed that education needed to be controlled by the established church.[49] The development of Sunday schools began in the 1780s and spread very quickly. The Manchester Sunday schools had 5,000 pupils in 1788. In England as a whole there were 1,086 Sunday schools with some 690,000 pupils, both adults and children, by 1797. The schools tended to place a strong emphasis on teaching morality as well as reading, writing and religious knowledge. An interdenominational London Sunday School Society was founded in 1785, though some Anglican bishops strongly disapproved of such initiatives. They saw, especially in the 1790s, dissenters as potential radicals whereas their primary goal was to use education as a means of preserving the established political and social order.[50] Anglicans preferred to promote church Sunday schools. Dean Kaye of Lincoln preached in their favour in 1785 and helped to establish them in his cathedral city. Some Lincolnshire parishes also established Sunday schools in the late 1780s and early 1790s. The fact that the schools were free and not held on a workday made them more attractive than day schools to poorer families, especially in rural areas where children were needed to help in agriculture.[51] In Wales and parts of England where Methodism was strong it tended to be Methodists who took the initiative in setting up Sunday schools and this could cause conflict with anti-Methodist Anglican clergy. Others were happy to allow Methodists to use their churches or day schools to run Sunday schools. In Scotland Sunday schools were started at Aberdeen and Glasgow in 1787; that at Aberdeen was intended 'for the instruction of poor children in reading English, learning the principles of Christian religion, and psalmody' and lasted from 8 a.m. until 7 p.m. with the aim of eliminating 'Sunday games and burglary of residents' homes during divine service'.[52] Sunday schools were also established in the highlands, at Inverness and Tain in 1790, and at Kiltearn in 1798.[53]

One of the great advantages of Sunday schools was that they were cheap and easy to establish and did not require the plant essential for a successful day school. The Sunday School Union, founded to coordinate the work of local Sunday school societies in 1803, encouraged its supporters to 'select a place in the country which had no Sunday school and spend their holidays there engaged in the good work'. Many individuals established Sunday schools at their own expense.[54] Although some of these were comparatively wealthy, Thomas Laqueur has produced a list of more than 50 small tradesmen and even labourers who established Sunday schools in different parts of England between 1780 and 1812.[55] Clergy, both high churchmen and Evangelicals, were also active in the promotion and direct establishment of Sunday schools. They included Archbishop Markham of York and Bishops Barrington of Salisbury and Durham, Horne of Norwich, Porteous of London, Pretyman-Tomline of Lincoln and Watson of Llandaff. Distinguished scholars and theologians, such as Thomas Burgess and William Paley, wrote textbooks for use in Sunday schools. They were also supported and established by Protestant dissenting ministers. In 1801, of the 2,290 English Sunday schools then in existence, 1,282 (56.4%) were Anglican foundations. By 1811 only 2,288 (48.8%) of 4,687 Sunday schools were in this category and the proportion of non-Anglican Sunday schools was to increase slightly in subsequent years. Laqueur has calculated that the proportion of all children between 5 and 15 attending Sunday schools in England increased from 10.3% to 18.2% between 1801 and 1811 and the proportion of working class children from 13.8% to 24.2%.[56]

The promotion of culture and learning

The established churches, and especially the clergy, were important figures in the general promotion of culture and learning between 1714 and 1815. This can be seen in the number of scholarly works in all fields of study produced by clergy, in the role of churches in promoting music and in the establishment of libraries. In Wales in particular the cultural contribution of the clergy was enormous, though from time to time rather idiosyncratic. Theophilus Evans, curate of Llangammarch (Brecs.), published *Drych y Prif Oesoedd* (Mirror of the First Ages) in 1716. This argued that the Welsh were descendants of Gomer, grandson of Noah, and popularised the idea that Joseph of Arimathea had visited Britain and 'the central role of Brutus in the history of the Britains'. Interest in the druidic tradition which, almost a century later, was to influence Iolo Morganwg, came from the publication of Henry Rowland's *Mona Antiqua Restaurata* in 1723. The centre of the Welsh antiquarian movement was London, where many of the leading Welsh families had houses. The Society of Ancient Britons was founded there in 1715, followed by the Honourable Society of Cymmrodorion in 1751. Both had members who were in holy orders. In 1764 one of them, Evan Evans, published some *Specimens of the Poetry of the Antient Welsh Bards*. Welsh Methodism made no contribution to this antiquarian and literary activity. Its protagonists were either Anglican clergy or gentry and leading members of 'old dissent', such as the Unitarian Iolo Morganwg. The *Myvyrian Archaiology*, three volumes of early Welsh literature, including some of Iolo Morganwg's forgeries, was published between 1801 and 1807. Informal *eisteddfodau*, festivals of Welsh culture, were held in north-east Wales from 1789. The *gorsedd* ceremony, invented by Iolo Morganwg, was first held in London, on Primrose Hill, in 1792, but was incorporated into the first formal eisteddfod, held at Carmarthen under the patronage of Bishop Thomas Burgess and Archdeacon Thomas Beynon in 1819. Antiquarian histories of the Welsh counties of Anglesey, Brecon, Caernarfon, Cardigan, Merioneth, Monmouth and Radnor were published between 1775 and 1818, many by local clergy.[57]

The role of the established church in promoting music was also considerable. An annual choral service, promoted by the 'Sons of the Clergy' Society, was held at Newcastle upon Tyne from 1722. The Three Choirs Festival, held in rotation in the cathedrals of Gloucester, Hereford and Worcester, was established in 1718, and from 1724 it raised money for the orphans of poor diocesan clergy and former choir members. Similar music festivals, with charitable objectives, were launched at Bristol in 1757, Winchester in 1760, Birmingham (to raise funds for a new hospital) in 1768 and Norwich in 1770. In many towns the organists of the parish churches effectively acted as municipal organists, 'organizing concerts, founding and promoting festivals and societies, teaching, composing, and writing'. Charles Avison, organist of St Nicholas, Newcastle upon Tyne, between 1736 and 1770, promoted concerts in nearby Durham and was a well-known composer of music for string orchestras. One of the great musical innovations of the eighteenth century, and one of its most popular, was the oratorio, which 'triumphantly reaffirmed the influence of the sacred in musical life' and maintained the influence of religion on English music.[58]

By far the most long-lasting religious contribution to the cultural life of the British Isles was the endowed or subscription library. The role of Dr Thomas Bray (1656–1730), one of the co-founders of both the Society for the Promotion of Christian Knowledge and the Society for the Propagation of the Gospel, was critical. It was Bray who persuaded the SPCK to make the establishment of parochial libraries one of its main priorities and who secured the passing of an Act for the Better Preservation of Parochial Libraries in 1708–9. A large number of such libraries were set up during the first half of the eighteenth century, and some thereafter. Many were designed for the use of the clergy but others, such as the library at Maidstone, established in 1716 and augmented in the 1730s by the deliberate purchase of Bray's own surviving books, operated as embryo public libraries. The library at King's Lynn received 'a handsome legacy of books left by the will of Dr Thurlyn', former President of St John's College, Cambridge, and rector of Gaywood (Norf.), in 1714. The corporation erected a new library building for it by public subscription to which the borough's two members of Parliament, Sir Robert Walpole and Viscount Townshend, contributed £75, and paid the usher of the town's grammar school to act as librarian. At Boston (Lincs.) the churchwardens built new bookcases to house the books bought by the corporation in 1720. The SPCK also encouraged the establishment of libraries in a central location for the four dioceses in Wales and these were eventually erected at Bangor, Carmarthen, Cowbridge and St Asaph. Cathedral libraries also offered borrowing rights to local people and were often well-stocked. That at Lichfield had 3,000 volumes. By 1745 the parochial library at St Nicholas, Newcastle upon Tyne, had 5,000 volumes. By the second half of the eighteenth century some of these early initiatives were being replaced by more secular book clubs and subscription libraries; the latter were founded at Liverpool in 1768, Sheffield in 1771, Hull in 1775 and Birmingham in 1779.[59] One of the most remarkable achievements in the establishment of libraries was undertaken by Bishop Thomas Wilson in the Isle of Man. During his long episcopate between 1698 and 1755 he established libraries in each of the island's 17 parishes, augmenting them on several occasions, and even larger libraries attached to the grammar schools at Castletown and Douglas. The Castletown library had 872 volumes in 1716. The Douglas library was smaller but was significantly enlarged by the bequest of 233 volumes from the library of Wilson's successor, Mark Hildesley, who died in 1772.[60]

The eighteenth-century emphasis on good works as a mark of true Christianity made an enormous contribution to the improvement of the lives of many ordinary families between 1714 and 1815. Education, the relief of poverty and the promotion of culture and learning all benefited from the desire of Christians to offer a practical demonstration of what their faith meant. Whilst clearly an element of social control was present in some of these initiatives, especially those aimed at the improvement of public morals, many of them were motivated largely by a genuine desire to improve social conditions and to make a contribution to the overall quality of life. In due course much of this philanthropy gave way to state provision, but it is important to emphasise that much of the achievement of this state provision, in the nineteenth and twentieth centuries, would have been very much more difficult had it not been for the layer of provision that had already been achieved by other means. It was an area in which secular society had good reason to owe a debt of gratitude to religion, for without the religious motivation behind these acts of charity that initial provision would never have been made.

Notes

1 N. Sykes, *From Sheldon to Secker*, Cambridge 1959, pp. 185–7.

2 W. Prest, *Albion Ascendant: English History 1660–1815*, Oxford 1998, p. 206; D. McClatchey, *Oxfordshire Clergy 1777–1869*, Oxford 1960, pp. 179, 220.

3 R. Porter, *English Society in the Eighteenth Century*, Harmondsworth 1982, pp. 295–9, 312–13.

4 *Ibid.*, pp. 278–83; R.B. Shoemaker, *Gender in English Society 1650–1850*, Harlow 1998, pp. 65–7, 72–85, quotation on pp. 76–7.

5 Porter, *English Society*, pp. 311–12; E.J. Bristow, *Vice and Vigilance: Purity Movements in Britain since 1700*, Dublin 1977, pp. 21–31, quotations on pp. 21, 26.

6 P. Langford, *A Polite and Commercial People: England 1727–1783*, Oxford 1989, p. 129.

7 W.M. Jacob, *Lay People and Religion in the Early Eighteenth Century*, Cambridge 1996, pp. 130–2.

8 *Ibid.*, pp. 135–54.

9 A. Warne, *Church and Society in Eighteenth-Century Devon*, New York 1969, p. 77.

10 *Ibid.*, pp. 74–86.

11 Porter, *English Society*, pp. 311–14, 325–8.

12 Bristow, *Vice and Vigilance*, pp. 33–41.

13 F. O'Gorman, *The Long Eighteenth Century: British Political and Social History 1688–1832*, London 1997, p. 298.

14 C.G. Brown, *Religion and Society in Scotland since 1707*, Edinburgh 1997, pp. 69–73.

15 N. Yates, R. Hume and P. Hastings, *Religion and Society in Kent, 1640–1914*, Woodbridge 1994, pp. 118–53.

16 R.A. Soloway, *Prelates and People: Ecclesiastical Social Thought in England 1783–1852*, London 1969, pp. 75–80.

17 D. Valence, 'Charity, custom and humanity: changing attitudes towards the poor in eighteenth-century England', in J. Garnett and C. Matthew (eds),

Revival and Religion since 1700: Essays for John Walsh, London 1993, pp. 59–78.

18 Porter, *English Society*, pp. 315–16.

19 Jacob, *Lay People and Religion*, p. 156.

20 P. Borsay, *The English Urban Renaissance: Culture and Society in the Provincial Town 1660–1770*, Oxford 1989, p. 297.

21 G.N. Evans, *Religion and Politics in Mid-Eighteenth Century Anglesey*, Cardiff 1953, pp. 40–1.

22 Warne, *Church and Society*, pp. 149–58.

23 *Ibid.*, pp. 159–61; Jacob, *Lay People and Religion*, pp. 179–82.

24 M.G. Jones, *The Charity School Movement: A Study of Eighteenth Century Puritanism in Action*, Cambridge 1938, p. 340. Despite its rather questionable subtitle this standard work on the topic has yet to be replaced. For the situation in Germany and Austria see J.G. Gagliardo, *Germany under the Old Regime, 1600–1790*, London 1991, pp. 188–9, 344, 392–3, and in France see E. Kennedy, *A Cultural History of the French Revolution*, New Haven and London 1989, pp. 353–6, 360–2.

25 P. Langford, *A Polite and Commercial People: England 1727–1783*, Oxford 1989, p. 130.

26 G. Holmes and D. Szechi, *The Age of Oligarchy: Pre-Industrial Britain 1722–1783*, London 1993, p. 191; W.K.L. Clarke, *A History of the SPCK*, London 1959, pp. 29–33, 46–8; Porter, *English Society*, pp. 181–2.

27 V.E. Neuburg, *Popular Education in Eighteenth Century England*, London 1971, pp. 1–2.

28 J. Rule, *Albion's People: English Society 1714–1815*, London 1992, pp. 142–5.

29 Yates, Hume and Hastings, *Religion and Society in Kent*, pp. 93–103.

30 R. Warne, *Church and Society in Eighteenth-Century Devon*, New York 1969, pp. 136, 139.

31 R.W. Ambler, *Churches, Chapels and the Parish Communities of Lincolnshire 1660–1900*, Lincoln 2000, p. 72.

32 Jacob, *Lay People and Religion*, pp. 161–3.

33 Porter, *English Society*, p. 244.

34 N. Hans, *New Trends in Education in the Eighteenth Century*, London 1951, pp. 117–18.

35 This section is based on the relevant drafts of chapters in my wife's forthcoming PhD thesis on the role of the churches in the provision of education for the poor in Wales between 1780 and 1840.

36 M.G. Jones, *The Charity School Movement*, Cambridge 1938, pp. 390–407.

37 *Ibid.*, pp. 235–6, 384–7; see also the excellent new study by K. Milne, *The Irish Charter Schools, 1730–1830*, Dublin 1997.

38 T.C. Smout, *A History of the Scottish People 1560–1830*, London 1969, pp. 450–9.

39 R.A. Houston and I.D. Whyte (eds), *Scottish Society 1500–1800*, Cambridge 1989, p. 135.

40 A.L. Drummond and J. Bulloch, *The Scottish Church 1688–1843: The Age of the Moderates*, Edinburgh 1973, p. 188.

41 Jones, *Charity School Movement*, pp. 377–82.

42 Smout, *History of the Scottish People*, pp. 463–4.

43 R.A. Houston, *Scottish Illiteracy and Scottish Identity: Illiteracy and Society in Scotland and Northern England 1600–1800*, Cambridge 1985, pp. 74–9.

44 Jones, *Charity School Movement*, pp. 195–7, 203–7.

45 D. Ansdell, *The People of the Great Faith: The Highland Church 1690–1900*, Stornoway 1998, pp. 92–4.

46 J. MacInnes, *The Evangelical Movement in the Highlands of Scotland 1688 to 1800*, Aberdeen 1951, pp. 234–48.

47 Smout, *History of the Scottish People*, pp. 467–78.

48 Jones, *Charity School Movement*, p. 339.

49 R.A. Soloway, *Prelates and People: Ecclesiastical Social Thought in England, 1783–1852*, London 1969, p. 371.

50 *Ibid.*, pp. 351–60; Porter, *English Society*, pp. 313–14.

51 Ambler, *Churches, Chapels and Parish Communities*, p. 73.

52 Brown, *Religion and Society*, pp. 96–7.

53 MacInnes, *Evangelical Movement*, pp. 257–8.

54 T.W. Laqueur, *Religion and Respectability: Sunday Schools and Working Class Culture*, New Haven and London 1976, pp. 25–6.

55 *Ibid.*, pp. 252–4.

56 *Ibid.*, pp. 30–2, 44.

57 J. Davies, *A History of Wales*, London 1994, pp. 302–6, 344–6.

58 Borsay, *English Urban Renaissance*, pp. 123–7.

59 *Ibid.*, pp. 132–3; Clarke, *History of the SPCK*, pp. 77–80; Jacob, *Lay People and Religion*, pp. 174–6; Porter, *English Society*, p. 244.

60 W.N. Yates, 'An opportunity missed? The provision of education and training for a non-graduate clergy: comparative case studies of the dioceses of St David's and Sodor and Man in the eighteenth and nineteenth centuries', *Dutch Review of Church History*, 83 (2003), pp. 323–4; see also J.P. Ferguson, *The Parochial Libraries of Bishop Wilson*, Douglas 1975.

CHAPTER 5

The Condition of the Established Churches

In this and the next chapter we will be looking at internal developments in the established churches of the British Isles. First we will analyse their state during the middle years of the eighteenth century between 1714 and 1780; in the next chapter we will look in detail at reform movements within the established churches between 1780 and 1815. In both cases the main emphasis will be on England, but there will also be separate sections on Ireland, Scotland and Wales.

The clergy: social background and education

By the beginning of the eighteenth century the Church of England had largely resolved the problems it had experienced in the immediate post-Reformation period in attracting men of adequate social standing and education to its ministry. Whereas in the seventeenth century it had not been considered 'honourable' for men from noble or gentry families to become clergymen, this was no longer the case by the eighteenth century. In the early seventeenth century a quarter of the bishops had been non-genteel in origin; by the reign of George III only 4% were.[1] However, whereas in France nobility alone was sufficient to gain a man a bishopric, in England only nobles who were able administrators or scholars were appointed to the episcopate.[2] Within the ranks of the clergy as a whole there was some social division with a minority, despite their university education, being 'permanently excluded from the style as well as the substance of the gentleman'.[3] However, there was in England nothing like the social gulf that existed in France between the higher and lower clergy and the clearly able could gain promotion even if they did not come from the upper levels of society. In many parts of the country clergy were frequently the sons of clergy, some parishes being served by members of the same family over several generations. The growing professionalisation of the clergy was manifested in the formation of local clerical societies and the service of clergy on such national bodies as the Society for the Promotion of Christian Knowledge (SPCK), Society for the Propagation of the Gospel (SPG) and societies for the reformation of manners or suppression of vice.[4]

This growing professionalisation was underpinned by the care with which diocesan bishops sought to recruit the clergy of their dioceses. Except in those areas in which it proved difficult to recruit clergy from families able to afford to send their sons to Oxford, Cambridge or Trinity College, Dublin, bishops normally insisted that clergy must have had a university education and they also, either in person or through one of their chaplains, examined all candidates for the ministry before agreeing to ordain them. Those who were deemed to be of unsuitable character, to have insufficient educational or theological qualifications, or to hold unorthodox opinions, were usually rejected. In 1769 Archbishop Secker of Canterbury published a set of *Instructions* in which he laid down the standards he expected from those seeking holy orders. They were to have been 'inwardly moved by the Holy Ghost', to show this by their lifestyle and to be the sort of person who could be an example to their parishioners in a 'profane and corrupt age'.[5] In the diocese of Sodor and Man, where it proved virtually impossible to recruit clergy who had been educated at the universities, potential ordinands had to rely on the education provided by the grammar schools established by Bishop Isaac Barrow (1663–71) at Castletown and Douglas. Bishop Thomas Wilson (1698–1755) sought to improve on this rather basic training by making his ordinands spend some time in the bishop's household, following a programme of prayer and study, and by licensing them as lay assistants to elderly or infirm clergy.[6]

The impact of all these provisions can be seen in the analyses that have been undertaken of the social background and education of the clergy in several English dioceses. In the diocese of Oxford Diana McClatchey calculated that of the 33 clergy in the rural deanery of Bicester in 1783 almost half (16) came from noble or gentry families, 1 was the son of a doctor, 8 the sons of clergy and 8 came from families below these social levels.[7] More recently an analysis of clergy in the dioceses of Hereford and Oxford has found that between 1680 and 1760 there was a considerable 'gentrification' of the clergy in both dioceses, those of plebeian origins having dropped from 55% to 35% in the diocese of Oxford and from 60% to 37% in that of Hereford.[8] Similar trends could be noted in the diocese of Canterbury as shown in Table 7. Although the balance of plebeian and

TABLE 7 *Social and educational backgrounds of clergy in the diocese of Canterbury 1720–1810*

	1720–50 (%)	1750–80 (%)	1780–1810 (%)
Social backgrounds			
Noble/gentry	40.5	33.0	36.6
Clergy	34.5	38.0	37.7
Professional	1.0	1.5	4.2
Plebeian	24.0	27.5	14.2
Educational backgrounds			
Oxford	43.9	51.0	53.0
Cambridge	53.8	48.0	37.5

Source: J. Gregory, *Restoration, Reformation and Reform, 1660–1828: Archbishops of Canterbury and their Diocese*, Oxford 2000, p. 73.

non-plebeian clergy remained fairly constant between 1720 and 1780, the number of plebeian clergy had been much higher (37.6%) in the period 1690–1720 and was to be further reduced after 1780. The overwhelming preponderance of university graduates among the clergy is also very clearly revealed. In the diocese of London Viviane Barrie-Curien found that, between 1714 and 1800, 39% of the clergy came from noble or gentry families, 35.4% were the sons of clergy, 6.2% the sons of professionals (doctors, lawyers, schoolmasters) and 19.4% were plebeians. A high proportion of the clergy also came from within the diocese or adjacent areas, with 17.6% from London and 21% from the Home Counties. The majority were university graduates with 54.3% having been to Oxford and 34.5% to Cambridge. Five clergy had degrees from universities in Ireland, Scotland or Europe.[9]

The clergy: incomes and social position

One of the reasons for the increasing social status of the clergy during the period 1714–1815 was the increase in the value of clerical and episcopal incomes.[10] In 1762 the annual value of English and Welsh bishoprics varied between £450 and £7,000. At the top of the scale were sees like Canterbury, York, Durham, London and Winchester, each worth over £4,000, and at the bottom those like Bristol, Chester, Gloucester, Oxford, Rochester, St David's and Llandaff, each worth less than £1,000. Holders of these bishoprics were usually permitted to hold another benefice *in commendam* as a means of increasing their income to the necessary level to meet their expenses. These were not inconsiderable, especially those of hospitality and charity, and it was estimated that some of the wealthier deans were considerably better-off than most of the poorer bishops.[11] Generally speaking, however, clerical and episcopal incomes increased dramatically as a result of a buoyant economy. The annual income of the chapelry of Cockthorpe (Norf.) increased from £69 in 1744 to £116 in 1777, that of the rectory of Long Melford (Suff.) from £303 in 1735 to £460 in 1790, £732 in 1800 and £1,219 in 1819.[12] Clerical incomes came from a number of sources: endowments of land which the clergyman either farmed himself, or rented out to somebody else to farm, tithes (technically a 10% tax on the gross agricultural product of a parish, though in practice not everything was tithed) and fees. Some clergy also supplemented their incomes by acting as schoolmasters. In some parts of the country tithes were still paid in kind but elsewhere they had been commuted by agreement to a fixed annual sum. Some clergy collected their tithes in person, others employed an agent or agents to collect them. The increase in income from land and tithes was the result of the improvements in the profitability of agriculture during the eighteenth century, but these improvements varied considerably from parish to parish with the result that the incomes of some clergy barely kept pace with inflation whereas those of others vastly exceeded it. In East Anglia especially the growth of enclosures and improvements in drainage could have a dramatic impact on the value of ecclesiastical benefices. The Cambridgeshire parish of Doddington was valued at £22 5s 0d in the 1530s. Three hundred years later it was valued at £7,306, and was worth more than the majority of bishoprics at the same time.[13] Enclosure comprised either the turning of open fields with the ancient manorial arrangement of 'strip' farming into newly hedged and ditched fields, or the bringing of farmers' waste or common land under cultivation. There were about 3,000 Enclosure Acts between 1760 and 1830 affecting about 10,500 parishes.[14]

Non-beneficed clergy appointed to curacies were paid rather differently, receiving a fixed stipend and sometimes a house for doing duty, frequently for a non-resident incumbent. Curates' stipends also increased in this period. Diana McClatchey has calculated that in Oxfordshire between 1782 and 1792, of the 70 curacies for which figures are available, 18 had annual stipends of between £20 and £29, 20 had ones of between £30 and £39, 21 had ones of between £40 and £49 and 11 had ones of £50 or above. Curates' stipends tended to rise in line with improvements in benefice income. Thus the curacy of Alvescot rose in annual value from £35 in 1787 to £50 in 1804, that of Westcote Barton from £27 6s 0d in 1791 to £40 in 1814, that of Charlbury from £31 10s 0d in 1790 to £50 in 1814, that of Cottisford from £27 16s 6d in 1747 to £50 in 1814, and that of Garsington doubled from £40 to £80 between 1790 and 1815. At Headington there was no change in the annual stipend of £20 between 1747 and 1790, but it had more than doubled, to £50, by 1814. At Weston-in-the-Green the curate's stipend was £25 in 1790, £40 in 1804 and £80 in 1816.[15]

During the course of the eighteenth century, as clergy ceased to be seen as potential Jacobites and therefore a threat to the state, their social and political role increased. One important role many of them exercised was as justices of the peace. Scholars are divided about the significance of clergy as magistrates, John Rule suggesting that only the better-off clergy with good connections became justices of the peace and that only 10% of the clergy were magistrates at any one time,[16] whilst William Gibson asserts that their presence was critical to local administration and the dispensing of justice. He notes that in the late eighteenth century 47% of the justices of the peace in Lincolnshire were clergy and that in Oxfordshire in 1780 82.6% of criminal convictions were signed by clerical magistrates.[17] Some clergy exercised very significant roles in county administration, such as John Foley, joint chairman of the Gloucestershire Quarter Sessions between 1796 and 1800, and Samuel Partridge, chairman of the Holland (Lincs.) Quarter Sessions in 1809.[18] Clergy also frequently exercised a more directly political role, acting as agents for candidates at parliamentary elections and serving on municipalities. Bishops, however, tended to be less active in the House of Lords than has sometimes been thought, with rarely more than eight, less than a third of the total number, present at the same sitting. Also, bishops did not always vote with the government despite the fact that they were government appointees.[19]

The social and political leadership expected of the clergy made it essential that, after ordination, their work should continue to be monitored on a regular basis. Archbishop Secker of Canterbury emphasised to his clergy that he expected them both 'to uphold the dignity and purity of the ecclesiastical character' and also 'not to be aloof from the life of their parishioners', and parishioners had similar expectations.[20] Bishops used the visitation process as their main means of controlling the clergy, encouraging churchwardens to report on any perceived deficiencies in their incumbents and curates. Research into the Norfolk clergy suggests that such complaints were very few. A small number were reported for non-residence or failure to appoint a curate to serve the cure, a rather larger number for failure to maintain their houses and outbuildings in good repair: there were 10 such complaints in 1716, 18 in 1725 and 5 in 1740. In 1743 Dudley Butts, vicar of Ludham and Potter Heigham was suspended for ante-nuptial fornication and his wife sentenced to do public penance. Such cases were, however, very unusual and the lack of serious indiscipline appears to have been replicated in other dioceses.[21]

Diocesan administration

Bishops between 1714 and 1815 exercised two very different roles. During the parliamentary session they were expected to reside in London so that they could attend the House of Lords and for the rest of the year, usually the summer months, they resided in their dioceses. Most conducted ordinations in their dioceses. Of the 388 clergy ordained for the diocese of Exeter between 1689 and 1792 only 26 were ordained in London.[22] The notion, widely held until recent years, that diocesan administration rather fell apart between 1714 and the 1780s can no longer be sustained. On the contrary there appears to have been no diminution in pastoral standards, the provision of public worship or the social role of the church in the parishes.[23] The only major failure was in the diocese of London where the bishop was notionally responsible, not just for his mainland diocese, but for all the clergy serving in foreign countries and the American colonies. This was despite pressure from the late seventeenth century from successive bishops of London that a bishopric or bishoprics should be established for North America. Bishop Gibson established a fund to provide a suitable endowment but the British government refused to pass the necessary legislation. Further pressure on the government in the 1760s was supported by the Archbishops of Canterbury and York and Archbishop Secker left £2,000 in his will to establish an American bishopric. In 1767 Bishop Ewer of Llandaff preached a forthright sermon for the Society for the Propagation of the Gospel advocating that such a bishopric should be established immediately.[24]

The evidence from surviving episcopal correspondence is that bishops were assiduous at following up evidence from their visitations and in responding to complaints from clergy or their parishioners. In 1738 Bishop Secker of Oxford required James Martin to reside and have two Sunday services at Heythrop. In 1740 he required Dr W.W. Ward to put the church of Cuddesdon into good order. In 1750 he was forced to intervene in two parishes. He initially rebuked William Reynolds for dismissing his curate at Shifford for no cause; however, when Reynolds told Secker that the curate's complaint was groundless he wrote to the curate, Thomas Middleton, asking him to justify his complaint as he thought Reynolds had made a good case for dismissing him. He also wrote to William Stockwood to criticise his absence from the last visitation and to explain why he had not provided him with the catalogue of the parochial library at Henley or applied for a licence for his curate. In 1752 Secker required John Land to reside on his living of Basildon and in 1756 instructed the principal landowner in the parish of Hampton Poyle, John Tilson of Watlington Park, to put the church into good repair. There was further trouble at Henley in 1756. Secker told Henry Hayman that he would not license him to the curacy and criticised him and the rector, William Stockwood, for their bad relations with each other.[25]

Diocesan administration was as efficient elsewhere. There were regular, triennial, episcopal visitations in the diocese of Chichester. In the diocese of Hereford there were usually two ordination services each year, and in the diocese of Oxford there were sometimes four. Bishop Secker of Oxford was rigorous in his preparations for conducting confirmations. Clergy were expected to present their candidates in person and to have instructed them beforehand. In 1748 Secker circulated 10,200 tracts for the preparation of confirmation candidates at his own expense and a further 15,000 in 1752. His confirmation tours normally included provision for services at all the major towns, and some of the larger villages, in the diocese. In 1738 he confirmed at Bampton, Banbury, Bicester, Bloxham, Burford, Chipping Norton, Ewelme, Haseley, Henley, Watlington and Witney.[26] The other aspect of diocesan administration which remained far more active than has previously been realised was that of the ecclesiastical courts, though some restrictions on their activities became unavoidable as a result of parliamentary legislation: this included measures in respect of the union of parishes in 1714 and 1733, Hardwicke's Marriage Act of 1753 and legislation in 1787 designed to prevent prosecutions for ante-nuptial fornication. In the diocese of London the ecclesiastical courts were still dealing with about 20 cases a year in the late eighteenth century. The last recorded case of 'spiritual death' or major excommunication took place as late as 1792. The main reason that the ecclesiastical courts remained active was not just the determination of the established church to maintain its jurisdiction but the support that the courts received from the community. They remained active because people wanted to use them 'as agents of moral and social reform'.[27]

Religious life in the parishes

The successful functioning of parish life in eighteenth-century England depended, certainly in the rural areas, on good relationships between the clergy, the lay parochial officers, the principal landowners and the patron of the living. By the late eighteenth century about 10% of patronage belonged to the crown, 25% to bishops, 55% to lay patrons (frequently one of the local landowners) and 10% to ecclesiastical or secular corporations, though there were significant variations from diocese to diocese. In the diocese of Oxford in 1777 46.6% of the advowsons were in the hands of private patrons, 11.5% in those of the bishop, 5.3% belonged to the crown and 36.7% to corporations, two-thirds of those patrons being Oxford colleges.[28] Clergy depended on the goodwill of patrons for promotion, either from a less to a more wealthy parish, or for the ability to hold more than one benefice. This was known as pluralism and was much criticised in the nineteenth century when bishops aimed at the idea of at least one clergyman in every individual parish. In practice pluralism, and the non-residence that could result from it, was much less of a problem for the eighteenth-century church than its critics have alleged. Indeed much pluralism and non-residence was highly technical in its nature and certainly did not lead to any serious lack of pastoral oversight in most parts of the country. In the diocese of Salisbury in 1783 only 90 out of 232 parishes had clergy who were technically 'resident', but of the 142 remaining 119 were served by clergy who lived less than five miles from their churches. In the diocese of Exeter in 1779 231 clergy were resident and 159 non-resident; of the non-residents 34 held parishes adjacent to the one in which they were non-resident and only 24 lived outside the diocese. Seventeen were unable to reside because there was no parsonage house. Bishops were keen to enforce residence wherever they could and the number of non-resident clergy decreased between 1714 and 1815. In the diocese of London in 1727 nearly a third of the parishes had neither a resident clergyman nor one living in an adjacent parish. This figure declined progressively to a fifth by 1738, to a tenth by the late 1760s and to virtually nil by the end of the century. The reasons for non-residence in the dioceses of England and Wales were revealed in responses to a series of Privy Council surveys as summarised in Table 8. The allegation that pluralism and non-residence resulted in pastoral neglect was disproved by the statistics for Sunday services and celebrations of Holy Communion in the late eighteenth century. In the diocese of Chester 78% of churches had two Sunday services; in that of Oxford the figure was 85%. In the

TABLE 8 *Reasons stated for the non-residence of clergy in England and Wales 1804–7*

	1804–5 (%)	1805–6 (%)	1806–7 (%)
No/inadequate house	30.3	32.4	17.2
Residence in another benefice	21.1	21.4	18.5
Ill-health	10.3	11.7	6.9
Employed as schoolteachers	10.1	11.0	6.4
University post	2.4	2.5	1.8
Cathedral post	11.3	4.5	6.3

Source: V. Barrie-Curien, *Clergé et Pastorale en Angleterre au XVIII*^e
Siècle: Le Diocèse de Londres, Paris 1992, p. 424.

diocese of Exeter in 1799 41 churches had a quarterly celebration of Holy Communion, the norm for most rural parishes in England, and 71 had between six and eight celebrations a year. In the diocese of Oxford, where about 60% of the clergy were non-resident in both 1778 and 1808, between about an eighth and a fifth were taking duty in person, about 16% employing a resident curate and between about a quarter and a third were relying on the services of clergy in adjacent parishes. In cases where two adjacent parishes were served by the same clergyman it was normal to have one Sunday service in each parish, alternating between the morning and the afternoon.[29]

That is the positive side of the picture and it is the one that currently finds favour with most ecclesiastical historians of this period. However, it is only fair to state that it is not shared by everybody. Peter Virgin still sees it as a real weakness of the pre-Victorian church:

It is one of the gentler ironies of history that the Augustan intellect, with its easy confidence in its own rationality and its corresponding contempt for the insights of every earlier age, should have permitted the regrowth – in the ecclesiastical sphere – of corruptions and decadences which, although they had luxuriated three or more centuries before, had already been cut down once by the sharpened sickles of Reformation and Renaissance reform.[30]

Virgin paints a picture of pluralism and non-residence in which the clergy are seen as financially grasping and the bishops administratively incompetent,[31] yet it is based on the same evidence as that used by others to defend the established church from these accusations. What is perhaps more to the point is that complaints about the inadequacies of pastoral care are largely lacking in diocesan archives. It could be argued that this was because contemporaries had such low expectations of the established churches, but this really does sound like special pleading.

The expectations of bishops in the eighteenth century were that each parish church should have, wherever possible, two Sunday services and at least a quarterly celebration of Holy Communion, but they recognised that in small rural parishes, with churches perhaps within one or two miles of each other, one service each Sunday was satisfactory, if such adjacent parishes were served by the same clergyman alternating the morning and afternoon services so that both sets of parishioners could attend two services if they wanted to.[32] Some scholars have cited evidence to suggest that church attendance declined significantly in the eighteenth century,[33] but it needs to be treated with caution and is not backed up by more recent diocesan studies. Donald Spaeth has criticised the eighteenth-century Church of England on the grounds that its services were boring and that a high proportion of even regular attenders were not regular, or even infrequent, communicants, but he does so precisely by comparing it with attitudes to worship and communion in the post-Victorian church where 'communion is administered frequently and virtually every adult who is present receives the sacrament'.[34] Judged, however, by the expectations of contemporaries all the evidence suggests that there was no demand for extra services and that when clergy sought to provide them they were not well attended. The *Book of Common Prayer* had assumed that morning and evening prayer would be said daily in church, with the litany on Wednesdays, Fridays, Sundays and Holy Days and Holy Communion on Sundays and Holy Days. This provision was only to be found, as it had been for most of the post-Reformation period, in cathedrals and some city churches. At Exeter cathedral there was Holy Communion every Sunday, on Good Friday and 29 May (Restoration of Charles II). Morning and evening prayer were sung daily and two sermons were preached every Sunday and on Christmas Day, 30 January (Execution of Charles I), Ash Wednesday, Good Friday, 29 May and 5 November (Gunpowder Plot). In both 1727 and 1790 about an eighth of the parishes in the predominantly urban diocese of London had regular weekday services.[35] Elsewhere weekday services were rare, especially in rural areas, where many parishes also had only one Sunday service, especially if they were served by the same clergyman as the neighbouring parish. Even so clergy could be hardworked on Sundays. The two brothers, John and James Evans, between them served the Wiltshire parishes of Fovant, Hindon and Teffont Evias, with the chapel of Pertwood. Each of the parish churches had two Sunday services, but only one sermon, and the chapel of Pertwood was served on alternate Sundays even though there was only one resident family. The morning service comprised the office of morning prayer, the litany and the first part of the communion service, extended on Sacrament Sundays, usually with a sermon. It probably took about 105 minutes. The afternoon service was shorter, about 85 minutes, and comprised the office of evening prayer with a sermon or catechising. Services were conducted with decency, the officiant wearing a surplice but changing into a black gown to preach the sermon. Copes were worn by bishops and ecclesiastical dignitaries on certain state occasions, and more regularly in some cathedrals until the end of the eighteenth century when such use appears to have been discontinued. Bowing to the altar, turning to the east for the Creed and the Gloria and making the sign of the cross are well-attested ceremonial gestures throughout the eighteenth century. Foreign visitors to English cathedrals and other large churches were generally impressed by the standard of worship on offer, one commenting in 1729 that 'the services are chanted in a tone resembling that used by the Roman Catholics in their services'.

Tables 9 and 10 show the comparison between the frequency of celebrations of Holy Communion in the dioceses of London and Canterbury with the latter also including evidence for normal Sunday worship in the diocese. What today would be seen as a severe lack of frequency in the celebration of Holy Communion was not so judged in the eighteenth century, when there was far greater emphasis on preparation for receiving the sacrament and a whole series of publications designed for the benefit

TABLE 9 *Frequency of celebrations of Holy Communion in the diocese of London 1738–90*

	1738 (%)	1742 (%)	1747 (%)	1778 (%)	1790 (%)
Weekly	–	0.5	–	0.3	0.9
Monthly	12.2	13.7	13.0	12.7	23.7
6–8 times pa	9.0	8.9	8.9	7.0	4.5
Quarterly	41.2	41.0	45.8	61.4	56.1
Major festivals	34.2	32.6	30.5	15.2	10.1
Rarely/never	3.4	3.3	1.8	3.4	4.7

Source: V. Barrie-Curien, *Clergé et Pastorale en Angleterre au XVIIIe Siècle: Le Diocèse de Londres*, Paris 1992, p. 431.

TABLE 10 *Frequency of Sunday services and celebrations of Holy Communion in the diocese of Canterbury 1716–1806*

	1716 (%)	1758 (%)	1806 (%)
Two Sunday services	31.5	42.0	38.7
One Sunday service	47.0	53.9	58.3
Less than one Sunday service	21.5	4.1	3.0
Monthly communion	6.9	6.5	6.9
Communion 9–12 times pa	3.4	6.9	6.5
Communion 5–8 times pa	16.0	9.5	4.3
Quarterly communion	41.7	72.0	67.0
Less than quarterly	32.0	5.1	15.3

Source: J. Gregory, *Restoration, Reformation and Reform, 1660–1828: Archbishops of Canterbury and their Diocese*, Oxford 2000, p. 263.

of intending communicants. Even in Roman Catholic countries, though the eucharist was celebrated at least weekly and often daily, few apart from the celebrant communicated. Since the *Book of Common Prayer* did not permit celebrations without communicants it was hardly surprising that communion services were less frequent. Even so the statistics for the dioceses of both Canterbury and London show a marked increase in the number of communion services as the century progressed. Progressive churchmen, like Bishop Secker of Oxford, encouraged clergy to 'advance from a quarterly communion to a monthly one' and privately would have supported liturgical reform aimed at reducing the length of the morning service so that it 'should not last longer than most people can be supposed to remain fervent'.[36]

Secker was also keen to encourage more and better singing in church as a means of making the services more enjoyable and there is considerable evidence that the standard of music in churches did improve during the eighteenth century. There was, however, some debate as to the type of singing that was most appropriate. Some bishops and clergy clearly felt that parish choirs should not endeavour to imitate those of cathedrals and tried to discourage them from attempting elaborate musical settings of the psalms and canticles. Bishop Gibson of London recommended a return to the older practice of 'lining out' whereby parish clerks would sing each line of the psalm or canticle which would then be repeated by the congregation. Bishop Sherlock of Salisbury tried to suppress the singing of anthems by parish choirs in his diocese. There was a concern that parish choirs would become in effect independent units in the parish, under-mining the authority of the clergy and excluding the congregation from any musical participation in the services. It was a battle that the parish choirs eventually won. They continued to occupy either special singing pews or galleries and often expanded to include a wide range of musical instru-ments. Several churches, especially in the towns and larger villages, purchased organs to replace or supplement parish orchestras: in Wiltshire they were introduced at Calne in 1736, Bradford-on-Avon by 1794, Horningsham in 1798 and Bishop's Cannings in 1810; and in Norfolk at Aylsham in 1769, East Dereham in 1785 and Wymondham in 1793. Surviving church music books for the Kent parishes of Kemsing and Trottiscliffe show that some parish choirs were performing a wide and ambitious range of music in the late eighteenth and early nineteenth centuries. The great bastions of English church music remained, however, the cathedrals and the churches in London and the major provincial towns.[37]

Church building and restoration

Another popular myth about the Georgian Church of England that can no longer be sustained is the notion that church buildings were in a state of serious disrepair and that little was done to address this problem. On the contrary the period between 1714 and 1815 was one in which substantial sums of money were spent on building, rebuilding, restoring and generally improving church buildings.[38] In Cumberland 17 churches were newly built or rebuilt between 1702 and 1768.[39] Peter Borsay notes the large number of such buildings in English provincial towns including two each in Liverpool and Whitehaven and three in Birmingham. All Saints at Derby, now the cathedral, was built in 1723–5 at a cost of £4,500. In 1755 it was noted that the church at Bideford had been 'partly new built; the whole has been repaired and beautified, and new seats have been made'.[40] In the planning of town redevelopments in the eighteenth century churches were very frequently built as focal points, often as part of a large square in which the church was situated.[41] In 1730 the parishes of Oldham and Saddleworth were served by four churches. In the next 50 years eight new chapels-of-ease were built, increasing the seating capacity of the estab-lished church from 2,300 to 6,255 in Oldham and from 517 to 2,517 in Saddleworth. In the case of Oldham the increase in church accommoda-tion significantly outstripped proportionally the increase in the popula-tion. In Saddleworth the churches could seat 30.4% of the population in 1730 but only 31.5% in 1790.[42] In some parts of England, especially in the larger cities, although new churches were built they were not built in sufficient quantities to provide the additional accommodation required.

The role of the laity in the programmes of church building and restoration was an important one since they had to provide the funding necessary for such programmes to be effective. They were spurred on by bishops, archdeacons and, in the diocese of Exeter, rural deans, who used the visitation process to check up on church fabrics and order repairs, or in some cases completely new buildings, if necessary. In some towns, such as Beverley and King's Lynn, the municipal corporations took on responsibility for the care of churches and frequently spent large sums on their repair and improvement. Landowners also gave sites for new churches or contributed to the repair of those on their estates. Some churches were rebuilt or repaired as a result of a bequest. Other churches were built or repaired by subscription. At Whitchurch (Salop) 204 inhabitants contributed to the rebuilding of the church in 1711–12 with contributions ranging from five shillings to £50. Other churches were rebuilt or repaired by brief, a royal warrant authorising a collection in churches across the country for a charitable purpose. Ravenstonedale church was rebuilt by these means in 1738–44 and the interior remains intact to this day (see Appendix 3). In many cases much expenditure was lavished on elaborate new altarpieces and pulpits as well as boards for the Ten Commandments, Creed and Lord's Prayer, the Royal Arms and gallery fronts. Some churches were even supplied with stained glass. Seating was normally provided by box pews or seats in galleries, the cost of which might be met either by the occupants of the individual pews or as part of a more general scheme of restoration and refurbishment. As well as expenditure on the fabric and furnishings between 1714 and 1815 many churches were provided with new pieces of communion plate, including chalices, patens, flagons, almsdishes and candlesticks. Altars and pulpits were frequently provided with new carpets, cushions, hangings and service books.[43]

A useful snapshot of the impact of this nationwide campaign for the improvement of accommodation for public worship is provided by the detailed research that has been undertaken on the dioceses of Canterbury and Exeter. In the former diocese the church of Leeds was rebuilt in 1753. Major repairs took place at St Peter-in-Thanet in 1758. The improvement of Faversham church in 1754 cost £2,700 including £400 spent on an organ. Chart Sutton church was rebuilt after lightning damage in 1779 at a cost of £1,810 raised by brief. Between 1765 and 1780 St Andrew's, Canterbury, was rebuilt by subscription, the subscribers including the city's two members of Parliament, who each gave £100, the mayor and the cathedral chapter.[44] In the diocese of Exeter and county of Devon 13 churches were newly built or rebuilt, including St George's, Tiverton (1714–33) and Filleigh, where a petition, signed by the patron, rector, churchwardens and the principal landowners, requesting permission to demolish the old church, which was 'very strait and incommodious', was sent to the bishop in 1730. Licence having been granted, the work was completed within 18 months and the bishop requested to consecrate the new building. At Buckerell the church was completely restored in 1783; both the pews themselves and the seating plan drawn up as part of the petition for a faculty for reseating still survive. Between 1737 and 1799 licences were granted for no fewer than 65 such reseating schemes in Devon as well as 51 licences for the erection of galleries to provide additional seating in churches. The churchwardens' accounts for the parish of West Alvington show that the church was ceiled and reseated in 1788, new windows put in and other windows glazed in 1790, the reading desk relocated and a new pulpit installed in 1799, a new altarpiece erected in 1803 and a new gallery erected in 1813, when the incumbent gave a new carpet, cushion and prayer book for the communion table.[45]

The church in Wales[46]

The four Welsh dioceses formed part of the province of Canterbury and thus to a large extent developments there were not that different from those in parts of England. However, particular problems were caused by the difficulties of communication in a largely mountainous country with few towns, and by the poverty of many benefices, particularly in South Wales. The Welsh bishops and clergy also had to take account of the fact that the majority of the laity, especially in rural areas, were Welsh-speaking and often totally or largely ignorant of English. Satisfactory pastoral provision in most parishes required the appointment of Welsh-speaking clergy capable of both reading the services and preaching in the native language. The geographical isolation of Wales undoubtedly made it unattractive to career-minded clergy, and bishops appointed to Welsh dioceses were usually successful in securing their translation to dioceses in England within a very short period of time. In the period between 1714 and 1815 there were no fewer than 17 bishops of St David's, 14 each of Bangor and St Asaph and 11 of Llandaff; the better than average tenure of this diocese was solely due to the failure of Bishop Richard Watson (1782–1816) to secure, largely on account of his dangerously radical opinions, translation to an English diocese. However, despite this quick turnover of bishops, there is plenty of evidence to suggest that the Welsh dioceses were as efficiently administered as their English counterparts. There was much criticism from the 1830s that the failure to appoint Welsh-speaking Welshmen to Welsh dioceses, after the translation of John Wynne of St Asaph to Bath and Wells in 1727, had been a major factor in the secessions to Calvinistic Methodism and other branches of Protestant dissent in Wales in the late eighteenth and early nineteenth centuries, but there is no evidence to support the view of such critics that ignorance of Welsh hampered diocesan administration or led to a wilful attempt to marginalise the language. Indeed William Jacob has suggested that, whereas some English dioceses suffered for years from elderly and infirm bishops in an age when there was no provision for retirement, 'Welsh dioceses may have benefited from the energetic episcopates of aspiring younger men'.[47]

Despite the difficulties of the terrain, Welsh bishops appear to have been assiduous in carrying out regular visitations of their dioceses. Bishop Herring of Bangor undertook a visitation of his diocese on horseback in 1739 and his successor, Bishop Pearce, repeated the process ten years later. In 1738 Bishop Maddox of St Asaph instructed his clergy to assist their churchwardens to compile presentments of things amiss in their parishes. In the dioceses of St Asaph and St David's rural deans compiled detailed reports on the state of the churches in their rural deaneries for onward transmission to their respective bishops. As a result of such reports and information gleaned from the replies to visitation queries, Bishop Drummond of St Asaph compiled in 1749 a detailed survey of every parish which was used by his successors in their administration of the diocese. In the diocese of Bangor the ability of the bishop to ensure that benefices were held by competent clergy was greatly assisted by the fact that, unusually, he was the patron of no fewer than 78 out of the 116 benefices, a position of power only exceeded by that of the Archbishops of Canterbury. Most bishops had considerably less patronage in their hands. The Bishop of St David's was able to present to about a quarter of the benefices in his diocese and the Bishop of Llandaff was the patron of only three benefices in that diocese. Bishops used the power that they had either to appoint, or insist that other patrons appointed, Welsh-speaking clergy to parishes in Welsh-speaking areas. The case brought against Thomas Bowles, rector of Trefdraeth and Llangwyfan on Anglesey, by a group of parishioners in 1770, alleging that he was incapable of ministering in Welsh in two Welsh-speaking parishes, though often quoted, seems to have been an exceptional circumstance. In this case the Dean of the Arches ruled that Welsh-speaking clergy should be appointed to

Welsh-speaking parishes, and that ignorance of Welsh was sufficient grounds for a bishop to refuse to institute an incumbent or license a curate. Bishop Smallbrooke of St David's encouraged the SPCK to produce a Welsh translation of the *Book of Homilies* and Bishop Claggett of St Asaph distributed a Welsh translation of Bishop Gibson's *Pastoral Letter on Methodism* throughout his diocese. Statistics from all four Welsh dioceses show that the diocesan and archdeaconry consistory courts continued to be active throughout the eighteenth century. Between 1750 and 1759 the archdeaconry court of Brecon heard 95 cases, the archdeaconry court of Carmarthen 63, the diocesan court of Llandaff 101 and that of Bangor 226; the majority of these cases involved allegations of either defamation or fornication.

In terms of clerical incomes there was a marked difference between the average value of benefices and curacies in the two northern dioceses of Bangor and St Asaph and the two southern ones of Llandaff and St David's. The poorest livings were those in the two archdeaconries of Cardigan and St David's where almost a quarter of benefices were valued at less than £10 per annum in the early eighteenth century. Pluralism was therefore essential for a clergyman to have even a modest income, but this was usually achieved by a clergyman holding two or more adjacent parishes which he served personally. Thomas Beynon, later archdeacon of Cardigan and estate agent to the Vaughans of Golden Grove, personally served the small neighbouring parishes of Llandyfeisant, Llanfihangel Aberbythych and Llanfihangel Cilfargen (Carms.) from 1770, adding to these in 1784 the rectory of Penboyr, where he employed a curate. He held a weekly Sunday service at 9 a.m. at Llanfihangel Cilfargen and 11.30 a.m. at Llanfihangel Aberbythych and a fortnightly afternoon service at Llandyfeisant. He established Sunday schools in the parishes of Llanfihangel Aberbythych, where he catechised the children personally, and Llanfihangel Cilfargen and Penboyr, where he employed a master to do so.[48] The real difficulty in the dioceses of Llandaff and St David's was that of attracting graduate clergy since the endowments, even by holding livings in plurality, were only sufficient to attract the sons of farmers and other men of modest means who could not afford the fees and living costs of Oxford or Cambridge. Such men had to rely on the education provided by either grammar schools or dissenting academies. Energetic attempts were made to increase the value of benefices in Wales through augmentation by Queen Anne's Bounty; between 1721 and 1780 no fewer than 372 Welsh parishes and chapelries benefited from such augmentations, to a total value of £132,800. Even so the incumbent of four neighbouring parishes in the Cardiganshire rural deanery of Ultra-Aeron in 1733 only had a combined annual income of £46 13s 4d.

Despite the difficulties caused by terrain, language and lack of finance, recent research has suggested that there was a real revival in the state of the parishes in Wales during the eighteenth century, much of which has been overlooked because of the attention paid to the Evangelical Revival and the eventual creation of a separate Calvinistic Methodist church. Much work seems to have been undertaken to put church fabrics and furnishings into a state of good repair. The surviving faculty book of the diocese of St Asaph for 1713–69 records 2 faculties for the installation of new organs, 2 for new pulpits, 15 for galleries and 80 for pews. Work took place on the fabrics of the cathedrals at St Asaph and St David's. In 1734 a new cathedral was built at Llandaff within the ruins of its predecessor and at Bangor Dean John Jones left 100 pounds for the purchase of a new altarpiece and altar cloth. Compared with the average English parish, the average Welsh one was more likely to have two Sunday services, services on holy days and monthly communion services. In the diocese of Bangor in 1749 114 parishes had two Sunday services and only 43 had one; 100 parishes had services on holy days; 46 parishes had a monthly communion service, 26 had a quarterly one and 26 had a celebration six times a year. In the same year in the diocese of St Asaph 120 parishes had two Sunday services and only 5 had one; 77 parishes had services on holy days; 74 parishes had a monthly communion service and only 15 a quarterly one. As in the Isle of Man communicant numbers were exceptionally high, frequently well in excess of the number of families in the parish. The vast majority of parishes had services only in Welsh. In the predominantly Welsh-speaking diocese of Bangor in 1749 111 churches had services only in Welsh, 3 only in English and 7 in both English and Welsh. In the diocese of St Asaph the comparative figures for the same year were 54, 18 and 37, reflecting the larger number of English-speaking parishes in north-east Wales. The decline in the use of Welsh as the century progressed reflected no disrespect for the native language but purely pragmatic decisions based on the fact that English was gaining ground as the language not just of business, but of everyday speech, in Flintshire, Monmouthshire, Radnorshire and the eastern parts of Montgomeryshire as well as in some of the larger towns. In some churches, where the congregation comprised a mix of English and Welsh speakers, services were held in a mix of the two languages, though this was not always deemed to be very satisfactory and led to complaints that one language was being favoured over the other.

There is no doubt that, though Wales had become a fully Protestantised country by the late sixteenth century, there was greater evidence for the survival of traditional customs and superstitions than in England. Many Welsh-speaking parishes observed *Plygain*, a pre-dawn service by candlelight on Christmas Day, and their patronal festivals. At Holyhead the alleged bones of St Cybi were carried through the town on three consecutive Sundays. The offerings at St Beuno's shrine at Clynnog Fawr were so substantial as to obviate the need for raising a church rate. There were also frequent pilgrimages to holy wells at which local clergy were usually present. The *Mabsant* or patronal festival service tended to be accompanied by public games, music, dancing, eating and drinking, often in the churchyard. Reforming clergy deprecated such survivals and some were suppressed during the second half of the eighteenth century. Often superstitious practices, such as the ringing of bells during funeral processions, saying prayers over the body of the deceased and frequent recourse to witches, astrologers and cunning men, survived much longer. In an attempt to disseminate a more restrained and orthodox theology among the Welsh clergy and laity, strenuous attempts were made by the SPCK and others to establish both diocesan and parochial libraries in Wales. As late as 1757–68, when such initiatives had largely ceased in England, the Associates of Dr Bray established no fewer than 45 parochial libraries in Wales.

The Church of Ireland[49]

The established church in Ireland was overwhelmingly the church of the English-speaking 'Protestant ascendancy'. In economic terms it was the wealthiest of the established churches in the British Isles. Its bishoprics were, on average, worth more than their English or Welsh equivalents, though the numerical weakness of the established church, and the political instability of Ireland, made them even less desirable to English candidates than bishoprics in Wales. The same was true in relation to other benefices. In 1787 Bishop Woodward of Cloyne estimated that the average benefice income in the Church of Ireland was £148 per annum though there were significant variations between one diocese and another. In Raphoe it was £250, in Clogher £187, in Cloyne £180, in Cork and Ross £150, in Waterford and Lismore £120, in Clonfert and Kilmacduagh £116, in Dublin £115 and in Killala and Achonry £90. The main difference between the Churches of Ireland and England was in the size and status of cathedrals. Most were very modest buildings which also acted as parish churches, their deans acting as incumbent of the parish. A majority of cathedral dignities and prebends had their endowment provided by a parochial living which the holder either had to serve personally or appoint and pay a curate to serve for him. The unions of dioceses which had taken place since the Reformation meant that some united dioceses had more than one cathedral, though a fair number had fallen into ruin. The dioceses of Kilmore and Meath had neither cathedrals nor cathedral chapters. The patronage of the diocesan bishops was generally more extensive than that of their counterparts in England and Wales with, overall, Irish bishops being able to present to 55% of the parishes in their dioceses and to 252 out of 268 of the dignities and prebends at the 28 Irish cathedrals. In England and Wales the diocesan average of episcopal presentation was only 11.7%.

During the second half of the eighteenth century the composition of the Irish episcopal bench began to change, with a higher proportion of bishoprics being filled by men of Irish birth, though the wealthier bishoprics still tended to be filled by men of English birth. As late as 1800 King George III blocked the translation of the obvious Irish candidate, Charles Agar, to the primatial see of Armagh and pressured a very unwilling William Stuart, then bishop of St David's, to accept the appointment. A high proportion of Irish appointees were, however, members of landed families. From 1805 three members of the Beresford family, major figures in Irish politics in this period, were bishops at the same time: William Beresford, Baron Decies, at Tuam and Ardagh; and his nephews George at Kilmore and John at Cork and Ross. Many of the bishops used their wealth to benefit their dioceses. Richard Robinson, archbishop of Armagh 1765–94, restored the cathedral, built a public library, a classical school and a new archiepiscopal palace and chapel, founded the Armagh observatory and was instrumental in securing the erection of a barracks, county gaol and public infirmary. It was estimated that in his lifetime he spent £35,000 on public works. At his death he bequeathed £5,000 to establish a university in Ulster but the bequest lapsed as it was not carried out within five years of his death as specified in his will. Robinson's contemporary, Bishop Chenevix of Waterford and Lismore, bequeathed £2,600 for charitable purposes, to be administered by his successors in the see. Bishop Hervey of Derry (1769–1803), despite his reputation for good living, foreign travel and womanising, was also a generous benefactor to his diocese, paying during his lifetime annual subscriptions of £30 and £60 respectively to the Poor of Derry and the Diocesan Clergy Widows' Fund. His ecumenical attitude caused him to contribute not just to Church of Ireland building projects, but also to Presbyterian and Roman Catholic ones in his diocese.

The weakness of the Church of Ireland and the fact that a significant number of parishes, especially in the west of Ireland, contained not a single Protestant inhabitant, had resulted in the formation of parochial unions. Most of these unions had at least one church but this was not always the case; in 1787 there were fewer churches than benefices in every diocese of the provinces of Cashel and Dublin, in two dioceses in the province of Tuam and one in that of Armagh. This meant that some benefices were in effect sinecures so that what looks like high incidences of pluralism and non-residence from the bald statistics can be very misleading. The average Church of Ireland incumbent was serving only about 500 parishioners compared with the 2,500 served by his Roman Catholic counterpart. A major reason for the high level of non-residence in Ireland was the paucity of glebe houses, though the number of these increased greatly as a result of grants or loans made by the Irish Board of First Fruits, which exercised similar functions to those of Queen Anne's Bounty in England and Wales. The evidence from Irish visitation returns is that the standards of public worship in the Church of Ireland were very high, though very few services were conducted in Irish. Most churches had two Sunday services, at least in the summer months, and monthly communion was frequent, not just in the towns, but in many rural parishes as well. Some town churches, especially in Dublin and Cork, had a fortnightly celebration of Holy Communion and they were so organised that, in both these cities, anyone familiar with the details would have been able to communicate every Sunday had they so wished. Few churches, however, had weekday services and daily services, even in cathedrals, were exceptionally rare. Christ Church Cathedral in Dublin had daily choral services in 1815 at 11 a.m. and 4 p.m.; in 1778 it was presented with an elaborate new set of altar plate comprising two chalices and patens, two large plates, an oval alms-dish and a pair of candlesticks. At Cashel Archbishop Agar endeavoured to put similar arrangements in place when the new cathedral was completed in 1788. He presented the cathedral with an organ and made provision for a choral establishment of an organist, six singing men and six choristers but the records show that, after Agar's translation to Dublin in 1801, the arrangements he had made began to disintegrate as the cathedral chapter could not afford to maintain them.

The last quarter of the eighteenth and the first quarter of the nineteenth centuries was a period of extensive church building and restoration for the Church of Ireland, much of it funded by the Irish Board of First Fruits, which from the late 1770s received substantial grants for this purpose from, initially, the Irish and, later, the British parliaments. Even before this date new churches were being built in Ireland, including 12 in Dublin and 4 in Cork. A good example of a handsome mid-eighteenth-century church was St Peter's, Drogheda, rebuilt in 1748–52 and enriched with elaborate plasterwork. New cathedrals had also been built before 1770 at Clogher and Cork. With the new resources available to the Board of First Fruits it was possible for a much larger number of new or replacement churches to be built, and Archbishop Agar of Cashel persuaded it to extend its system of grants and loans to include the purchase of glebes and the building of glebe houses. Between 1791 and 1803 no fewer than 116 new glebe houses had been built with financial aid from the Board of First Fruits. Some of the Irish bishops thought that the building of glebe houses was a better use of the Board's money than the building of churches, which discouraged parish vestries from raising money for the repair of existing buildings. There was also a worry that some incumbents were milking the Board's resources to build unnecessarily elaborate churches. The Board originally granted £2,500 to the rebuilding of Collon church in County Louth and was reluctantly persuaded to offer a further £2,500 when the costs began to spiral out of control. The final cost of the new church was £6,500 and the incumbent, unable to repay the loan element of the financial support from the Board of First Fruits, was under threat of sequestration and imprisonment for debt at the time of his death in 1821. The impact of the system of financial support provided by the Board can be seen, both in the vast number of late eighteenth- and early nineteenth-century churches still in use in Ireland and in the formal statistics for church building and restoration: in 1830 it was estimated that of the 1,100 Church of Ireland churches then in existence 474 had been built or rebuilt since 1800, 134 had been erected during the eighteenth century and the dates of 492 were unknown. The majority of those in the last group had undergone at least substantial restoration in the century before these calculations were made. One of the most important group of Church of Ireland buildings to benefit from this programme of rebuilding and restoration was the church's cathedrals, almost all of which had substantial work done on them between 1770 and 1820. One of the best examples, the furnishings of which have remained largely intact, was the cathedral at Downpatrick. This had been destroyed in 1538 and had remained in ruins ever since. In 1790 it was decided to rebuild it and King George III and the Marquess of Downshire, who a decade earlier had rebuilt the church of Hillsborough at his own expense, both contributed 1,000 pounds to the project, as did the Board of First Fruits. The total cost of rebuilding was £13,000 and the new cathedral was opened for worship in 1818.

The Church of Scotland

When Samuel Johnson and James Boswell visited Scotland in 1773,

we talked of the assiduity of the Scotch clergy in visiting and private instructing their people, and how in this they exceeded the English clergy.[50]

Nevertheless there is little doubt that before the early nineteenth century there was an enormous difference between the effectiveness of the Church of Scotland in the lowland parishes of Scotland compared with that in the highland parishes. Boswell and Johnson noted that there was no church on the island of Raasay but that the minister of Portree on the neighbouring island of Skye preached occasionally in the laird's house. The same was true on Coll where worship was held in a private house conducted by the minister of Coll and Tiree who was then 77. He had no manse but lived in his own farmhouse combining his ministerial responsibilities with agricultural ones.[51] Even where there were churches, the size of many highland and island parishes, and the lack of roads and bridges, meant that many parishioners were unable to attend them weekly or even monthly. Some ministers held services at outlying preaching stations, occasionally even in the open air, for the benefit of those parishioners unable to get to the parish church. Such services tended to be irregular, perhaps three or four times a year. The minister of the Small Isles parish officiated, weather permitting, once a month on Muck, once a quarter on Canna and on all other Sundays on Eigg, where the parish church was located. With such irregular services establishing Sabbath observance often proved difficult. In 1750 the minister of Laggan had to wait until shinty was finished before the service could begin and in 1810 the presbytery of Lochcarron 'proposed withdrawing baptism and communion from those who went fishing on the Sabbath'.[52]

Many of the problems of the Church of Scotland were blamed by Evangelicals on what they considered to be the shortcomings of Moderate ministers, 'neglecting their spiritual functions and pastoral duties . . . more worldly-minded than spiritually minded', and therefore as a result showing 'little concern for the eternal welfare of their parishioners'.[53] Such charges, however, need to be treated with caution. Principal Burleigh considered that 'the charge of moral laxity brought against the Moderates . . . probably amounts to little more than that they abandoned the Puritan ways still followed by the old-fashioned'.[54] They were accused of, and indeed openly admitted, going to dances and the theatre and playing cards, but there is no evidence that this produced the sort of irreligion among their par-ishioners that some critics alleged. Church attendance seems to have been far from universal, and various attempts were made by the General Assembly to enforce it, but this simply replicated a situation repeated elsewhere in the British Isles and throughout mainland Europe. On the other hand the maintenance of discipline through the kirk sessions seems to have had a strongly moderating effect on sexual behaviour in Scotland. Compared with the situation in England most fathers acknowledged, when accused, paternity of their bastard children and accepted financial respons-ibility for them so that they did not need to be supported from poor relief. There was, however, some evidence of increasing 'insolence towards ministers, parish schoolteachers and members of the kirk session', though this was far from widespread. The main problem, as it was in Ireland and Wales, was the widespread retention of superstitious beliefs including a morbid fear of witchcraft.[55] Unlike the Anglican churches in England, Wales and Ireland, the Presbyterian Church of Scotland did not have a major problem with pluralism and non-residence. Only one type of plural-ism was permitted, the holding of a parochial charge at the same time as a university professorship, and only then because the endowments of the latter were usually very low. Parish clergy were obliged to reside on their charges and presbyteries were strict at enforcing this provision. However, Scottish clergy had much lower stipends than those in England as the tiends, the Scottish equivalent of tithes, had been appropriated by the heritors who used then to pay the clergy. Most only used about half the income from tiends to pay the stipends, keeping the rest for themselves. As a result, at the beginning of the nineteenth century, it was estimated that no fewer than 273 parochial charges, over 38% of the total number in Scotland, were worth less than £50 a year.[56]

In most parts of Scotland church services were conducted in English but in the Gaelic-speaking areas, which until the nineteenth century comprised most of the highlands and islands, excluding eastern Caithness, Orkney and Shetland, parish churches tended to have one service in English and one in Gaelic on Sundays. A few, such as that at Tongue, had two Sunday services in Gaelic and one in English.[57] Communion services were rare in the Church of Scotland, usually four times a year in urban, and twice in rural, parishes. However, the normal highland and island practice by the end of the eighteenth century was for a single communion service each year, spread out over several days and conducted in the open air. What was termed 'the communion season' normally began on a Thursday with a solemn fast, followed by self-examination on Friday, preparation and distribution of communion tokens on Saturday, the communion service on Sunday and a service of thanksgiving on Monday. Before this date communion services had been even more infrequent, with gaps of several years in some parishes. The following description of an early nineteenth century communion service in the Skye parish of Sleat gives some impression of the solemnity of the occasion:

the tables . . . made of long planks of wood about two feet in breadth . . . rested on clods of earth, were about a foot off the ground and were covered by a white cloth . . . the ministers took their places at the head of the tables and gave a short message, distinct from the sermon, before the bread and wine were passed around. When this was done, the ministers would address each table again and those at each table would then rise to make way for the others who would again be spoken to and served by the ministers.

Though many attended the communion services the process of examination and the awarding of tokens meant that not all communicated, the total number of communicants depending on how exacting the standards for reception imposed by the ministers were. Although each parish had only one such season each year, ministers and parishioners from neighbouring parishes usually took part, and seasons were staggered so that people in a particular area would have more than one opportunity, if they so wished, to communicate each year. The normal Sunday service consisted largely of preaching. No form of musical accompaniment was permitted and the singing of metrical psalms was conducted by a precentor who would sing out each line which was then repeated by the congregation.[58] This practice of 'lining out' the psalms was also practised in the Calvinist Netherlands and in some Anglican churches which had no choir and organ or orchestra.

A major problem for the Church of Scotland was a serious shortage of church accommodation in some of the larger cities and in large rural parishes, especially in the highlands and islands. Some of the larger pre-Reformation town churches and former cathedrals had been divided into two or more churches served by separate ministers. In lowland parishes, where outdoor communion was not the normal practice, tables were incorporated in the seating in such a way that the seats could be converted into table pews when required. In some towns, such as Edinburgh, the town council took on responsibility for building new churches to serve a growing population. The council then appointed the minister and recouped the cost of erecting and maintaining the churches from pew rents. In rural areas a temporary solution was found in the erection of chapels-of-ease to serve the outlying areas of large parishes, but there was a lot of opposition to this practice. Since they had either to be funded by the heritors (landowners) or from church door collections, which then reduced the amount given for poor relief and resulted in an assessment being made on the heritors, the cost was seen to lie unfairly on those who did not always have the financial resources to meet it without serious detriment to their own incomes. In 1798 the General Assembly passed a series of regulations to be observed in the erection of chapels-of-ease: the decision had to be taken by the assembly and not the presbytery, the qualifications of the minister had to be established, the amount of the stipend and the security for its payment had to be agreed and it had to be clear that the parish was capable of both paying for the new church and maintaining collections for poor relief. Chapels-of-ease had no ecclesiastical area allocated to them and no separate kirk session; the minister was not a member of the presbytery and the congregation was subject to the discipline of the parish church's kirk session. These stringent conditions made it difficult to establish chapels-of-ease. Between 1799 and 1826 only 27 such chapels-of-ease were established and it was not until 1824 that efforts were made to increase them through the provision of a parliamentary grant of £100,000 to build and endow some 40 new churches in the larger highland and island parishes.[59]

Notes

1 R. Porter, *English Society in the Eighteenth Century*, Harmondsworth 1982, pp. 76–7.

2 W. Gibson, *Church, State and Society, 1760–1850*, Basingstoke 1994, pp. 11–12.

3 J. Rule, *Albion's People: English Society 1714–1815*, London 1992, p. 48.

4 Gibson, *Church, State and Society*, pp. 14–15. See also G. Holmes, *Augustan England: Professions, State and Society 1680–1730*, London 1982, pp. 83–114.

5 J. Gregory 'Standards for admission to the ministry of the Church of England in the eighteenth century', *Dutch Review of Church History*, 83 (2003), pp. 283–95.

6 W.N. Yates, 'An opportunity missed? The provision of education and training for a non-graduate clergy: comparative case studies of the dioceses of St David's and Sodor and Man in the eighteenth and nineteenth centuries', *Dutch Review of Church History*, 83 (2003), pp. 322–3.

7 D. McClatchey, *Oxfordshire Clergy 1777–1869*, Oxford 1960, p. 27.

8 W.M. Marshall, 'The dioceses of Hereford and Oxford, 1660–1760', in J. Gregory and J.S. Chamberlain (eds), *The National Church in Local Perspective: The Church of England and the Regions, 1660–1800*, Woodbridge 2003, pp. 214–16.

9 V. Barrie-Curien, *Clergé et Pastorale en Angleterre au XVIIIe Siècle: Le Diocèse de Londres*, Paris 1992, pp. 369, 376, 394.

10 J. Black, *Eighteenth-Century Britain 1688–1783*, Basingstoke 2001, p. 135.

11 G. Holmes and D. Szechi, *The Age of Oligarchy: Pre-Industrial Britain 1722–1783*, London 1993, pp. 107–9, 395–6.

12 W. Gibson, *Church, State and Society, 1760–1850*, Basingstoke 1994, pp. 29–30.

13 P. Virgin, *The Church in an Age of Negligence: Ecclesiastical Structure and Problems of Church Reform 1700–1840*, Cambridge 1989, p. 47.

14 *Ibid.*, pp. 54–5.

15 McClatchey, *Oxfordshire Clergy*, pp. 71, 76.

16 Rule, *Albion's People*, p. 41.

17 Gibson, *Church, State and Society*, p. 13.

18 Virgin, *Church in an Age of Negligence*, p. 120.

19 Gibson, *Church, State and Society*, pp. 5–6.

20 J. Gregory, *Restoration, Reformation and Reform, 1660–1828: Archbishops of Canterbury and Their Diocese*, Oxford 2000, p. 87.

21 W.M. Jacob, 'Supervising the pastors: supervision and discipline of the clergy in Norfolk in the eighteenth century', *Dutch Review of Church History*, 83 (2003), pp. 296–308.

22 W.A. Speck, *Stability and Strife: England 1714–1760*, London 1977, pp. 96–7.

23 F. O'Gorman, *The Long Eighteenth Century: British Political and Social History 1688–1832*, London 1997, pp. 166–8.

24 N. Sykes, *From Sheldon to Secker*, Cambridge 1959, pp. 205–10; Gibson, *Church, State and Society*, p. 42.

25 A.P. Jenkins (ed.), *The Correspondence of Bishop Secker*, Oxfordshire Record Society 57 (1991), pp. 4–5, 50, 180–2, 192–5, 218, 265, 271.

26 Gregory and Chamberlain (eds), *National Church*, pp. 78, 205–7.

27 W. Gibson, *The Church of England 1688–1832: Unity and Accord*, London 2001, pp. 127–36; W.M. Jacob, *Lay People and Religion in the Early Eighteenth Century*, Cambridge 1996, p. 135.

28 Gibson, *Church, State and Society*, p. 9; D. McClatchey, *Oxfordshire Clergy 1777–1869*, Oxford 1960, p. 3.

29 Gibson, *Church, State and Society*, pp. 19–25; Barrie-Curien, *Clergé et Pastorale*, pp. 418–19; McClatchey, *Oxfordshire Clergy*, p. 31.

30 Virgin, *Church in an Age of Negligence*, p. 191.

31 *Ibid.*, pp. 191–252.

32 This section is based on N. Yates, *Buildings, Faith and Worship: The Liturgical Arrangement of Anglican Churches 1600–1900*, new edn, Oxford 2000, pp. 55–65, together with reference to some more recent studies.

33 For example, R.A. Soloway, *Prelates and People: Ecclesiastical Social Thought in England, 1783–1852*, London 1969, pp. 50–1; A.D. Gilbert, *Religion and Society in Industrial England*, London 1976, p. 27.

34 D.A. Spaeth, *The Church in an Age of Despair: Parish and Parishioners, 1660–1740*, Cambridge 2000, p. 191.

35 Barrie-Currien, *Clergé et Pastorale*, p. 430.

36 Marshall, 'Dioceses of Hereford and Oxford', pp. 211–12.

37 D.A. Spaeth, *The Church in an Age of Danger: Parsons and Parishioners 1660–1740*, Cambridge 2000, pp. 237–52; Yates, *Buildings, Faith and Worship*, pp. 64–5; see also the very detailed study of the topic in N. Temperley, *The Music of the English Parish Church*, 2 vols, Cambridge 1979, i, pp. 100–267.

38 See especially Yates, *Buildings, Faith and Worship*, pp. 48–55, 66–123 and B.F.L. Clarke, *The Building of the Eighteenth-Century Church*, London 1963.

39 Speck, *Stability and Strife*, p. 112.

40 P. Borsay, *The English Urban Renaissance: Culture and Society in the Provincial Town 1660–1770*, Oxford 1989, pp. 110–12.

41 *Ibid.*, pp. 78–9.

42 M. Smith, *Religion in Industrial Society: Oldham and Saddleworth 1740–1865*, Oxford 1994, pp. 34–6.

43 Jacob, *Lay People and Religion*, pp. 186–222.

44 Gregory, *Restoration, Reformation and Reform*, pp. 173–7.

45 A. Warne, *Church and Society in Eighteenth-Century Devon*, New York 1969, pp. 51–63.

46 This section is based on chapters 4–6 of G. Williams, W.M. Jacob, N. Yates and F. Knight, *The Welsh Church from Reformation to Disestablishment 1603–1920*, Cardiff 2007.

47 *Ibid.*, forthcoming.

48 N. Yates, 'Archdeacon Thomas Beynon and Lampeter College', *Trivium*, 35 (2004), pp. 88–90.

49 This section is based on Chapters 3–6 of N. Yates, *The Religious Condition of Ireland*, Oxford 2006.

50 F.A. Potter and C.H. Bennett, *Boswell's Journal of a Tour to the Hebrides with Samuel Johnson, LLD*, London 1936, p. 215.

51 *Ibid.*, pp. 143, 255–6, 282.

52 D. Ansdell, *The People of the Great Faith: The Highland Church 1690–1900*, Stornoway 1998, pp. 22–3, 114.

53 *Ibid.*, pp. 47–8.

54 J.H.S. Burleigh, *A Church History of Scotland*, London 1960, p. 304.

55 R.A. Houston and I.D. Whyte (eds), *Scottish Society 1500–1800*, Cambridge 1989, pp. 30, 219; C.A. Whately, *Scottish Society 1707–1830: Beyond Jacobitism, Towards Industrialisation*, Manchester 2000, pp. 164–6.

56 S.J. Brown, *The National Churches of England, Ireland and Scotland 1801–46*, Oxford 2001, pp. 30–1, 66.

57 C.W.J. Withers, *Gaelic in Scotland 1698–1981*, Edinburgh 1984, p. 177.

58 Ansdell, *People of the Great Faith*, pp. 114–16, quotation on p. 115. See also D. Johnson, *Music and Society in Lowland Scotland in the Eighteenth Century*, Oxford 1972.

59 Yates, *Buildings, Faith and Worship*, pp. 28–9; Burleigh, *Church History of Scotland*, pp. 319–20; see also G. Hay, *The Architecture of Scottish Post-Reformation Churches*, Oxford 1957.

CHAPTER 6

The Beginnings of Ecclesiastical Reform

In the last chapter we began with the situation in England and ended up by looking at the state of the established churches in Wales, Ireland and Scotland. In this chapter we will begin with Ireland and Wales and move on to other parts of the British Isles. The reason for this is that the latest research on the ecclesiastical reform movement in the British Isles is showing that, far from emanating, as one might expect, from London and the south-east, this movement began in the western extremities of the British Isles and gradually moved eastwards.

Ecclesiastical reform in Ireland[1]

By the last quarter of the eighteenth century the established Church of Ireland was under some pressure from the changing political balance in Ireland. Though the Irish Parliament was happy to preserve the Protestant ascendancy as it had been constituted in the early part of the century, the British government recognised that the numerical strength of both Roman Catholicism and Presbyterianism made it essential that some concessions were made to these two groups. The moves from the 1770s towards giving them a larger economic and political stake in the nation, whilst strongly resented by many members of the established church, was recognised as essential by some of its more enlightened leaders, such as Bishop Hervey of Derry, and led to an acceptance by him and some of the other bishops that, if the Church of Ireland was not to be damaged by this process, the new political situation had to be addressed by reforming the established church from within. The Church of Ireland was, however, greatly assisted in this process by the decision of the Irish and British governments to provide financial assistance to the Irish Board of First Fruits, a decision not replicated in England and Wales until the provision of parliamentary grants for new churches in 1818, or in Scotland until 1824. Nevertheless this largesse alone would not have been sufficient to induce the changes that took place in the Church of Ireland in the last quarter of the eighteenth, and the first quarter of the nineteenth, centuries. It is always very difficult to establish the instigator of any widespread reform movement but insofar as it is possible to do so in this instance the credit must go to Charles Agar (1735–1809),[2] from 1768 successively Bishop of Cloyne, Archbishop of Cashel and Archbishop of Dublin. The office of rural dean had been restored in the diocese of Cloyne by one of Agar's predecessors, the philosopher George Berkeley, and provided an element of diocesan middle management lacking elsewhere in Ireland, where the post of archdeacon carried no administrative functions. On his translation to the united diocese of Cashel and Emly in 1779, Agar revived the office there as well, and within two years it had been revived in virtually every diocese in the province of Cashel. Following Agar's example, the office of rural dean was reconstituted in several dioceses in other parts of Ireland, including Armagh, Dromore and Ossory in the 1790s, and by 1820 there were rural deans in 16 out of the 22 Irish dioceses. Agar was also a moving force in trying to secure the better preparation of candidates for ordination in the Church of Ireland. In 1790 he organised a meeting of 14 Irish archbishops and bishops at which it was agreed that they would only ordain those who could produce a certificate from Trinity College, Dublin, stating that they had attended specified lectures in divinity. At a later meeting the bishops agreed which books would be prescribed for ordination examinations. As a diocesan Agar promoted clerical residence, refusing to institute candidates unwilling to reside on their benefices in all his dioceses; rebuilt or repaired the cathedrals at Cashel, Cloyne and Emly; organised the building of 6 new churches in the diocese of Cloyne and 11 in the diocese of Cashel and Emly; repaired the archbishop's palace at Cashel; and increased the number of glebe houses in the dioceses of Cashel and Emly from 3 to 24. He was, in old age, rather less energetic as archbishop of Dublin but he still delivered a primary charge in 1802 in which he urged his clergy to visit the sick, to keep their churches in repair and to reside constantly on their cures. The system of rural deans was introduced into the province with appointments being made every three years from among the resident clergy in each diocese.

Agar's example was emulated by his successor at Cashel and Emly, Charles Brodrick, and by Thomas Lewis O'Beirne, Bishop of Ossory 1795–8 and Meath 1798–1822. Brodrick appointed John Jebb, the future

Bishop of Limerick, as one of his principal advisers and in 1814 commissioned him to carry out a survey of the condition of the parishes in the dioceses of Cloyne, Cork and Ross. Brodrick was keen to promote monthly communion services and Jebb noted that at last these were being introduced. O'Beirne was a convert from Roman Catholicism and of more modest social origins than most of his fellow bishops in Ireland. Possibly because of this he was keen to promote reform in the parishes, especially the desirability of clerical residence. At both Ossory and Meath detailed evidence of episcopal visitation survives and attests to the thoroughness of this process under Bishop O'Beirne. In 1818 O'Beirne calculated that, in his 20 years as bishop of Meath, 25 new glebes had been purchased, 67 new glebe houses had been built or acquired, 25 new churches built and 32 existing churches rebuilt. Another reformer was Bishop Percy of Dromore (1782–1811). He repaired and enlarged his cathedral and enforced a rota whereby each of the six dignitaries and prebendaries had to preach twice a year or incur a fine. Clergy who neglected their duties, such as the curate of Waringstown who intended to spend Christmas 1791 in Bath, were severely reprimanded. The surviving visitation diaries of Bishop Lindsay of Kildare for 1804–8 and Bishop Stock of Waterford and Lismore for 1811 also provide excellent illustrations of the average bishop's attention to detail when carrying out his visitations and his determination to promote best practice throughout his diocese.

Ecclesiastical reform in Wales[3]

The initiatives in ecclesiastical reform manifested in Ireland from the 1770s began to be manifested in Wales from the 1780s and between then and 1815 all four Welsh dioceses were held by bishops committed to ecclesiastical reform: John Warren (1783–1800) and H.W. Majendie (1809–30) at Bangor; Richard Watson (1782–1816) at Llandaff; Samuel Horsley (1801–6) and William Cleaver (1806–15) at St Asaph; and Horsley (1788–93) and Thomas Burgess (1803–25) at St David's. At Bangor Warren resided for part of each year, only appointed graduates to benefices in his gift, persuaded the cathedral chapter to have two Sunday services instead of one, improved the bishop's palace and enforced clerical residence. Majendie used the visitation process as a means of promoting reform, successfully encouraging the repair of churches and the establishment of day and Sunday schools and, rather less successfully, the provision of two Sunday services. Horsley was an exemplary reformer at both St David's and St Asaph. He personally examined candidates for ordination, maintained a strict discipline over clerical appointments and issued instructions for the proper observance of holy days and a monthly celebration of Holy Communion. Shortly before his death in 1806 his charge to the clergy of the diocese of St Asaph contained new regulations to prevent non-resident incumbents appointing unlicensed curates to serve their benefices at stipends below what Horsley considered acceptable. In 1807 Bishop Cleaver commissioned a meticulous survey of the parishes in his diocese which was still being updated by his successor two decades later. Cleaver was also a strong supporter of the National Society for Education, established in 1811, and encouraged the establishment of schools in his diocese. Another strong supporter of education was Thomas Burgess. His first charge to the clergy of the diocese of St David's announced the establishment of a Society for Promoting Christian Knowledge and Church Union in the Diocese with five primary objectives: to distribute Bibles, prayer books and religious tracts in both English and Welsh; to establish libraries for the use of the clergy; to enable ordinands to obtain a decent education; to establish schools for the education of the poor; and to promote the setting up of Sunday schools. He also encouraged his rural deans to form clerical societies in their deaneries 'to organize Sunday schools, to promote theological study, and to support each other in their clerical work', in essence a precursor of the ruridecanal conferences established in some English dioceses before 1850. Both Horsley and Burgess were strong disciplinarians, taking action against clergy for neglect of duty or improper behaviour. Horsley had attempted to improve the education of ordinands in the diocese of St David's by insisting that they attend 'a reputable public school' and providing them with lists of books on which he would 'examine them and expect to find them expert'.[4] Unfortunately the chief result of this policy was a drop in the number of ordinands, from about 25 a year in the period 1750–87 to six in the period 1788–1800. Burgess initially announced that he would only ordain non-graduates who had studied divinity at one of nine licensed grammar schools in the diocese and then, in 1804, that he proposed to found a college for the training of ordinands. Although a good deal of money was raised in the first few years, it proved difficult to obtain a site and the project kept being delayed. Eventually the foundation stone of St David's College (now the University of Wales) at Lampeter was laid in 1822 and the first students admitted five years later.

Undoubtedly one of the most interesting of the episcopal reformers in Wales was Bishop Watson of Llandaff. He was in fact both a pluralist and a non-resident, though he justified both on the grounds that the income of

the see was insufficient to meet his expenses as bishop, that his income
from his total preferment was never more than £2,000 *per annum*, and
that the diocese had no episcopal residence. Watson, however, confirmed
regularly and increased the number of confirmation centres in the diocese
from four to eight. He also carried out nine full visitations of his diocese.
He required his clergy to reside, wherever this could be achieved, and that
each church should have two Sunday services and services on holy days.
In his 1802 charge he encouraged his clergy to read widely and to take
seriously their responsibilities for schools established in their parishes. He
also insisted that clergy should dress in a manner suitable to their station
and not emulate secular fashions. Watson's wider concerns for the reform
of the established church in England and Wales were expressed in a letter
to Archbishop Cornwallis of Canterbury, dated 12 November 1782 and
later published,[5] in which he recommended

*the utility of bringing a Bill into Parliament to render the Bishopricks
more equal to each other, both with respect to income and patronage,
by annexing part of the estates, and part of the preferments of the richer
Bishopricks, as they become vacant, to the poorer . . . By a Bill of this
kind, the poorer Bishops would be freed from the necessity of holding
Ecclesiastical preferments* in commendam *with their Bishopricks; a
practice which bears hard upon the rights and expectations of the rest
of the clergy; which is disagreeable to the Bishops themselves; which
expose them to much, perhaps, undeserved obloquy.*[6]

He argued that the desire for translation, thus caused,

*influences the minds of the Bishops too powerfully, and induces them to
pay too great an attention to the beck of a Minister.*[7]

The equalisation of episcopal incomes would reduce the desire for translation and make the episcopate a more independent lobby in the House of
Lords. He also believed that

*a third probable effect, of the proposed plan, would be a longer
residence of the Bishops in their respective Dioceses; from which the
best consequence might be expected.*[8]

As far as the clergy were concerned Watson recommended

*the introduction of a Bill into parliament for appropriating, as they
became vacant, one third or some other definite part, of the income of
every Deanery, Prebend or Canonry, of the Churches of Westminster,*

*Windsor, Christchurch, Canterbury, Worcester, Durham, Norwich, Ely,
Peterborough, Carlisle, &c, to the same purposes,* mutatis mutandis, *as
the First Fruits and Tenths were appropriated by the Act passed in the
fifth of Queen Anne. Dignities which after this deduction would not
yield one hundred a year, should not I think be meddled with.*[9]

As things stood at present,

*the whole provision for the church is as low as it can be, unless the State
will be contented with a beggarly and illiterate Clergy, too mean and
contemptible to do any good either by precept or example, unless it will
condescend to have Taylors and Coblers for its Pastors and Teachers . . .
But though the whole Revenue of the Church is so inconsiderable, as not
to admit any diminution of it; yet a somewhat better distribution of it
might be introduced with much, it is apprehended, advantage to the State,
and without the least injustice to any individual.*[10]

Watson used statistics produced by the ecclesiastical lawyer, Richard
Burn, to argue that there was still a total of 5,597 livings eligible for
augmentation under the rules of Queen Anne's Bounty, and that

*computing the clear amount of the Bounty to make 55 augmentations
yearly it will be 339 years from the year 1714 (which was the first year in
which augmentations were made) before all the said livings can exceed
£50 a year. And if it be computed that half such augmentations may be
made in conjunction with other benefactions (which is improbable) it
will require 226 years before all the livings already certified will exceed
£50 a year.*[11]

Such views, combined with Watson's rather radical political opinions,
were not calculated to appeal to either bishops or ministers and they were
completely ignored. Nor was Watson to be translated from his poor Welsh
see. However, it is perhaps ironic that when the major financial reform
of the Church of England was at last undertaken by the government in
the 1830s the measures that were put in place included several very similar
to those that Watson had advocated 40 years earlier.

One of the major elements in the reform process in all the Welsh dioceses
was the increased use of rural deans by reforming bishops to implement
reform programmes. Unlike most parts of England and Ireland, where
the office had to be revived, rural deans had survived in most of the Welsh
dioceses, though the level of their activity clearly varied from diocese
to diocese. In that of St Asaph they had remained active throughout the

eighteenth century and the surviving reports of fabric inspections in the diocesan archives bear witness to this. In the dioceses of Bangor and St David's the powers of rural deans were substantially increased from the first decade of the nineteenth century. Bishop Majendie of Bangor used them as the principal agents of his well-documented reform programme, particularly in his campaign for church restoration. Similarly, in the diocese of St David's, Bishop Burgess was relying on regular reports from his rural deans to inform him of the state of the parishes in his diocese and so that he could take disciplinary action against incompetent or recalcitrant clergy.

Ecclesiastical reform in England

Critical to the moves for ecclesiastical reform in England, which to some extent lagged behind that in Ireland and Wales, was a growth of confidence among churchmen who had felt marginalised by the Whig governments of George I and George II. From the 1760s this confidence began to be regained, assisted by the promotion of high churchmen to high office 'after a fifty year drought'.[12] Peter Virgin has identified the major problems facing the church in the late eighteenth and early nineteenth centuries as the lack of a professional training for the clergy or indeed any concept of vocation, the laxity of standards for ordination, serious inequalities in the career structure for clergy, an outdated parochial geography, clerical poverty and lack of affordable housing, 'an expectation of lethargy', and the difficulties of removing incompetent, sick or elderly clergy.[13] Some elements of Virgin's analysis need challenging; others fail to recognise that bishops and churchmen generally were well aware of the problems but could do nothing without parliamentary legislation to tackle them. The lack of specific training for the clergy beyond a good classical education including philosophy and theology was not seen as a defect at the time and criticism of such a lack reflects a concept of ministerial preparation which, together with the emphasis on spiritual calling, did not really become accepted until well into the second half of the nineteenth century. The training of Anglican clergy before then was, on the whole, replicated by other Protestant churches in Europe. It was only the Roman Catholics who had developed seminaries for the training of priests and even these were considered to be not without their faults. Some of the other abuses of the pre-Victorian church were greatly exaggerated. Only about a fifth of the clergy, even on Virgin's own statistics, failed to gain a benefice within five years of ordination in the first decade of the nineteenth century.[14] The inflexibility of the parochial structure was certainly a weakness and was a real problem in some of the rapidly expanding urban areas. Energetic bishops, as we have already seen in Ireland and Wales, and such were also appointed in England, made strenuous attempts to improve the conditions of the clergy in relation to both incomes and housing, refusing for example to license curates without guarantees of a reasonable stipend.[15] Virgin criticises the arrangement whereby, in neighbouring parishes, either one incumbent served two or more cures, or else served one parish as an incumbent and another as curate to a non-resident rector or vicar, but he fails to recognise that many of these parishes were very small and their churches close together and they could just as easily be served by a single clergyman as they are today, when pluralism and non-residence, even if not defined as such, in rural parishes is both widespread and accepted as providing a perfectly acceptable measure of pastoral oversight. One clergyman serving a parish of 50 or 100 inhabitants almost certainly, as Virgin suggests, would not have had enough to do and the system of clergy serving more than one parish rather undermines his charges relating to 'an expectation of lethargy'. Even when clergy did not have to serve more than one benefice the evidence, to which Virgin somewhat inconsistently alludes, shows that the late eighteenth and early nineteenth centuries witnessed

a surprisingly vigorous spiritual revival. Services, especially celebrations of Holy Communion, were becoming more frequent; congregations were growing; catechising was on the increase; and schools were springing up everywhere.[16]

The difficulties in dealing with inadequate clergy were largely caused by the legal difficulties of doing so. In the case of those who were medically unfit, either through illness or senility, this was entirely the fault of there being no provision for the payment of pensions. There is, however, plenty of evidence in diocesan records that most clergy in these categories employed curates to act for them or that, when they did not do so, bishops endeavoured to persuade them that it was their duty to make proper pastoral provision for their parishioners.

Although Samuel Horsley spent some of his episcopal career in Wales, he was also Bishop of Rochester and Dean of Westminster (the two being held in plurality to provide an adequate income) between 1793 and 1802. Since he had to spend the winter months in London in order to attend to his parliamentary duties, Horsley could also then reside on his deanery, with the result that he was able to implement reform in both the offices he held. He devoted his first visitation charge to the clergy of the diocese of Rochester in 1796 to the evils of neglecting parochial duty and, despite a period of serious illness in the late 1790s, was as strong a disciplinarian at Rochester as he had been at St David's and was to be at St Asaph. At Horsley's second visitation of his diocese in 1800 he issued a printed circular to his clergy instructing them on the proper method of preparing candidates for confirmation. They were to be at least 14 years of age, capable of saying the Lord's Prayer, Apostle's Creed and Ten Command-dments and have been properly instructed in both the church catechism and the significance of the confirmation rite. As Dean of Westminster, Horsley was nearly always present at chapter meetings and he increased their frequency. He undertook a major restoration of King Henry VII's Chapel, though this was not completed in his lifetime. He also made important contributions to the improvement of the services, especially the music, in Westminster Abbey and to increasing the efficiency of its financial management, almost doubling its annual income from £5,139 13s 2d in 1793 to £9,380 10s 10d in 1804.[17]

This emphasis on liturgical renewal was not just confined to Horsley but was a marked feature of the late Georgian Church of England, rather overlooked in the past because of the greater attention paid to the cere-monial innovations resulting from the Oxford Movement. In a sermon preached before the University of Oxford in 1801, Thomas Saunders 'condemned the modern practice of congregations sitting when they should kneel'. Archdeacon Daubeny erected a plain cross over both the altar and the pulpit in his Bath church at about the same time. Somewhat earlier, in the 1780s, George Horne had placed lighted candles on the altar of Magdalen College Chapel in Oxford during celebrations of Holy Communion and, in his Bampton Lectures of 1786, George Croft had 'called for the reintroduction of a richer ceremonial' into Anglican wor-ship.[18] Such liturgical considerations also impacted on the design of church buildings, and the desire to give greater prominence to the altar, after about 1780. One of the earliest of such buildings is the church at Shobdon (Herefs.), rebuilt between 1752 and 1756. Although pulpit, reading and clerk's desk are grouped together in the traditional manner, they are positioned so as to give a clear view of the sanctuary from most seats in the church. More common, especially by the early years of the nineteenth century, was to place the pulpit and the reading desk on opposite sides of the sanctuary, or entrance to the chancel, so that the altar was placed at mid-point between them and to raise it on a small flight of steps to give it greater prominence. Early examples of this arrangement have been noted at Wolverton (Hants) in 1717, Saxby (Lincs.) in 1775 and Yarwell

(Northants) in 1782. It became very common after 1800 for the altar to be raised at least two or three steps above the rest of the church and frequently rather more.[19]

The most notable feature of the ecclesiastical reform programme in England, probably copied from the earlier experiments in Ireland and Wales, was the reintroduction of a system of effective rural deaneries, with rural deans exercising a level of supervision, below that of the bishop and the archdeacon, over the other clergy in the deanery. In 1800 the only English diocese in which rural deans were active was Exeter. They had been revived at Gloucester by Bishop Benson in 1734 but had ceased to be effective by the late eighteenth century. In 1811, John Fisher, recently translated from Exeter, revived the office and functions of the rural dean in the diocese of Salisbury. His initiative was copied by Bishop Buckner at Chichester in 1812. It appears that Bishop Yorke of Ely also appointed rural deans to inspect parishes for him in the 1780s and 1790s but the arrangement was not continued thereafter. Although the other English dioceses did not follow the example of Chichester, Exeter and Salisbury until after 1815, progress thereafter was rapid: Bath and Wells (possibly before 1815, certainly by 1820), Peterborough (1820), Bristol (1824), Lincoln (1829), Oxford (1831), Canterbury and London (1833), Worcester (1834).[20] Although it took a while to be implemented, the revival of rural deans was clearly a late Georgian initiative. Along with the introduction of rural deans, Arthur Burns has noticed a much greater efficiency in the carrying out of episcopal and archdiaconal visitations in the first quarter of the nineteenth century and the growing use of the visitation charge to instruct the clergy on ways to improve their pastoral activity. Although the average length of episcopal charges did not increase significantly until after 1825, those of archdeacons did so dramatically between 1801 and 1815. As early as 1741 Bishop Secker used his second visitation charge to refer to information he had acquired about deficiencies in his diocese at his primary visitation and in 1770 Bishop Terrick of London specifically targeted his visitation articles at clergy who had failed to make a return at his 1766 visitation. In 1790 Bishop Porteous of London used his primary visitation charge to highlight those abuses he intended to address as bishop. In some dioceses societies were set up for educational purposes, such as those for Durham in 1811 and York in 1812.[21]

The one part of the British Isles in which our understanding of the process of ecclesiastical reform is limited by the lack of research on the topic is Scotland. Historians of the Church of Scotland have tended to the view that the Moderate majority in the General Assembly was only interested in preserving the political and religious status quo and that there was therefore little emphasis on any reform agenda. Reform in the Church of Scotland was seen as being primarily associated with the Evangelicals and being largely confined, as has been noted earlier, to the western highlands and islands. However, exactly the same line used to be taken by older historians of the established churches in England, Ireland and Wales, and we now know that this portrait of corrupt and lethargic institutions is simply not borne out by the available evidence. It should also be emphasised that recent research into the main Presbyterian body in Ireland, always strongly influenced by events in Scotland, has shown that there was certainly a reform movement at synod and presbytery level, not exclusively associated with Evangelicalism, and it is likely that this was the case in Scotland as well. There is, however, a strong need for new research in this area to complete our understanding of ecclesiastical reform movements across the British Isles in the late eighteenth and early nineteenth centuries. What, however, is certainly the case in Scotland is that there was a greater willingness on the part of those dissatisfied with the established church to secede from the Church of Scotland and set up their own religious organisations, compared with the much greater unwillingness of those in England, Ireland and Wales to secede from their established churches. It may have been the case that these acts of secession in a sense absolved the Church of Scotland from taking the sort of action to try to retain the malcontents undertaken, admittedly with only partial success, by the Anglican established churches.

Government and parliament

Although the major reform of ecclesiastical institutions in England, Wales and Ireland did not take place until the 1830s, and the internal reforms that took place within the established churches were largely those promoted by bishops, archdeacons and rural deans, there was plenty of government consideration of, and parliamentary debate on, ecclesiastical issues in the late eighteenth and early nineteenth centuries. This was notably the case during the long ministry of William Pitt the Younger between 1783 and 1801. William Wilberforce took the view that Pitt had

given little reflection to religious matters. On one occasion he prevailed on Pitt to join him in listening to a sermon by a noted evangelical preacher, Richard Cecil, evidently hoping that it would stir Pitt into a stronger commitment to religion. He was disappointed when Pitt turned

*to him on the way out of church and said, 'You know, Wilberforce, I have
not the slightest idea what that man has been talking about.'*[22]

Nevertheless Pitt's ministry, and parliament during this period, took more
interest in religious issues than any ministry since Walpole's in the 1720s
and 1730s. Partly this was due to the presence from 1788 of Bishop
Horsley in the House of Lords. Whilst not making some of the radical
proposals suggested earlier by Bishop Watson of Llandaff, he had some
sympathy with ideas put forward by Francis Maseres in his pamphlet *The
Moderate Reformer*, published in 1791. In this, Maseres suggested the
annexing of certain benefices to poorer bishoprics to avoid the practice
of having to seek government permission to hold them *in commendam*;
an increase in some benefice incomes by restoring the great tithes of
bishoprics, deaneries and prebends to parishes; a reduction in clerical
non-residence by requiring clergy suing for tithes to prove that they had
done duty in their churches for at least 40 Sundays each year and permitting only a partial allocation of tithe arrears if they could not show that
they had done so; and the division of some of the larger parishes in the
north of England.[23]

    Pitt's earliest initiative in ecclesiastical legislation was a series of meas-
ures passed in 1785–9 to provide compensation to dispossessed American
loyalists, many of them clergy, who had refused to support American
independence. This was balanced in 1784 by the passing of legislation to
permit the English bishops to ordain as deacons or priests in 'countries out
of His Majesty's Dominions' without taking the oath of allegiance to the
crown, and a similar provision of 1786 permitting the archbishops of
Canterbury and York to consecrate bishops for such areas.[24] In 1798 Pitt
and Horsley collaborated on proposals to reform the land-tax and to make
provision for landowners to redeem some of their tax obligations through
the sale or mortgaging of parts of their estates to purchase stock which
would then be transferred to the Commissioners of the National Debt.
The short-term advantage to the government in reducing the national debt
charge, and the long-term advantage to landowners when the price of
stock was at a record low level, suited everybody. The result was that in
1788–9 a quarter of the national debt charge was redeemed through the
scheme. The original scheme, however, offered few advantages to ecclesiastical landowners, since it had not removed the restrictions on the sale of
ecclesiastical property, and in February 1790 Horsley submitted to Pitt a
paper on how it could be amended so as to benefit both the government
and the established church. A month later Pitt brought forward measures

which both removed the existing restrictions and set up a Commission for the Sale and Redemption of the Land Tax on Church and Corporation Estates. The resulting sales of land provided further benefit to the government's revenues and long-term advantages to ecclesiastical landowners in relief from land-tax. By 1813 sales of ecclesiastical land totalling £1,061,600 had taken place, of which about a quarter were episcopal estates, 45% those of deans and chapters, a fifth those of parochial clergy and the remaining tenth those of collegiate institutions.[25] In 1800 Pitt put forward proposals for the augmentation of all ecclesiastical benefices and curacies in England and Wales to a minimum of £70 per annum, to be linked to provisions for residence to be supervised by the bishops. Archbishop Moore of Canterbury supported the financial aspects of the proposals, but had some reservations about the enforcement of the residence provisions, and discussions about these were still taking place when Pitt's ministry fell in 1801.[26]

The issue was not, however, allowed to drop. In his 1796 charge to the clergy of the diocese of Rochester, Bishop Horsley had identified clerical non-residence as an evil which needed to be tackled. Horsley did not consider all non-residence to be a problem. Whilst he condemned clergy who used non-residence to pursue what he defined as 'secular pleasures', he thought the church benefited from using its livings to provide an income for those pursuing scholarly activity, even when it was not strictly theological. Horsley's remedy was a simple one. To raise benefice incomes to a level sufficient to enable any incumbent who had a legitimate reason for non-residence to pay a curate a stipend adequate to enable him to serve only that parish. The attitude of Horsley and some other bishops in condemning non-residence encouraged the taking out of prosecutions for non-residence against some clergy by anti-clericalist laity, under the archaic provisions of an Act of 1529, which had never been implemented, in 1800. In one case, the vicar of Norham (Northumb.) was convicted for taking lodgings in his own parish whilst his vicarage was being rebuilt, since the requirement for residence specified in the Act was taken to mean living in the parsonage house. Clearly such prosecutions were vexatious and in 1801–2 a series of bills were passed in Parliament to suspend the provisions of the Act whilst measures to enforce residence, or at least mitigate the problems of non-residence, were being considered. Bishop Horsley felt that this was no more than a delaying tactic and in March 1803 he elicited a promise from the government that no further suspension bills would be brought forward but that legislation would be produced to both repeal and replace the provisions of the 1529 Act, though when the new measures were introduced he was far from enthusiastic about them. The bill, which was the work of the Lord Chancellor's brother, Sir William Scott, MP, was passed by both Houses of Parliament and received the royal assent in July 1803. It permitted clergy to be non-resident under certain, strictly specified, conditions, but it also increased the powers of bishops to enforce residence where these conditions were not met, and it required bishops to submit to the Privy Council annual returns of non-residence, and various other statistics, for their dioceses.[27]

Following the success of his clerical non-residence bill, Sir William Scott tried in both 1803 and 1804 to introduce a further bill which would have forced non-resident clergy to pay their curates a stipend which would have equated to a specified percentage of the benefice income. His attempts were unsuccessful. There was criticism that such a measure would lead to wholesale interference by Parliament in ecclesiastical affairs and that, if clergy could be forced to pay their curates a 'minimum wage', then such a provision could be extended to other employers. It was a concept far too radical for the age and smacked of the sort of attitude that had recently been adopted by revolutionary governments in France and other parts of Europe. Whilst Scott dropped his attempts to introduce legislation, the cause was taken up by the Evangelical attorney-general, and future prime minister, Spencer Perceval. Perceval believed that curates

were a largely impoverished and exploited body of men whose treatment by unscrupulous incumbents disgraced the church. Legislation was required to force incumbents to pay their curates a fair share of the income of the living. If incumbents were unhappy with this, they should reside in their parishes and do the duty themselves. The purpose of Church property, he insisted, was not to provide incomes for the clergy, but to provide religious instruction and pastoral care for the parishioners.[28]

He had no more success than Scott, his three curacy bills being defeated in 1805, 1806 and 1808. When he became prime minister in 1809, Perceval decided that, rather than seeking to introduce another curacy bill, the answer might be to concentrate on the augmentation of poorer benefices. He calculated that it would take Queen Anne's Bounty at least 40 years to raise the annual income of all benefices to at least £50, but that if Parliament voted an annual grant of £100,000 for four years, this minimum level could be achieved within the timespan of the grant. He further proposed that, following such a grant being made for England and Wales, enquiries should be undertaken into the number of poor livings in Ireland and Scotland to see whether similar grants should be considered. The proposal was approved and indeed extended beyond Perceval's original time limit, his objectives being supported, not just by fellow Evangelicals, but by high churchmen such as Lord Liverpool, who succeeded him as prime minister after his assassination in 1812. Between 1809 and 1821 11 annual grants were made to increase the benefice incomes of poor livings in England and Wales. In 1810 the annual parliamentary grant to the Irish Board of First Fruits was dramatically increased from £10,000 to £60,000, continuing at this level until 1816.[29]

In 1808 Parliament followed up the provisions on clerical residence in England and Wales by passing somewhat more draconian legislation for Ireland. Bishops were empowered to sequester the benefice incomes of non-resident incumbents and use a fifth of it to pay the annual stipend of a curate. After three years of persistent non-residence bishops could declare a benefice vacant and organise the appointment of a new incumbent. The passing of this measure resulted in the number of resident incumbents increasing from about 46% to over 65% of the total number of incumbents between 1806 and 1819. Additional subsidies from the British government also resulted in a significant increase in the number of parochial schools in Ireland, which rose from 361, with 11,000 pupils, in 1788 to 549, with 23,000 pupils, in 1810. Annual grants were made to the Association for Discountenancing Vice and Promoting the Practice of the Christian Religion, an Evangelical body which also supported parochial schools in Ireland, with the result that by 1819 the Association was educating some 8,000 pupils in its schools. In 1810 the government also made provision for poorer ministers in the Church of Scotland by making an annual grant of £10,000 which could be used, where the heritors were unwilling to increase stipends from the revenue of tiends, the Scottish form of tithes, to increase the minimum annual stipend of a parish minister to £150.

The progress of ecclesiastical reform was continued under Lord Liverpool. In 1812 Lord Harrowby, an Evangelical whose brother was later to become, as Bishop of Gloucester, the first Evangelical to be raised to the English episcopate, revived Perceval's curates bill which, despite episcopal opposition to some of its provisions, passed both Houses of Parliament. Harrowby also drew attention to the serious problems for religious observance posed by the paucity of church accommodation in some of the expanding urban areas of England.[30] Here his fellow Evangelicals had the support of Anglican high churchmen. In a pamphlet entitled *The Church in Danger*, Richard Yates pointed out the impossibility of a single parish clergyman providing pastoral care for between thirty and forty thousand parishioners, as was the case in some urban areas, and that in

central London there was Anglican church accommodation for only 216,000 people whereas the total population was 1,162,300. He felt that 'a large urban underclass was emerging, with no religious and moral instruction . . . driven to join the ranks of injurious opposition, either in Dissent, and Sectarian Enthusiasm; or in the infinitely more dangerous opposition of Infidelity, Atheism, and ignorant depravity'.[31] Yates may have exaggerated, but there is no doubt that his complaint was listened to by both bishops and politicians. In 1815 John Bowdler drafted a memorial to Lord Liverpool, signed by 120 other prominent laymen, demanding that Parliament address the serious shortage of church accommodation in some urban areas by providing funds for the erection of new churches in which there would be substantial free seating for the poor. Although the government announced its commitment to such a measure in 1816 it was not until two years later that the government announced that it would provide a million pounds to build new churches in towns and cities where these were needed.

Although the reform measures adopted by parliament in the first two decades of the nineteenth century were modest compared with the full-scale reform programme of the 1830s, they did provide a precedent on which future governments could build. It is also important to stress that the initial emphasis for reform before 1800 had come from the bishops and that it was the government and Parliament that had to be persuaded to bring forward measures for reform. When the bishops criticised some of these measures it needs to be emphasised that they were not opposing the principle of reform but simply the detail. Occasionally parliamentary legislation could be so poorly framed that it simply did not achieve what it aimed to achieve, or in solving one problem it merely created others which had either not been foreseen or demonstrated that warnings given at the time had been unwisely disregarded. Above all support for reform crossed the boundaries of churchmanship. Both high churchmen and Evangelicals believed that reform was necessary and were prepared to collaborate in order to achieve it.

Notes

1 This section is based on Chapters 3 and 5 of N. Yates, *The Religious Condition of Ireland*, Oxford 2006.

2 See the excellent biography by A.P.W. Malcolmson, *Archbishop Charles Agar: Churchmanship and Politics in Ireland, 1760–1810*, Dublin 2002.

3 This section is based on Chapter 9 of G. Williams, W.M. Jacob, N. Yates and F. Knight, *The Welsh Church from Reformation to Disestablishment 1603–1920*, Cardiff 2007.

4 T. Burgess, *A Charge Delivered to the Clergy of the Diocese of St David's in the Year 1804*, Durham 1805.

5 R. Watson, *A Letter to His Grace the Archbishop of Canterbury*, 2nd edn, London 1783.

6 *Ibid.*, pp. 7–8.

7 *Ibid.*, pp. 10–11.

8 *Ibid.*, pp. 19–20.

9 *Ibid.*, p. 25.

10 *Ibid.*, pp. 29, 31.

11 *Ibid.*, pp. 36–7.

12 W. Prest, *Albion Ascendant: English History 1660–1815*, Oxford 1998, p. 207.

13 P. Virgin, *The Church in an Age of Negligence: Ecclesiastical Structure and Problems of Church Reform 1700–1840*, Cambridge 1989, pp. 131–70.

14 *Ibid.*, p. 139.

15 W. Gibson, *Church, State and Society, 1760–1850*, Basingstoke 1994, p. 31.

16 Virgin, *Church in an Age of Negligence*, p. 155.

17 F.C. Mather, *High Church Prophet: Bishop Samuel Horsley (1733–1806) and the Caroline Tradition in the Later Georgian Church*, Oxford 1992, pp. 177–91.

18 P.B. Nockles, *The Oxford Movement in Context: Anglican High Churchmanship 1760–1857*, Cambridge 1994, pp. 210–12.

19 N. Yates, *Buildings, Faith and Worship: The Liturgical Arrangement of Anglican Churches 1600–1900*, new edn, Oxford 2000, pp. 115–22.

20 R.A. Burns, 'A Hanoverian legacy? Diocesan reform in the Church of England c.1800–1833', in Walsh, Haydon and Taylor (eds), *The Church of England c.1689–c.1833*, pp. 267–8; R.A. Burns, *The Diocesan Revival in the Church of England c.1800–1870*, Oxford 1999, pp. 75–9.

21 Burns, *Diocesan Revival*, pp. 26, 30, 48, 116.

22 W. Hague, *William Pitt the Younger*, London 2004, pp. 237–8.

23 Mather, *High Church Prophet*, pp. 141–2.

24 G.M. Ditchfield, 'Ecclesiastical legislation during the ministry of the younger Pitt', in J.P. Parry and S. Taylor (eds), *Parliament and the Church 1529–1960*, Edinburgh 2000, pp. 68–9.

25 Mather, *High Church Prophet*, pp. 145–9.

26 Ditchfield, 'Ecclesiastical legislation', p. 71.

27 Mather, *High Church Prophet*, pp. 149–55.

28 S.J. Brown, *The National Churches of England, Ireland and Scotland 1801–46*, Oxford 2001, p. 63.

29 *Ibid.*, pp. 64–5.

30 *Ibid.*, pp. 65–8.

31 *Ibid.*, p. 69.

CHAPTER 7

The Threat of Revolution

British society, at least at its upper levels, was rocked by two traumatic events in the late eighteenth century: the loss of the American colonies and the revolution in France. Both made it fear that equivalent traumatic events might take place in the British Isles and the existence of radical groups in some British cities, and the almost permanent threat of politically motivated disturbances in Ireland, made it extremely nervous of any pressure for change. In this final chapter we will look at how this fear and anxiety impacted on religion, and particularly the church–state relationship, in the British Isles between 1780 and 1815.

Religious dissent and political radicalism

The crucial matter that dominated the political debate about religious issues in the late eighteenth and early nineteenth centuries was the status of the established churches in the British Isles, particularly in England, Wales and Ireland, where there were significant groups of non-episcopalian Protestant dissenters, and, in the case of Ireland, the additional complication of a large Roman Catholic population. Jonathan Clark has emphasised the stability of traditional views about the nature of the church–state relationship throughout this period and such opinions are certainly backed up by the known views of leading politicians. William Pitt the Younger described the established church in 1796 as 'so essential a part of the constitution that whatever endangered it would necessarily affect the security of the whole'.[1] Not surprisingly most Anglican bishops took a similar line and were vociferous in expressing their opposition to the demands of Protestant dissenters for the repeal of the Test and Corporation Acts. In the late eighteenth century only two of the Welsh bishops, Shipley of

St Asaph and Watson of Llandaff, supported repeal, though some Anglican clergy were more sympathetic.[2] A number of other scholars have suggested that Clark's line of widespread support for the political and religious status quo may have been overestimated and certainly underestimates the strength of political radicalism among Protestant dissenters. Bradley argues that a large number of dissenters supported the American colonists' demand for independence in the 1770s and that by the last decade of the century some were even demanding the complete disestablishment of the Church of England, which they viewed as an institution blocking political and social reform.

Nonconformity amounted to a substantial challenge to the constitution in Church and State that was woven into the very fabric of English society.[3]

Nonconformists had felt that the Whig dominance of British politics in the reigns of George I and George II, whilst not delivering all their political objectives, did at least offer them protection from any further efforts by Anglican high churchmen to marginalise them. This meant that the more inclusive political agenda under George III, and in particular a willingness to promote high churchmen to positions of power, was a serious cause for concern.

After the accession of George III, the Dissenters' old loyalties shifted away from the House of Hanover. Their dissatisfaction did not represent a uniform alienation in every congregation, but on the whole, the events of the 1760s and 1770s witnessed an increasingly coherent opposition, and the antipathy toward specific policies became in time a permanent undercurrent of criticism toward the state.[4]

The extent to which this undercurrent represented a serious threat to the political and religious establishment is by no means clear.

Clark and others would argue that, though political and religious radicals might have made a lot of noise, this was not a genuine reflection of the strength of their opinions among the populace at large:

The Church of England retained the overwhelming support of the English people in all ranks of society. The political power and widespread influence of the Church rested on firm foundations. Its bishops sat in the House of Lords and its communicants dominated the many offices in central and local government. The church still possessed considerable wealth, property and patronage, and it played a major role in education, charity and the dissemination of news and views. Its parish structure

remained a basic unit of local government and administration . . . The
Church of England also played a central role in conservative political
ideology. Throughout the eighteenth century conservatives agreed that
government in general was ordained by God and that the workings
of civil society were at the mercy of divine providence. It was a view
propagated not only by the Tories, but by the majority of Whigs.[5]

Nevertheless the political and religious establishments were deeply worried
about the views and influence of some of the radical Whigs. Orthodox
high churchmen, such as William Jones of Nayland, produced a series of
publications aimed at undermining radical polemic. Jones' *The Scholar
Armed*, the first edition of which appeared in 1780, was a collection of
tracts designed to promote an orthodox understanding of the church–state
relationship and a defence of the powers of the church justified by the
doctrine of apostolic succession. Similar arguments were used by a future
bishop, John Randolph, the Regius Professor of Divinity at Oxford, in
1792 and by another future bishop, William Van Mildert, in his Boyle
Lectures of 1802–5. In 1798 Charles Daubeny used the first edition of
his *Guide to the Church* to condemn schism from the Church of England
and the pragmatic arguments in the defence of the church–state relationship used by Bishop Warburton and others. Daubeny emphasised, as
seventeenth-century high churchmen had done, that the Anglican religious
and political establishment was to be 'justified not on principles of private
judgement, or the expediency of *any* establishment, but, ultimately,
because its doctrine was *true*.'[6]

From the 1770s radical views of not just the church–state relationship,
but other aspects of the British constitution, were being put forward by a
number of critics. Thomas Paine, who had been brought up in the Society
of Friends, argued in *Common Sense* (1776) that monarchy was far from
an ideal form of government even when it was not absolute. He pushed
these views a good deal further in *Rights of Man* (1791–2), a detailed
criticism of Edmund Burke's defence of monarchy and attack on the French
Revolution. In *Rights of Man* Paine 'is taken up not with an exposition of
the theory or practice of democracy, but with a denunciation of the two
central features of ancien régime governments, including England's: the
hereditary principle, underpinning monarchy and aristocracy, and
"priestcraft", offering a divine sanction for authority and hierarchy.' In
The Age of Reason (1794–5) Paine pushed even further, arguing that
scripture was not divinely inspired and that 'God existed, but only as an
abstract first cause'. William Godwin, a former dissenting minister, was

advocating outright atheism by 1787.[7] The Unitarian Joseph Priestley had condemned Warburton's pragmatic view of the church–state relationship as early as 1768; by the 1790s he was seeing the French Revolution as the precursor to 'the imminent fall of the Papacy and the Ottoman Empire and the return of the Jews to Judea' as preliminaries to the 'Second Coming of Christ'.[8] It was an intellectual expression of a mood that had its emotional expression in the prophecies of Richard Brothers and Joanna Southcott. Similar views were also to be found among the new Methodist groupings by the late eighteenth century. Among the leading Methodist radicals were Henry Moore and Samuel Bradburn. Bradburn, a strong supporter of the leading radical Whig politician, Charles James Fox, was sympathetic to the French Revolution and in 1794 preached a sermon on equality at Bristol.[9] It was opinions such as those of Bradburn that led to bishops such as Horsley of Rochester comparing the Methodists to the French Jacobins in 1801 and to the Methodist leadership being anxious to demonstrate their political loyalty. In 1798 the Methodist Conference, the Connexion's governing body, passed a resolution condemning the Irish rebellion of that year and in 1814 Joseph Sutcliffe, in a published sermon entitled *The Divine Mission of the People called Methodists*, argued that Methodism was essentially 'unrevolutionary' in its political beliefs, that it strongly disapproved of 'anarchy and revolt' and that it had made a positive contribution to British commerce and industry.[10]

Just as both old and new dissent were divided in their political attitudes, it is important to note that Anglicans, even bishops, were as well. The support of the bishops for the political and religious status quo did not mean that they unreservedly supported government policy on all matters. Bishops Hinchcliffe of Peterborough, Keppel of Exeter and Shipley of St Asaph were strong opponents of the war against the American colonies, and most bishops were anxious to press the government to outlaw slavery. James Ramsay, vicar of Teston in Kent, had published an essay arguing for abolition in 1784 and in 1786 Bishop Porteous of Chester encouraged William Wilberforce to raise the issue in Parliament. Those clergy who argued that slavery was consistent with the teachings of scripture were roundly disabused, even by conservative bishops such as Horsley. Relations between the government and the episcopate were also severely strained by the slowness with which the former responded to requests for the consecration of bishops for the independent American church.[11] Indeed, an analysis of the voting record of the bishops in the House of Lords between 1788 and 1805 shows that although a majority of the bishops voted with the government in most significant divisions, they were notable dissentients on several occasions. Brownlow North of Winchester, Watson of Llandaff and Wilson of Bristol voted against the regency proposals in 1788; Horsley voted against the preliminary negotiations for peace with France in 1801; Madan of Peterborough, Pretyman of Lincoln and Vernon of Carlisle voted against the Irish militia bills in 1804; and Cleaver of Bangor voted against measures for the defence of the country in 1805.[12] There was also a very strong measure of episcopal support for social reform in the late eighteenth and early nineteenth centuries with even conservative bishops like Horsley taking up the causes of popular education and the relief of poverty.[13]

Opposition to tithes

Donald Spaeth has noted that 'the payment of tithes was the issue over which parsons and parishioners quarrelled most often',[14] and the abolition of tithes, which formed a major part of most clergymen's incomes, was central to the radical reform agenda in the late eighteenth century.[15] Tithes were 'meant to link pastors with the productive toil of the community in symbiotic relationship'.[16] They were divided into the great tithes, paid either to the rector or a lay impropriator, usually a landowner whose predecessors in the estate had acquired this right with the purchase of monastic lands at the Reformation, and the small tithes paid to the vicar. Great tithes usually comprised those on corn, hay and wood and small tithes those on everything else, especially wool, livestock and garden produce, though rectors (often university colleges or cathedral chapters) and impropriators could legally claim that any item that provided the chief product in the parish should be regarded as forming part of the great tithe. This in itself could lead to disputes. By the end of the eighteenth century most tithes were paid in cash, rather than kind, through what were known as composition agreements. However, these agreements also led to potential disputes and they tended to benefit the richer clergy who could afford to employ professional agents to value and collect their tithes. Occasionally composition agreements were subject to annual review, but this was expensive so valuation tended to be periodic, with clergy agreeing composition payments at a fixed annual amount for a number of years. As well as having to bear the cost of collecting the tithes, the clergy were expected to reward the payers with an annual tithe feast and this could also prove expensive. As tithes were liable to tax it was essential for the clergy to extract fair compositions or payments in kind from their parishioners. Those who refused to pay could be taken to court but the suit against them had to be taken by the clergy or lay impropriators and this was a further added expense, though most suits for non-payment seem to have been successful.

There had always been opposition to the payment of tithes from the Society of Friends, arguing their case on religious rather than economic grounds. Their view was that 'the ministry of the Gospel is to be without pecuniary remuneration'.[17] Quakers who paid tithes, which some did in order to avoid prosecution for non-payment, could be expelled from the Society. There were several unsuccessful attempts in Parliament between the 1730s and the 1790s to pass legislation that would have exempted Quakers from paying tithes. A solution was finally achieved in 1813 when the power of excommunication was removed from the ecclesiastical courts. Prior to this the initial suit for non-payment had been made under ecclesiastical legislation with the result that, as Quakers refused to accept this jurisdiction and to appear before the ecclesiastical courts, they had been excommunicated and therefore made subject to the secular courts which had sought to recover the unpaid tithes. Even so, many courts took a fairly lenient stance and very few Quakers were imprisoned for non-payment. More widespread opposition to the payment of tithes began in the 1790s, especially in Devon and Cornwall where fishermen were particularly hostile. Part of the cause of this increased opposition to the payment of tithes, which had always been seen as something of an irritant by both collectors and payers, was the perception that tithe-owners were benefiting from the results of enclosure. There was a good deal of evidence to support this perception. After enclosure in 1772 the annual value of the tithes at Slattenham and Ditchingham (Bucks.) increased from £60 to £85; at Raventhorpe (Northants) from £108 to £225 in 1795; at Harrold (Beds.) from £60 to £100 in 1796; and, even more spectacularly, from £192 to £550 at Clophill (Beds.) in 1808.[18]

The impact of the French Revolution

Revolution against the monarchy and its ministers broke out in France in 1789. Whereas the American Revolution was an embarrassment for the British government, and certainly had a traumatic effect on British public opinion, it was not seen as having any long-lasting ramifications for the way in which Britain was to be governed in the future. The French Revolution was a very different matter. Initially its full impact was not realised but by the time the king and much of the aristocracy had been executed, a reign of terror had been launched and any form of Christianity attacked, with churches being turned into Temples of Reason, there were few in Britain who did not fear its consequences, not just for mainland Europe but for Britain as well. The determination to prevent revolution in Britain was to result, not in a programme of political repression, but certainly in the placing of blocks in the way of political and social reform for fear that modest change, such as had initially been expected in France, should provide a catalyst for a full-scale political, religious and social upheaval.

Whereas by the end of the 1790s virtually all Anglican and Roman Catholic opinion was hostile to the Revolution and its aftermath in France, this had not been so a decade earlier. In 1789 Anglicans like Bishop Watson of Llandaff and Roman Catholics like Joseph Berrington were far from hostile to the Revolution, though some Anglicans such as Bishops Horsley of St David's, Porteous of London and Warren of Bangor, William Jones of Nayland and Hannah More expressed their horror at the outset. The massacre of September 1792, the abolition of the monarchy, the trial and execution of Louis XVI, the Edict of Fraternity and its suggestion 'that the revolution should be spread to other countries' and above all the declaration of war between Britain and France in February 1793, finally made support for the Revolution highly dangerous and Loyalist Associations were established all over the country to combat the radical societies. Even Bishop Watson, despite his earlier sympathy for the Revolution, used his 1798 visitation charge to condemn support for events in France.[19] The principal early support, and certainly continued support after 1792–3, for the Revolution came from the radical nonconformists. In Wales especially there were a few who, following the example set by the French revolutionary government, lapsed into deism and cults of reason and nature. This example was not lost on Iolo Morganwg and strongly influenced his invention of the *Gorsedd*, which later became a feature of the national *eisteddfodau*. One of the London Welsh societies with which Iolo was connected, the Gwyneddigion founded in 1770, strongly supported the Revolution in France and published radical political literature in Welsh. The Welsh Calvinistic Methodists, fearful that they would be accused of similar radicalism, reacted by emphasising their own political loyalty. Thomas Charles vigorously promoted this non-radical stance in *The Welsh Methodists Vindicated* published in 1802. Concerned that their meeting houses might be attacked, the Welsh Methodists began registering them as dissenting meeting houses so as to protect them under the provisions of the 1689 Toleration Act. Previously they had been unwilling to do this as they wanted to emphasise that they were loyal Anglicans, but unlicensed chapels did not enjoy the protection of the law.[20]

The gradual shift of public opinion from some support, and much ambivalence, towards the Revolution in France, was greatly influenced by the publication in 1790 of Edmund Burke's *Reflections on the Revolution in France* and his decision to speak and vote against a motion in Parliament for the repeal of the Test and Corporation Acts in March of that year. Previously Burke had been seen as a moderate Whig whom dissenters could have counted on to support them. Burke, however, had been horrified by the Revolution in France and saw the makings of a potential revolution in Britain. He saw dissenters as providing the catalyst for such a revolution and this made him determined to continue to exclude them from office if they would not, at the very least, agree to occasional conformity. He used the *Reflections* to defend both the political and the religious components of the British constitution and to argue that these were under threat from radical dissenters.[21] The bishops of the Church of England were only too happy to jump on the bandwagon that Burke had provided for them:

Most of them thought of themselves as rational, suspicious of enthusiasm and advocates of a natural theology conformable to a balanced mind that found it difficult to give credence to agitated prophets ranting about the apocalypse or the second coming.

They then applied this principle to the Revolution in France which they saw, not as 'millenarian expectations of the disintegration of European Society', but as the result of human wickedness and misguided notions about the structure of that society. They saw the events in France as a 'grand conspiracy' organised by the opponents of religion.[22]

The attacks on churches and clergy by the revolutionary government confirmed their worst fears:

Conservative opinion was bitterly hostile to the French Revolution precisely because it sought to undermine Christianity and organised religion. The French were accused of forsaking truth and virtue and of substituting the unrestrained will of man for the providential dispensations of God. The ideological crusade against them involved a struggle for religion against atheism.[23]

Anglican bishops and clergy were fully seized of the situation. Anglican high churchmen such as Jones of Nayland 'sought to refute natural right theories by a vigorous reassertion of the patriarchal theory of the origin of

government which they derived from Scripture'.[24] Hannah More and
Sarah Trimmer argued that increasing provision for Christian education
was the best means of ensuring social control and preserving the social
hierarchy. It is not without significance that a major expansion of Sunday
schools took place in the period between 1790 and 1815; 'the most
eloquent opponents of religious education for the poor were not, in fact,
clerical reactionaries but infidel radicals'.[25] Bishops and clergy equated
religious dissent and potential revolution in the same breath. Bishop
Randolph of Oxford argued in 1800 'that Unitarianism was as responsible
for the French revolution as deism'. Bishop Horsley thought the
Methodists were using their Sunday schools to spread revolutionary ideas.
Hostility towards the French government was such that most Anglican
bishops and clergy were critical of Napoleon's Concordat with the papacy
in 1802, even though this created a remarkably similar constitutional
position between church and state in France as that which existed in most
parts of the British Isles.[26]

The trouble with violent rhetoric was its tendency to lead to violent
action. Just as Roman Catholics had suffered violence in the Gordon riots,
so it was now the turn of the nonconformists, particularly the Unitarians,
to suffer the attacks of the mob. In July 1791 there were three days of
rioting in Birmingham. Three meeting-houses were destroyed and Joseph
Priestley's house was burnt down with the loss of a vast quantity of
scientific papers and apparatus. There were anti-dissent demonstrations
in Manchester in 1792 and 1795. In Liverpool the Unitarians were
described as Jacobins by their enemies; a dissenting Sunday school was
attacked in Warwick; the Baptist minister of Bromsgrove (Worcs.) was
forced to flee; and the Unitarian minister in Exeter was under pressure
from his own congregation, fearing persecution, to tone down his radical
opinions. Dissenters responded by publishing loyal addresses to crown and
parliament, by conforming to the established church or by emigrating to
America. In the long run, of course, the action taken against dissenters
proved counterproductive. It eventually encouraged the more radical
Methodists, such as Alexander Kilham, to press for secession from the
Church of England and resulted in an increase in support for radical
dissent. By the late 1790s the Church of England was noting a draining
away in the enthusiasm for church and king, which had been the cry of the
mob a decade earlier, and a serious drop in the size of congregations at
Anglican services. Bishop Pretyman of Lincoln appointed a commission of
enquiry into the state of 100 parishes in his vast diocese in 1799. It found
that only a third of the population were regular attendants and only about

a sixth were regular communicants. Many of those who had ceased to attend their parish churches were, however, to be seen at cottage prayer meetings conducted by the more radical itinerant preachers, some of whom were Methodists and some of whom belonged to no denomination. By the late 1790s county associations to promote, mostly undenominational, itinerant preaching had been set up in Berkshire, Dorset, Hampshire, Kent, Surrey and Wiltshire and in 1798 an undenominational Northern Evangelical Society had been set up to promote preaching in Cumberland, Durham, Northumberland and Westmorland.[27]

Whilst the aftermath of the French Revolution worsened relations between Anglicans and Protestant dissenters it, at least temporarily, improved them between Anglicans and Roman Catholics. Among those forced to flee from Revolutionary France were large numbers of Roman Catholic clergy. A Committee for the Relief of the Suffering of the Clergy and Laity of France raised a total of £41,314 for French exiles in England. Support for the French émigré clergy came not just from high churchmen but also from Evangelicals.[28] By the end of 1792 there were some 1,500 French émigré clergy in England and a further 1,000 in the Channel Islands. Between 1793 and 1800 it has been estimated that there may have been as many as 5,000 émigré clergy on the British mainland at any one time. Many were destitute. English colleges and convents in France and Belgium relocated to the British Isles, as did some members of French monastic orders. There is no doubt that the need to assimilate so many exiles, even though most returned to France after the Concordat of 1802, caused major problems, especially in those areas in which the largest number of exiled priests settled. There were nearly 1,000 in Winchester in the 1790s, where they supplemented a long-established recusant community in the city and its neighbourhood. Despite the support offered to them by the cathedral chapter, there was a major scandal in 1795 when one of the priests, Jacques Couvert, was found to be trying to proselytise among the local Protestant population. The cathedral authorities raised the matter, through the SPCK, with the Archbishop of Canterbury, who arranged with the Home Secretary for Couvert to be deported under the provisions of the Aliens Act.[29]

The role of the Anglican bishops during the period following the Revolution in France can be seen in the activities and pronouncements of Bishop Horsley. Horsley was the acknowledged leader of the high church party among the episcopate and his lead was generally followed by the majority of his episcopal colleagues. He had condemned the Revolution from the beginning and by the time that Britain and France were officially at war was an enthusiastic supporter of that war. He defended the government over measures to increase taxation to pay for the war in 1796. The serious threat of a French invasion in 1797–8 led to the recruitment of armed local volunteer associations across the south of England and calls for the clergy to enrol in these. There was some division among the bishops as to whether such service was consistent with the clerical profession and, after some debate, each bishop was allowed to issue his own pastoral letter to the clergy if he wished to do so. Archbishop Moore of Canterbury issued one stating that it was permissible for the clergy to involve themselves in military action in a state of national emergency. Horsley's pastoral letter was much more aggressive, denouncing 'an enemy, who threatens to come with a prodigious army, to depose our King, to plunder our property, to enslave our persons, and to overturn our altars'. Defensive war, in these circumstances, was 'neither contrary to the general spirit of the morality of the Gospel nor forbidden by any particular precept nor discouraged by the example of the first Christians', and it was not just permissible, but a clear moral duty, for the clergy to support, physically if necessary, the war effort. Horsley's visitation charge in 1800, after the immediate crisis had passed, was full of denunciations of the situation in France and in 1801, when consideration was being given by Addington's ministry for peace with France, Horsley spoke against the government when the preliminary proposals were debated in the House of Lords. On this occasion none of his fellow bishops supported him.[30]

Although Horsley and the other bishops, even the usually unreliable Watson of Llandaff, supported, with slightly varying degrees of enthusiasm, the war with France, this was not the line taken by all the clergy. Among the anti-war minority was John Henry Williams, vicar of Wellesbourne in Warwickshire from 1778 until his death in 1829. As part of the Church of England's contribution to the war effort fast days had been instituted, as they had been periodically during other conflicts, rebellions or natural disasters, and special services were drawn up for them containing appropriate psalms, scripture readings and prayers. Those during the war against France condemned the Revolutionary government for 'horrible iniquities, and cruelties, which astonish the Christian World' and as 'declared Enemies to all Christian Kings, Princes and States, the impious and avowed Blasphemers of Thy Holy Name and Word' who threatened 'destruction to Christianity, and desolation to every Country where they . . . erect their bloody Standard'.[31] Williams suffered from sincere doubts about the ethics of a Christian minister promoting bloodshed. Not only was he required to read the prescribed services on fast days but he was also expected to preach a sermon supporting the texts he was reading. In 1793 he preached an anti-war sermon and then compounded his offence in the eyes of orthodox Anglicans by arranging for its publication under the title *Piety, Charity and Loyalty*. Williams was not a total pacifist. He believed in the concept of a just war. It was just that he could not bring himself to believe that the war against France fell into that category. He repeated this view in further fast day sermons in 1794 and 1795 and again in 1802 in his thanksgiving service for the Peace of Amiens, which concluded the first phase of the war against France. He published these sermons as well, keen that his views should be known, not just to his parishioners, but to the world at large. Whilst Williams received support from a few other Anglican clergy, and from radical dissenters, the majority of the clergy, including his neighbours in Warwickshire, were appalled by his opinions.[32] The war against France was not just a military and political event. It was a national crusade of a Christian nation against a heathen one that threatened not just Britain but the rest of the Christian world.

Rebellion in Ireland

From the 1760s onwards there had been periodic outbreaks of violence in Ireland, most of it perpetrated by secret societies dedicated to the overthrow of British rule. The ecclesiastical leadership of all the churches in Ireland had condemned such events and several Roman Catholic bishops had excommunicated the members of the societies that promoted them. The bishops of the province of Cashel issued pastoral letters denouncing the Whiteboys in the 1750s, the Bishops of Ferns, Kildare and Leighlin and Ossory excommunicated their members during the disturbances of 1775, and Bishop Troy of Ossory took similar action against them in 1779 and 1784. The Irish Roman Catholic bishops were as horrified by the post-Revolutionary events in France as their Anglican counterparts. Nevertheless the radical elements in Ireland which came together to form the Society of United Irishmen in 1791 were able to count on the support of a small but active minority of both Roman Catholic priests and Presbyterian ministers. The Presbyterian leadership was, however, as desirous as the Roman Catholic hierarchy to distance itself from political radicals among their clerical and lay membership and to express their loyalty to the British crown and constitution. Radical actions and opinions were formally condemned by the Synod of Ulster in 1790. For some Presbyterians, however, the events in France and, in particular, the attacks on the French Roman Catholic church 'seemed to be the key to unlock the treasure chest of biblical prophecy . . . Calvinists and Covenanters with an extravagant cosmology believed that God was hastening the downfall of popery and prelacy'.[33] Other Presbyterians had been influenced by more political arguments:

One strand had its origins in the Commonwealth tradition . . . This antique republicanism stressed the right of resistance, electoral reform and equality before the law . . . Yet another strand drew its ideas and encouragement from the American and French Revolutions, Paine's Rights of Man *and the democratic corresponding societies.*[34]

These different influences were to lead to some fragmentation among radical Presbyterians by the mid-1790s.

Many Ulster liberals began to feel that the French revolutionary government was deviating from the principle of liberty in both politics and religion. The French were accused of exercising a despotic power over the small nations within their control, and of setting up an irreligious regime.[35]

Thus many of those who might have been counted potential radicals in the 1780s were not supporters of the rebellion that eventually broke out in Ireland.[36]

The Society of United Irishmen, under the leadership of Wolfe Tone, a lay member of the Church of Ireland, aimed to unite all radicals in Ireland, irrespective of religious affiliation. It established its own newspaper, the *Northern Star*, in 1792. However, tensions between Protestants and Roman Catholics were to lead to outbreaks of sectarian violence from 1795. Some Protestants were fearful that political change in Ireland might give too much power to Roman Catholics and their determination to resist this was to lead to the establishment of the Orange Order. Roman Catholics responded to Protestant attacks on their homes by joining the Secret Society of Defenders and sectarian passions were further enflamed when this society entered into a formal alliance with the Society of United Irishmen. With Britain now at war with France, a group of Irish radicals, including Wolfe Tone, joined a French expeditionary force which tried, unsuccessfully, to land in Bantry Bay in December 1796. The government responded with a policy of ruthless coercion, aimed at the elimination of Irish radicalism, supported by the leadership of the Church of Ireland, the Roman Catholic hierarchy and the Synod of Ulster. The defeat of the French invasion force was celebrated with a solemn High Mass and *Te Deum* of thanksgiving at the Francis Street Chapel in Dublin attended by six bishops; Archbishop Troy preached a sermon, attacking the political situation in France, as vociferous as those preached by the Anglican bishops and clergy in England. Unfortunately, just as the policy of coercion increased rather than decreased the extent of political radicalism in England and Wales, it was similarly counterproductive in Ireland and can be said to have contributed directly to the Irish rebellion which broke out in the summer of 1798 in a series of local, and not very well organised, risings, some of which also involved a high degree of sectarian violence. Of the religious groups in Ireland the one most heavily implicated in the rebellion was the Presbyterians. Only 14 Roman Catholic priests were indicted, and 6 executed, compared with 13 indictments and 3 executions among the much smaller number of Presbyterian ministers. Involvement was, of course, much more widespread than this, on both sides. Recent research has identified 63 Presbyterian ministers and licentiates suspected of involvement and 57 Roman Catholic priests. In the south-eastern diocese of Ferns the sectarian violence was extreme, with massacres of Protestants at Scullabogue and Wexford Bridge, attacks on Roman Catholic chapels and the murder of Roman Catholic parish priests at Arklow and Wicklow. Both the Roman Catholic hierarchy and the Synod of Ulster unreservedly condemned the rebellion and the involvement in it of their clergy.

The 1798 rebellion was the final straw that determined the British government to push through, against the wishes of the Irish parliament, the full political union of Ireland with the rest of the British Isles, though some political opinion at Westminster had favoured union since the 1780s. Although the passage of the Act of Union required the support of politicians in both houses of the Irish parliament, the attitude of the Church of Ireland and Roman Catholic hierarchies was crucial. The votes of the former might turn out to be decisive in the Irish House of Lords and the support of the latter would be important in securing more general Roman Catholic support for the Act of Union. The Church of Ireland hierarchy was divided on the issue and the support of some bishops, and several laymen in the Irish parliament, had to be bought with a mixture of threats and bribes, euphemistically referred to as 'union engagements'. The Roman Catholic hierarchy was much more supportive. Archbishop Troy went so far as to encourage the parish priest of Newry to mobilise the Roman Catholic vote for the pro-union candidate at a by-election in 1799. Although some of the bishops had always been in favour of union, believing that Roman Catholics in Ireland would receive better treatment from a British Protestant rather than an Irish Protestant parliament, what finally decided the hierarchy as a whole to support the Act of Union was the indication given to them by Pitt and other ministers that it would be quickly followed by legislation to give full political emancipation to Roman Catholics, allowing them to be elected to and take their seats in a British parliament without being required to subscribe to an oath which no self-respecting Roman Catholic could take with a clear conscience.

As a result of the pressure exercised by the British government, both houses of the Irish parliament reluctantly voted themselves out of existence in 1800 and the Act became operative on 1 January 1801. The Church of Ireland lost influence as a result of the legislation. Whereas all its arch-bishops and bishops had sat and voted in the Irish House of Lords, only one archbishop and three bishops were given, on the basis of rotation, seats and votes at Westminster. However, both Church of Ireland and Roman Catholic bishops were generally positive about the likely benefits of union. Charles Brodrick, the Church of Ireland archbishop of Cashel, thought that a British parliament would legislate to break up some of the parochial unions in Ireland and increase the number of benefices. Francis Moylan, the Roman Catholic bishop of Cork, thought that it would lead to stronger action to prevent 'Civil and religious disorders'. What Pitt and other ministers had not foreseen was that their clear hint to the Roman Catholic hierarchy that union would be followed by emancipation could not be acted upon. They had genuinely thought that they could deliver the promise but they had not taken into account the opposition of King George III, who believed that it was impossible for him to assent to an emancipation measure without breaking his coronation oath to uphold the Protestant religion throughout his realm. When it was clear that the king could not be persuaded to change his mind Pitt and his ministers tendered their resignations. Lord Cornwallis, the Lord Lieutenant of Ireland, who considered emancipation a matter of honour in view of the thinly veiled promises he had given to the Roman Catholic hierarchy, also resigned.

The limits of toleration

George III's opposition to Catholic emancipation was widely shared in early nineteenth-century England. Roman Catholicism was still seen as a foreign and potentially traitorous religion and there was a feeling that any legislation to permit Roman Catholics to participate fully in the British political process might have undesirable consequences, though few people had a clear idea of what these might actually be. William Pitt, on the other hand, took a much more pragmatic view. He argued that measures taken against Roman Catholics in the seventeenth century had been necessary at the time but that they were now inappropriate as Roman Catholics no longer posed a threat to the constitution. Other ministers such as Viscount Castlereagh, the Chief Secretary for Ireland, argued that the growing wealth of the Roman Catholic community demanded political concessions that would make them ardent supporters of that constitution. Neither Pitt nor Castlereagh saw emancipation as a question of 'natural right'. Even so their view was not shared by many, both in parliament and the country, who took the view that, because the pope was both a secular ruler and a religious leader, Roman Catholics had divided political loyalties and were not therefore to be trusted in any position of political power.[37] Though the Anglican bishops had generally been seen to be as hostile to Catholic emancipation as they had been to the repeal of the Test and Corporation Acts, to assist the political aspirations of Protestant dissenters, their attitude began to change in the 1790s, largely as a result of their sympathy for émigré French clergy forced into exile in Britain. A compromise measure acceptable to the bishops of the United Church of England and Ireland after 1801, and also to the Roman Catholic hierarchy in Ireland, was that full Catholic emancipation should be accompanied by a measure which imposed a British government veto on Roman Catholic episcopal appointments in Ireland.[38] The views expressed by Pitt and Castlereagh continued to be supported by a significant number of ministers even after the collapse of Pitt's administration in 1801. The general election of 1807 was fought largely on the issue of Catholic emancipation, with disastrous effects as far as the reformers were concerned. The Whigs, who were generally more likely to support emancipation than the Tories, lost more than 50 of their members and their strength in the House of Commons was reduced to a rump of 155. Even so Catholic emancipation was not entirely removed from the political agenda. A motion in favour of emancipation in the House of Lords in 1811, though defeated, secured the support of 62 peers and a speech in favour from Bishop Bathurst of Norwich.[39]

Nevertheless the situation in the British Isles after 1801 was less conducive to the cause of Catholic emancipation than it had been beforehand. If Pitt and his ministers had not been faced with the complete intransigence of George III there is little doubt that an emancipation measure would have secured parliamentary support in 1799–1800. A decade later many of those who would earlier have supported emancipation had changed their minds. Partly this was due to the stand that had been taken by the king; partly, also, it was the result of the growing strength of Evangelical opinions in government and parliament. Spencer Perceval was an implacable opponent of emancipation and it would have been impossible to get his government to introduce the necessary legislation. The Roman Catholic cause was not assisted by the growing militancy of Roman Catholics in Ireland, frustrated that the promises they had been given were not to be honoured, though the major campaign to secure emancipation did not happen until after 1815. Evangelicals did not just oppose emancipation. They also promoted campaigns to convert Irish Roman Catholics to Protestantism, though these were not to reach their full force until the Second Reformation movement of the 1820s. In addition to the charges of divided political allegiance levelled against Roman Catholics there was hostility to them on other grounds. Their Latin liturgy and what was considered to be a neglect of scripture was considered offensive in a Protestant country. It was alleged, despite constant denials that this was true, that the Roman Catholic church was guilty 'of absolving its adherents from the necessity of keeping faith with heretics'. It was also alleged, with perhaps more justification, that the Roman Catholic church taught that salvation was exclusive to its own faithful; in their defence, however, Roman Catholics could, with equal justification, accuse some Protestants of describing their religion as 'false Christianity' and the pope as 'Anti-Christ'.[40]

The Evangelical anti-Roman Catholic lobby was greatly strengthened by the growth of Methodism. In a sense this is surprising since, in the early days of Methodism, its leadership was seen to be politically in tune with radical political opinion in the British Isles which supported increased toleration. Before the French Revolution most of those who supported relief measures for Protestant dissenters accepted that toleration for one minority had to be balanced by greater toleration for Roman Catholics as well. David Hempton argues that as a result of the political situation in the 1790s the Methodist leadership throughout the British Isles shifted its political position.

Of central importance for Methodist political development was the fact that opposition to radical politics and the Catholic claims came to precisely the same point – a shift towards popular Toryism. This was reinforced by a growing desire for respectability and a rekindled enthusiasm for the Established Church, after it had been leavened by the Evangelical Revival . . . the history of Methodist opposition to Catholic claims shows how the leadership of the connexion was forced to abandon its Whiggish advocacy of religious toleration in order to defeat heresy.[41]

In Ireland 'the true significance of . . . Methodism . . . lay not in its numbers, nor in its impact on Irish society, but rather in its front-line position in the evangelical crusade against Roman Catholicism'.[42] In 1799 the Methodist Conference agreed to send out three full-time Gaelic-speaking missionaries to preach to Roman Catholics in the west of Ireland. As a result of Methodist initiatives a number of interdenominational Protestant societies were established, specifically to proselytise among the Irish Roman Catholic population: the London Hibernian Society in 1806, the Sunday School Society in 1809, the Religious Tract and Book Society in 1817 and the Irish Society in 1818; the British and Foreign Bible Society sent its publications to Ireland for distribution from 1804; Anglican Evangelicals set up an Irish branch of the Church Missionary Society in 1814. Methodist experience in Ireland was to lead to Methodists becoming much more actively involved in the campaign to prevent the passing of emancipation legislation by the Westminster parliament after the assassination of Spencer Perceval in 1812. There was a fear that a government led by the high church Lord Liverpool might be tempted by the pragmatic arguments in favour of emancipation. In 1813 two prominent Methodists, Joseph Butterworth, MP for Coventry, and Thomas Allen, a London solicitor, were instrumental in setting up the Protestant Union for the Defence and Support of the Protestant Religion and the British Constitution. Allen published two anti-Catholic pamphlets in the same year. He and Butterworth were to lay down the principle of Methodist opposition to Catholic emancipation that was to continue until its final concession, in very different political circumstances, in 1829.[43]

The attacks on political radicalism in the 1790s, in response to the events in France, combined with the increasing strength of anti-Catholicism in Britain after the passing of the Act of Union, was to mean that the growing sympathy for religious toleration, notable in the 1770s and 1780s, was to be, in effect, frozen for a generation. There were still powerful lobbies pressing for toleration but they did not have popular support. Britain seems to have been, certainly in the quantity of published polemic, a less tolerant society in 1815 than it had been 30 years earlier. The expression of hostility towards Roman Catholicism was replicated in attitudes to both Jews and those regarded as 'infidels'. The Jewish community in Britain was very small but it was targeted as a candidate for proselytising activity with the foundation in 1808 of the London Society for Promoting Christianity among the Jews, set up by members of the Evangelical London Missionary Society. Jewish leaders protested that this was an outrage and they were supported by some non-Evangelical Anglicans who published pamphlets advocating the adoption of measures that would extend greater toleration to the Jewish community, though the community itself took no steps to secure legislation to this effect.[44] The attacks on religion that took place in France in the 1790s were to lead to repressive measures being taken against those who were thought to be opponents of organised religion in the British Isles. In 1812 Daniel Eaton was sentenced to stand in the pillory, a punishment abolished in 1816, for publishing an edition of Thomas Paine's *The Age of Reason*. There were several prosecutions for blasphemy as a result of which the government introduced the Trinity Act of 1813 in order to extend the provisions of the Toleration Act to Unitarian belief and worship. There was, however, general reluctance to move beyond this and to grant protection to deists, agnostics or atheists. Evangelical Anglicans generally supported the existing concessions made to Protestant dissenters since most of them shared their doctrinal stance in many respects, but they distinguished between them and 'Dissenters hostile to all religion, or at least attached to a religion subversive of the greater truths of Christianity'.[45]

The political developments of the 1790s and their aftermath were to have a major impact on the debate about the 'confessional state'. Whereas the concept seemed to be weakening in the 1770s and 1780s, this was no longer true by the first two decades of the nineteenth century. From very different perspectives churchmen of different religious opinions found the concept a convenient one. The high church revival in the Church of England from the 1760s had re-established in substantial sections of that church, and its sister church in Ireland, a new respect for the doctrines of the divine nature of monarchy and of non-resistance to lawful authority, which had been rather downplayed in the second quarter of the eighteenth century. The Evangelical revival had produced a desire to defend Protestantism against the Roman Catholic attempts to seek a share of political power. This had the effect of making Evangelicals comfortable with the concept of a 'confessional state' dedicated to the Protestant cause. Even many Protestant dissenters felt that accepting limits on their own political power was a price worth paying to withhold it from Roman Catholics. Many Roman Catholics themselves would have been happy to subscribe to the concept of a limited 'confessional state', for example by accepting a veto on episcopal appointments, in return for emancipation. Unfortunately emancipation, whether of Roman Catholics, Jews or those opposed to organised religion, was a step too far for most politicians, and there is good evidence to suggest that their attitude was shared by the public at large.

Notes

1 J. Rule, *Albion's People: English Society 1714–1815*, London 1992, p. 93.

2 W. Gibson, *Church, State and Society*, 1760–1850, Basingstoke 1994, p. 68.

3 J.E. Bradley, *Religion, Revolution and English Radicalism: Nonconformity in Eighteenth-Century Politics and Society*, Cambridge 1990, pp. 416–19; quotation on pp. 417–18.

4 *Ibid.*, p. 422.

5 H.T. Dickinson, *The Politics of the People in Eighteenth-Century Britain*, London 1977, pp. 261–2.

6 J.C.D. Clark, *English Society 1688–1832*, Cambridge 1985, pp. 247–9, 270–2; quotation on p. 272.

7 *Ibid.*, pp. 324–30; quotation on pp. 328–9.

8 *Ibid.*, pp. 332–5.

9 B. Semmel, *The Methodist Revolution*, London 1974, pp. 113–21.

10 *Ibid.*, pp. 125–6, 128, 135–6.

11 Gibson, *Church, State and Society*, pp. 43–4, 46–7.

12 F.C. Mather, *High Church Prophet: Bishop Samuel Horsley (1733–1806) and the Caroline Tradition in the Late Georgian Church*, Oxford 1992, pp. 223–4.

13 *Ibid.*, pp. 270–2, 278–83.

14 D.A. Spaeth, *The Church in an Age of Danger: Parsons and Parishoners 1660–1740*, Cambridge 2000, p. 133.

15 The section that follows is largely informed by the seminal study of E.J. Evans, *The Contentious Tithe: The Tithe Problem and English Agriculture 1750–1850*, London 1976.

16 *Ibid.*, p. 6.

17 *Ibid.*, p. 58.

18 *Ibid.*, p. 105.

19 R. Hole, *Pulpits, Politics and Public Order in England 1760–1832*, Cambridge 1989, pp. 98–104; quotation on p. 101.

20 J. Davies, *A History of Wales*, London 1994, pp. 338–40.

21 U. Henriques, *Religious Toleration in England 1787–1833*, London 1961, pp. 99–135.

22 R.A. Soloway, *Prelates and People: Ecclesiastical Social Thought in England, 1783–1852*, London 1969, p. 36.

23 Dickinson, *Politics of the People*, p. 263.

24 P.B. Nockles, *The Oxford Movement in Context: Anglican High Churchmanship 1760–1857*, Cambridge 1994, p. 48.

25 R. Hole, *Pulpits, Politics and Public Order in England 1760–1832*, Cambridge 1989, pp. 138–9.

26 Gibson, *Church, State and Society*, pp. 49–51.

27 W.R. Ward, *Religion and Society in England 1790–1850*, London 1972, pp. 23–5, 34–9, 47–9.

28 Gibson, *Church, State and Society*, p. 49; Hole, *Pulpits, Politics and Public Order*, pp. 107–8.

29 Mather, *High Church Prophet*, pp. 103–6.

30 *Ibid.*, pp. 250–60; quotation on p. 256.

31 C. Haydon, 'The "most horrid and unnatural state of man": John Henry Williams and the French Wars, 1793–1802', in W. Gibson and R.G. Ingram (eds), *Religious Identities in Britain, 1660–1832*, Aldershot 2005, p. 256.

32 *Ibid.*, pp. 258–75.

33 D. Hempton, *Religious and Political Culture in Britain and Ireland*, Cambridge 1996, p. 98.

34 *Ibid.*, pp. 95–6.

35 *Ibid.*, pp. 96–7.

36 The rest of this section is based on the accounts in D. Keogh, *The French Disease: The Catholic Church and Irish Radicalism, 1790–1800*, Dublin 1993; I.R. McBride, *Scripture Politics: Ulster Presbyterians and Irish Radicalism in the Late Eighteenth Century*, Oxford 1998; and N. Yates, *The Religious Condition of Ireland 1770–1850*, Oxford 2006, Chapter 2.

37 J. Derry, 'Governing temperament under Pitt and Liverpool', in J. Cannon (ed.), *The Whig Ascendancy: Colloquies on Hanoverian England*, London 1981, pp. 134–6.

38 Gibson, *Church, State and Society*, pp. 71–2.

39 Clark, *English Society*, pp. 359–64.

40 Henriques, *Religious Toleration*, pp. 136–58.

41 D. Hempton, *Methodism and Politics in British Society 1750–1850*, London 1987, pp. 117–18.

42 *Ibid.*, p. 119.

43 *Ibid.*, pp. 120–1, 127–30.

44 Henriques, *Religious Toleration*, pp. 175–9.

45 *Ibid.*, pp. 206, 209; quotation on p. 221.

Conclusion

While it is clear that the strength of the Anglican tradition during the eighteenth century had been underestimated by a generation of historians with primary interests in social, political and economic change, that does not negate the fact that England, and by extension Britain, was different from the rest of Europe in the proportion of its population which was participating in a commercial economy, and who consequently might be seen as an incipient middle class . . . It is clear that both elements are present and that the debate is over which to give precedence; continuity or change.[1]

In the preceding pages we have endeavoured to address this issue and overall we have come to the conclusion that there was a good deal of similarity between the state of religion in the British Isles in 1815 compared with a century earlier, whereas someone familiar with the religious state of Britain in 1815 would have found the situation in 1865 almost unrecognisable. Britain experienced a major change in religious attitudes between the 1820s and the 1850s, which was cataclysmic compared with the very modest changes that took place between 1714 and 1815. Nevertheless change did occur and we have tried to document and explain it. If we return to the five core themes of the book outlined in the introduction we need to attempt the construction of a change versus continuity balance sheet for each of them.

The first theme is the relationship between church and state and the assessment of whether or not Jonathan Clark is correct in his analysis that Britain remained a 'confessional state', or more correctly a series of such states, throughout the eighteenth century. I think that we would need to conclude that, overall, Clark's case was a sound one. Indeed there is a sense in which the belief in a 'confessional state' was perhaps even more secure in 1815 than it had been in 1714. Then the concept seemed quite fragile, with major political differences between Whigs and Tories over the precise nature of the church–state relationship and the security of the Church of England's position to some extent undermined by the non-juring schism. In the 50 years that followed the concept seemed to be getting even shakier with real fears that it would be undermined by parliamentary measures to provide relief to Roman Catholics and Protestant dissenters. In practice, very little in the way of real change was ever accomplished and from the 1760s there was much more common ground between Whigs and Tories on religious policy. This was further strengthened by the isolation of the more radical Whigs as a result of the anti-radical backlash caused by events in France after 1789 and the subsequent war. The determination to preserve the established churches as essential bulwarks of the British constitution ensured that the concept of the 'confessional state' was both maintained and strengthened. Even ideas of divine monarchy seemed more acceptable in the early nineteenth century than they had been in the mid-eighteenth. The British establishment had looked at change, tinkered a bit at the edges but, in the light of events elsewhere in Europe, decided that the status quo must be maintained at all costs. In terms of its church–state relationship, Britain was still in 1815 a largely *ancien régime* country. It is true that exact parallels cannot be made between Anglican beliefs in the late seventeenth and early nineteenth centuries. The concepts of divine monarchy and the doctrines of passive obedience were that much weaker, but they had certainly not totally disappeared. The motto of the Tory provincial newspaper, the *Leeds Intellingencer* (God, the Church and the Throne), still reflected the political and religious outlook of Anglican Tory high churchmen.

The second theme is the extent to which religious pluralism developed in the British Isles between 1714 and 1815. Here again the changes that took place seem, with hindsight, to have been fairly modest. We have seen that in England and Wales Protestant dissent was in decline during the first half of the eighteenth century. It began to revive during the second half, though in statistical terms the major bodies of 'old dissent' had by 1815 barely reached the numerical strength that they had had a century earlier. Roman Catholics in England and Wales had similarly experienced a period of both decline and recovery, which just about balanced one another in terms of numbers. What had really changed the religious structure of the British Isles was the impact of Evangelicalism. Within England and Wales, and eventually in Ireland, the Evangelical revival, and particularly the various bodies of Methodists, were to create 'new dissent'. By the first quarter of the nineteenth century various groups of Evangelicals that had emerged from the Anglican churches had seceded from them to set up their own denominations, with a consequent weakening of the episcopalian branch of Protestantism. In Scotland the Evangelical revival was largely contained within a Presbyterian established church until the Disruption of 1843. In terms of their status Protestant dissenters throughout the British Isles had achieved little, despite their active attempts to promote various relief measures, especially the repeal of the Test and Corporation Acts. Here a majority in parliament had stood firm and it was, legally at least, no easier for a Protestant dissenter to be active politically in 1815 than it had been for the whole of the previous century and more. Roman Catholics had, however, secured measures that had made their lives considerably easier, though they still had not achieved full political emancipation. However, by the end of the eighteenth century they could worship in public without the threat of action being taken against them, professions which had been closed were now open to them and the economic restrictions under which they had been placed, and which had led to some Roman Catholics seceding to the established churches, had been lifted. A similar relaxation of the laws which restricted the activities of Scottish Episcopalians had also taken place. Even Unitarians had been freed from fear of prosecution for denying the doctrine of the Trinity, but free-thinkers, whether deists or atheists, still suffered the threat of prosecution under the laws against blasphemy. In this area the balance between change and continuity was certainly on the side of change, though not the level of change that members of non-established churches, or those who disapproved of any form of organised religion, would have liked.

The third theme is the theological balance between different doctrinal positions within the Protestant churches, especially the established ones. In 1714 most Anglicans were rather dry Arminians and most other Protestants equally dry Calvinists. Among all the Protestant churches there was a liberal or rationalist element, but whereas this was largely snuffed out in the Anglican established churches, it developed into Moderatism in the Church of Scotland, and to full-blown Unitarianism among some Presbyterians, Independents and even Baptists. Overall there were probably no more religious radicals in the Protestant churches in 1815 than there had been in 1714, but their distribution within them was rather different. The Churches of England and Ireland experienced a real high church, though still strongly anti-Roman Catholic, revival in the late eighteenth century, which was to be found chiefly in their interpretation of doctrine, but also, to some extent, in the design of church buildings and even in some modest ceremonial innovations. The greatest difference between 1714 and 1815, however, was in the impact that Evangelicalism had made to all the Protestant churches. It had led to significant secessions from the Church of England to create Methodist churches, some of which were Arminian and some of which were Calvinist, in doctrine. It had also led to the formation of Evangelical lobbies within the Churches of England and Ireland which, though still limited in strength in 1815, were to grow thereafter. Although Evangelicals never became a majority within the established church in England and Wales, where many had seceded to the Methodist churches, they had become a majority within the Church of Ireland by the 1840s. The same had occurred within the Church of Scotland; Evangelicalism before the nineteenth century had largely been confined to the highlands and islands; by the 1830s Evangelicals had become a majority within the General Assembly. A similar pattern could be observed within the Presbyterian Synod of Ulster where Evangelicals had effectively taken control by the 1820s. In questions of doctrine and churchmanship change had definitely won over continuity in the theological make-up of the Protestant churches in the British Isles between 1714 and 1815.

The same is true as far as the fourth theme, the role of the churches in the provision of education and social welfare, was concerned. In 1714 there was investment in charity schools, parochial libraries and societies for the reformation of manners. The societies lost support in the 1720s and 1730s but were revived by Evangelicals as societies for the suppression of vice at the end of the eighteenth century. The opportunities for a limited type of formal education, especially for the sons and daughters of the poor, were vastly more plentiful in 1815 than they had been in 1714, especially in England and Wales. Charity schools, contrary to some earlier opinion, continued to be established and maintained throughout the eighteenth century. By the 1780s this provision was being supplemented by the Sunday schools and, by 1815, the British schools, technically non-denominational but normally set up by Protestant dissenters, and the National Society for the Education of the Poor, an Anglican body, had been established. Progress had been less marked in Scotland, where provision for schools in 1714 had been noticeably better than in England and Wales, and in Ireland, where educational initiatives had all too often fallen victim to sectarian tensions, the economic exploitation of Roman Catholic children, or just plain mismanagement. Throughout the British Isles, despite much private charity, rather less had been done to alleviate the sufferings of the poor whose lot depended a great deal on the parish in which they happened to be located. On the other hand some parishes, in many cases motivated by Christian notions of charity, spent considerable sums on poor relief, and there were many parts of England and Wales where the poor were considerably better off under the somewhat ramshackle arrangements of the late eighteenth and early nineteenth centuries than they were under the new systems of relief provided by the poor law unions set up under the Poor Law Amendment Act of 1834. Although the Church of England as an institution cannot claim credit for this, its clergy, through the influence of their sermons on the laity, probably could.

The fifth and final theme of this book is that of reform movements within the churches in the last two decades of the eighteenth, and the first two decades of the nineteenth, centuries. This is an area in which scholars are now suggesting that, despite some limitations, a great deal was achieved. There is little doubt that the established churches of England, Ireland and Wales were in considerably better shape administratively in 1815 than they had been in 1714. From the reforms of Bishop Wilson in the diocese of Sodor and Man in the middle decades of the eighteenth century, through the initiatives of the Irish bishops from the 1770s, the Welsh bishops from the 1780s and the English bishops from the 1790s, steps had been taken to tighten up clerical discipline, to regulate as far as legislation permitted pluralism and non-residence, to repair churches and to build new parsonage houses, and to improve the provision of church services, preaching and catechising. Similar initiatives were taking place in the Church of Scotland, though here relatively little research has been done and it is still much more difficult to quantify the results than it is in other parts of the British Isles. In Ireland the reform movement within the established church was replicated by similar movements within the Roman Catholic and Presbyterian churches. There is no doubt that this reform movement, especially within the established churches, was less thorough than was needed. Whilst parliamentary grants for church and parsonage building in Ireland were provided from the late 1770s and the Irish Roman Catholic church benefited from government support to establish the seminary at Maynooth in 1795, it was not until after 1815 that similar support was made available to the established churches in England, Scotland and Wales. Whilst those who criticised the state of the Anglican established churches in the 1830s, and historians who have agreed with them, may have been correct in their analysis of some of the shortcomings, they were undoubtedly wrong in laying the blame for this at the feet of bishops and clergy. Anyone who has read contemporary episcopal correspondence and other surviving material, cannot fail to have noticed that bishops and clergy were only too well aware of the problems that existed and of their own powerlessness to address them without parliamentary legislation. The attempts of bishops to promote the necessary legislation was all too often blocked by those with vested financial interests in preserving the status quo. It is a fact that parliamentarians and ministers found it easier to resist the rational arguments of the bishops before 1815, than the much more emotional, and frequently inaccurate, attacks on the established churches by the anti-clericalists in the 1820s and 1830s. The established churches had done their best to set their houses in order and their achievement in this respect deserves to be recognised.

On balance therefore, though the constitutional position of the established churches and those who dissented from them, remained much the same in 1815 as it had been in 1714, in many other respects change had been greater than continuity. There was marginally more religious toleration in 1815 than there had been in 1714. Profound changes in doctrinal stances had taken place over the intervening period. There had been a vast increase in the role of the churches in the provision of education. There had been a strong reform movement within the established, and some other, churches which had increased their effectiveness in preaching the Gospel. Whilst change in respect of religion, and its role in politics and society, was clearly far less dramatic in the eighteenth than it was in the nineteenth century, change certainly did take place and it must be recognised that this was so. The continuity in the church–state relationship, the survival of the 'confessional state', must not be allowed to disguise the fact that religion, politics and society were not the same in 1815 as they had been in 1714.

Note

1   A. Murdoch, *British History 1660–1832: National Identity and Local Culture*, Basingstoke 1998, pp. 96–7.

Chronology of Principal Events

1714	Accession of George I
1715	First Jacobite Rebellion
1717	Prorogation of Convocations of Canterbury and York
1718	First Three Choirs Festival
1719	Repeal of Occasional Conformity and Schism Acts
1720	South Sea Bubble
1721	Walpole becomes First Lord of the Treasury
1722	Knatchbull's Poor Law Act
1723	Deprivation and banishment of Bishop Atterbury; *regium donum* first paid to dissenting ministers in England and Wales
1727	Accession of George II
1729	John Wesley's Holy Club meetings at Oxford
1732	Formation of Protestant Dissenting Deputies
1733	Establishment of Incorporated Society for Promotion of English Protestant Schools in Ireland
1735–6	Passing of Mortmain and Quaker Tithe Bills in House of Commons; Witchcraft Act prevents suits for witchcraft and sorcery
1742	Resignation of Walpole
1745–6	Second Jacobite Rebellion
1753	Hardwicke's Marriage Act
1760	Accession of George III

1766	Death of 'James III' the Old Pretender
1772	Feathers Tavern Petition
1776	American Declaration of Independence
1778	First Catholic Relief Act
1780	Anti-Catholic Gordon Riots
1782	Gilbert's Poor Law Act; establishment of Society for Distribution of Religious Tracts
1783	Peace of Versailles ends War of American Independence; Pitt the Younger becomes First Lord of the Treasury
1785	Establishment of London Sunday School Society
1787–8	Establishment of General Evangelical, London Abolition, Philanthropic and Proclamation Societies
1788	Death of 'Charles III' the Young Pretender
1789	Outbreak of Revolution in France
1791	Second Catholic Relief Act
1792	Establishment of Baptist Missionary Society
1792–3	Catholic Relief Acts in Ireland
1793	Catholic and Episcopalian Relief Act in Scotland; outbreak of French Revolutionary Wars
1795	Establishment of Seminary at Maynooth and London Missionary Society
1796	Attempted French Invasion of Ireland; establishment of Methodist New Connexion and Society for Bettering the Condition and Increasing the Comforts of the Poor
1798	Irish Rebellion; Establishment of Ulster Evangelical Society
1799	Establishment of Church Missionary Society
1800–1	Act of Union between Great Britain and Ireland
1801	Resignation of Pitt the Younger
1802	Concordat between France and the Papacy
1803	Establishment of Sunday School Union
1804	Establishment of British and Foreign Bible Society
1806	Establishment of Hibernian Bible and London Hibernian Societies

1807   Abolition of slave trade

1808   Establishment of London Society for Promoting Christianity
            among the Jews

1809   Establishment of Sunday School Society

1810   Lord Sidmouth's Bill; establishment of Royal British School
            Association and Belfast Academical Institution

1811   Calvinistic Methodist Schism in Wales; establishment of Gaelic
            School Society and National Society for Educating the Poor

1813   Trinity Act

1814   Establishment of Hibernian Missionary Society

1815   Congress of Vienna ends French Revolutionary Wars

Biographies of Political and Religious Leaders

Charles Agar (1736–1809)

Leading figure in Irish politics and Church of Ireland ecclesiastical reformer. Dean of Kilmore 1765–8, Bishop of Cloyne 1768–79, Archbishop of Cashel 1779–1801 and Dublin 1801–9. Reluctant supporter of Act of Union. Created Baron Somerton 1795, Viscount Somerton 1800 and Earl of Normanton 1806.

Francis Atterbury (1663–1732)

Leading Anglican high churchman, Tory politician and Jacobite supporter. Dean of Carlisle 1704–11 and Christ Church, Oxford, 1711–12. Bishop of Rochester and Dean of Westminster 1713–23. Disillusioned by the political situation after 1715, he became a Jacobite and was involved in Jacobite invasion conspiracy of 1721. Arrested in 1722 and sentenced to deprivation from office and banishment in 1723, later acting as Secretary of State to 'James III' in Paris.

Shute Barrington (1734–1826)

Leading ecclesiastical reformer of the late eighteenth and early nineteenth centuries. Bishop of Llandaff 1769–82, Salisbury 1782–91 and Durham 1791–1826. Friend of Wilberforce and Hannah More and opponent of slave trade. Supporter of Sunday schools, of the National Society (1811), the Proclamation Society (1788) and the Society for Bettering the Condition and Improving the Comforts of the Poor (1796). More willing than most high churchmen to work with Evangelicals and across denominational boundaries.

Hugh Boulter (1672–1742)

Leading figure in Church of Ireland from 1724, though born and educated in England. Bishop of Bristol and Dean of Christ Church, Oxford, 1719–24. Archbishop of Armagh 1724–42. Argued strongly for strengthening of English interest in Ireland and strong supporter of the Irish charter schools.

Samuel Bradburn (1751–1816)

Radical Methodist minister. Travelling preacher from 1774. Strong opponent of Church Methodists. President of Methodist Conference 1799–1800 but suspended from ministry in 1802–3 for debt and drunkenness.

Thomas Bray (1658–1730)

Anglican divine and co-founder of both the SPCK and the SPG. Rector of St Botolph, Aldgate, London 1708–30. Instrumental in encouraging the parochial library movement in early eighteenth century, he established the Associates of Dr Bray to carry on this work after his death. Strong opponent of Roman Catholicism publishing *Papal Usurpation and Persecution* in 1712.

Richard Brothers (1757–1824)

Self-styled prophet. Served in Royal Navy 1772–83 and later in mercantile marine. Had series of visions in 1791 and prophecies published in 1794 by his supporters. Arrested and declared insane though continuing to attract wealthy supporters.

Thomas Burgess (1756–1837)

Distinguished classical scholar and ecclesiastical reformer. Domestic and examining chaplain to Bishop Shute Barrington from 1785. Bishop of St David's 1803–25 and Salisbury 1825–37. Established St David's College at Lampeter 1822–7. Supporter of Welsh culture and antiquarianism. First President of Royal Society of Literature. Strong opponent of Roman Catholicism and Unitarianism.

Edmund Burke (1729–97)

Moderate Whig writer and politician. Editor of *Annual Register* from 1758. Elected MP for Wendover in 1765 and quickly became one of the leading speakers in the House of Commons. Elected MP for Bristol in 1774. Opposed war with American colonies. Supported concessions to Roman Catholics and Protestant dissenters. Appointed paymaster-general of the army in 1782. Strong opposition to French Revolution led to a gradual change in Burke's stance on church–state relations and he opposed the repeal of the Test and Corporation Acts in 1790; later that year he published *Reflections on the Revolution in France*.

Edmund Calamy (1671–1732)

Leading Presbyterian divine. Educated at Utrecht and Leiden, he was ordained in London in 1694. Published a history of dissent, including an account of ministers ejected in 1662, attacked by John Walker's *Sufferings of the Clergy* in 1714. Principal spokesman for English dissent by this date and one of the original trustees of Dr Williams's Library.

Richard Challoner (1691–1781)

Roman Catholic writer and ecclesiastic. Educated at Douai. Administrator of the London district from 1737 and consecrated Bishop of Debra in 1741. Vicar-apostolic of the London District 1758–81. Published *The Garden of the Soul* in 1740 and produced a revised version of the Rheims–Douai Catholic Bible in 1749–50. Much distressed by the Gordon Riots of 1780, which were rumoured to be the cause of his death.

Thomas Charles (1755–1814)

Leader of Welsh Calvinistic Methodists. Ordained deacon and priest in the Church of England 1778–80. Married Sally Jones in 1783 and settled in Bala. Preacher in North Wales and at Spa Fields Chapel in London. Established circulating schools in North Wales from 1784 and later Sunday schools. Opposed to secession from the Church of England but reluctantly agreed to ordination of first Calvinistic Methodist ministers in 1811.

Samuel Clarke (1675–1729)

Anglican theologian. Rector of St James, Westminster, 1709–29. Delivered Boyle Lectures 1704–5. Published *The Scripture Doctrine of the Trinity* (1712), regarded as an attack on orthodox beliefs about the divinity of

Christ, and agreed compromise with bishops not to publish anything further on Trinitarian theology.

Thomas Coram (1668–1751)

Merchant and philanthropist. Involved in various shipbuilding and other projects for American colonies from 1694 and later regarded as an expert on colonial affairs. Petitioned for the establishment of a Foundling Hospital for illegitimate children in 1737; charter granted in 1739 and hospital opened in 1741.

Charles Daubeny (1745–1827)

Anglican high church writer. Student of Roman Catholic and Eastern Orthodox theology. Rector of North Bradley (Wilts.) from 1776 and Archdeacon of Salisbury from 1804. Introduced weekday services at North Bradley and founded an almshouse, school and poor-house at his own expense. Published *A Guide to the Church* (1798) and *Appendix to the Guide to the Church* (1799). Strong opponent of Evangelicals in Church of England.

Philip Doddridge (1702–51)

Dissenting minister and writer. Minister at Kibworth 1723–9 and Northampton 1729–51. Established famous dissenting academy at Northampton in 1730. Well known as preacher and writer of hymns. Also published *The Rise and Progress of Religion in the Soul* (1745) and *The Family Expositor*, a paraphrase and commentary on the New Testament in several volumes, from 1739. Remnant of his extensive collection of books is preserved in Dr Williams's Library.

Henry Fielding (1707–54)

Author and magistrate. Published *Joseph Andrews* (1742) and *Tom Jones* (1749) having previously written largely for the theatre. Called to the bar in 1740 he practised intermittently on the western circuit. High Steward of the New Forest 1746–8. Appointed to Middlesex magistracy in 1748 and chairman from 1749; extremely active in this role publishing *An Enquiry into the Causes of the Late Increase of Robbers* in 1751 and *A Proposal for Making an Effectual Provision for the Poor* in 1753.

Charles James Fox (1749–1806)

Whig politician. First elected to parliament in 1768 and MP for Westminster from 1780. Supported American independence and opposed the resulting war. Foreign Secretary 1782–3. Led Whig opposition to Pitt administration. Sympathetic to French Revolution and strong opponent of Burke's views, though later modified this standpoint in response to reign of terror. Supported Peace of Amiens in 1802. Foreign Secretary in 1806 in 'ministry of all the talents'. Hostile to organised religion and a deist in his religious opinions.

Edmund Gibson (1669–1748)

Whig scholar and episcopal reformer. Author of treatise on Roman antiquities and editor of a new edition of Camden's *Britannia*. Librarian of Lambeth Palace from 1696 and rector of Lambeth from 1703. Appointed archdeacon of Surrey in 1710. Published *Codex Juris Ecclesiastici Anglicani* in 1713. Bishop of Lincoln 1715–23 and London 1723–48. Principal ecclesiastical adviser to Walpole ministry 1723–36. Strong supporter of SPCK and charity schools. Early opponent of Methodism.

Lord George Gordon (1751–93)

Anti-Catholic leader. Entered parliament in 1778. Opponent of government's American policy. President of the Protestant Association from 1779, he led opposition to Roman Catholic relief measures and effectively stimulated the London riots in 1780, though took no active part in them. Tried for high treason in 1781 but acquitted. Later successfully prosecuted for libel and sentenced to five years in prison, where he died. Converted to Judaism in 1787.

Georg Friederich Handel (1685–1759)

German-born composer resident in England from 1713 and naturalised in 1727. Made major contributions to English church music including anthems and canticle settings for the Chapel Royal. Also composed major religious oratorios including *Samson, Messiah, Joseph and his Brethren, Belshazzar, Judas Maccabeus, Susannah* and *Solomon*. Presented an organ to the Foundling Hospital and became one of its governors in 1750.

Howell Harris (1714–73)

Calvinistic Methodist preacher who underwent a conversion experience in 1735. Refused Anglican orders, he preached to groups of Methodists in South Wales and England. Had a difficult relationship with the other South Wales Methodist leader Daniel Rowland and estranged from him for long periods, though the two worked together after 1762. Established college at Trefeca, with support of Countess of Huntingdon, in 1750s.

Thomas Herring (1693–1757)

Reforming churchman and Whig supporter. First came to prominence in 1728 when attacked John Gay's *Beggar's Opera* as immoral. Dean of Rochester 1731–43, Bishop of Bangor 1737–43, Archbishop of York 1743–7 and Canterbury 1747–57. A reforming archbishop at York notable for his detailed visitation of his diocese but a nonentity at Canterbury where he was overshadowed by Bishop Sherlock of London.

Frederick Hervey (1730–1803)

Leading figure in Church of Ireland, despite well-known eccentricities. Inveterate traveller in Europe from 1765. Bishop of Cloyne 1768–9 and Derry 1769–1803. Sympathetic to Roman Catholic claims and much involved in Irish politics in 1770s. Succeeded his brother as fourth Earl of Bristol in 1779. In his early days as bishop he had used his wealth to support not just Church of Ireland, but Roman Catholic and Presbyterian building projects. During the latter part of his episcopate he was largely absent from his diocese, either on his English estates or travelling in Europe.

Benjamin Hoadly (1676–1761)

Whig polemicist and churchman. Crippled by smallpox whilst at Cambridge. Published pamphlets and sermons in early 1700s arguing for greater comprehension in the established church and concessions to Protestant dissenters. Denied the necessity of episcopal ordination and the real presence of Christ in the eucharist. Bishop of Bangor 1716–21, Hereford 1721–3, Salisbury 1723–34 and Winchester 1734–61. Unfairly condemned for the poor pastoral administration of his dioceses though not a major reforming bishop. Loathed by high churchmen especially after his sermon on *The Nature of the Kingdom, or Church, of Christ* in 1717, which was the origin of the Bangorian Controversy.

William Hogarth (1697–1764)

Painter, engraver and moralist. His moral subjects included *A Harlot's Progress* and *The Rake's Progress* but he also painted religious subjects such as *The Good Samaritan* and *The Pool of Bethesda*. Later moral subjects included *Marriage à-la-Mode, Industry and Idleness* and *The Four Stages of Cruelty*. Commissioned to paint a new altarpiece for St Mary Redcliffe, Bristol, in 1755. Governor of the Foundling Hospital from 1750.

George Horne (1730–92)

Leading Anglican high church theologian and disciple of John Hutchinson. Vice-Chancellor of Oxford University 1776–80 and President of Magdalen College 1768–91. Dean of Canterbury 1781–90. Bishop of Norwich 1790–2. Strong supporter of Sunday schools and opponent of Unitarianism.

Samuel Horsley (1733–1806)

Leading Anglican high church reformer and Tory supporter. His strong interests in science resulted in his becoming a member of the council of the Royal Society in 1771. Led ecclesiastical opposition to repeal of Test and Corporation Acts. Rector of Newington Butts 1759–93, Bishop of St David's 1788–93, Rochester (and Dean of Westminster) 1793–1801 and St Asaph 1801–6. Strong opponent of Methodism and political radicalism. Active episcopal reformer in all three of his dioceses.

David Hume (1711–76)

Scottish philosopher and historian. Published *A Treatise of Human Nature* (1739) and *Essays, Moral and Political* (1741–2). Appointment as professor of moral philosophy at Edinburgh vetoed by city clergy, on grounds of Hume's unorthodoxy, in 1745. Published *Philosophical Essays Concerning Human Understanding* (1748), *An Enquiry Concerning the Principles of Morals* (1751) and *Political Discourses* (1752). Keeper of the Library of the Faculty of Advocates from 1752. Completed his several volume *History of England* in 1762. Visited Paris 1763–5 and established friendship with Rousseau.

Selina, Countess of Huntingdon (1707–91)

Founder of group of Methodist dissenters from the Church of England. Married Theophilus Hastings, ninth Earl of Huntingdon (died 1746) in 1728. Became Methodist supporter in 1739. Initially supported the Wesleys but transferred her allegiance to George Whitefield and Howell Harris in 1743–4. Established chapels at Brighton in 1761, Bath in 1765 and Tunbridge Wells in 1769. Establishment of Spa Fields chapel in London in 1770s led to dispute with the bishop of London and she formally seceded from Church of England in 1782. At her death the Connexion she had established had about 60 chapels.

William Huntington (1745–1813)

Evangelical preacher. Illegitimate son of Kentish farmer. Experienced visions in 1773 which he published as *The Kingdom of Heaven Taken by Prayer* in 1784. Established a chapel in London in 1783 with support of several rich Evangelical patrons. Opened further chapels at Lewes (1802), Brighton (1805), Newark and Sleaford (1806), Chichester (1809) and Bristol (1810).

Francis Hutcheson (1694–1746)

Presbyterian philosopher. Born in Ireland and educated at Glasgow University. Licensed as probationer by presbytery of Armagh in 1719. Supported those ministers who argued for voluntary subscription to the Westminster Confession and moved to Dublin where he published *An Enquiry into the Original of Our Ideas of Beauty and Virtue* (1725) and *Essay on the Nature and Conduct of the Passions and Affections* (1728). Elected professor of moral philosophy at Glasgow in 1729, and later offered chair of moral philosophy at Edinburgh, which he declined, when David Hume was vetoed for post in 1745, partly on his advice.

John Hutchinson (1674–1737)

Natural philosopher and theologian. Privately educated and in service of Duke of Somerset from late 1690s. Published his *Observations* on nature in 1706 and later developed interests in natural philosophy as an opponent of the ideas of Isaac Newton and Samuel Clarke. Published *Moses's Principia* (1724–7) and collected volumes of previously unpublished *Works* published posthumously in 1748–9. Hutchinson's ideas strongly influenced both Anglican high churchmen and Methodists.

Samuel Johnson (1709–84)

Author and Anglican layman. Commissioned to produce a new English dictionary in 1746 and work published in 1755. Edited *The Rambler* 1750–2 and *The Adventurer* 1752–4, both publications dealing with political and religious issues. Member of the Society of Arts from 1756. Published new edition of Shakespeare in 1765. Founder member of the Literary Club in 1764. Travelled the highlands and islands of Scotland with James Boswell in 1773. Johnson was a deeply religious man exemplifying the high church piety of the late eighteenth century.

Griffith Jones (1684–1761)

Anglican clergyman and educator. Non-graduate who became rector of Llanddowror in 1716. Married the sister of his patron, Sir John Phillips of Picton Castle, in 1720. Notable preacher regarded as influential by Welsh Methodists though he was never one of their number. Began his scheme of circulating schools in 1731 and published accounts of them in an annual report entitled *Welch Piety*.

William Jones (1726–1800)

Anglican clergyman and polemical writer known as 'Jones of Nayland'. A strong high churchman and disciple of John Hutchinson who published *Catholic Doctrine of a Trinity* (1756). Perpetual curate of Nayland from 1777, having previously held livings in Kent. Published *Essays on the Church* (1780). Strong opponent of Unitarianism and the French Revolution.

Alexander Kilham (1762–98)

Founder of Methodist New Connexion. Became Methodist local preacher in 1782. Helped establish first Methodist mission in Jersey in 1783–4. Supported celebration of Holy Communion in Methodist chapels. Superintendent of Aberdeen circuit 1792–5, using his position to argue for separation of Methodists from established churches. Dismissed as preacher and established New Connexion in 1796.

William King (1650–1729)

Former presbyterian who became an Anglican whilst at Trinity College, Dublin. Dean of St Patrick's, Dublin, 1689–91. Bishop of Derry

1691–1703, Archbishop of Dublin 1703–29. A committed pastoral reformer and supporter of the Protestant ascendancy in Ireland, though after his conversion a strong opponent of both presbyterianism and Roman Catholicism. Leading spokesman for the Church of Ireland 1703–24 until supplanted by Hugh Boulter.

William Law (1686–1761)

Popular Anglican devotional writer. Held clerical and university appointments at Cambridge until he became a non-juror in 1716. Published strong response to Benjamin Hoadly's *The Nature of the Kingdom, or Church, of Christ* in 1717 and two popular devotional works, *A Practical Treatise upon Christian Perfection* (1726) and *A Serious Call to a Devout and Holy Life* (1729). Much admired by Charles and John Wesley. Lived from 1740 in a quasi-religious community at King's Cliffe where he continued to produce devotional and theological works.

John Milner (1752–1826)

Leading Roman Catholic antiquarian, polemicist and reformer. Educated at Douai. Parish priest of Winchester from 1779. Led Ultramontanists against Cisalpine party of Joseph Berrington. Published *History and Survey of the Antiquities of Winchester* in 1798–1801. Collaborated with high church Anglicans in 1790s in opposition to French Revolution and political radicalism. Vicar-apostolic of Midland District from 1803 where he imposed Ultramontanist reforms on the clergy and the strictest observation of ecclesiastical, including moral, discipline on the laity.

Hannah More (1745–1833)

Evangelical writer and philanthropist. Early career as dramatist before undergoing gradual conversion to Evangelicalism in 1780s. Friend of John Newton, Sarah Trimmer and William Wilberforce. Published *Thoughts on the Importance of the Manners of the Great to General Society* in 1788. Set up schools in Cheddar and neighbouring villages from 1790. Regarded by many, both supporters and opponents, as 'moral guardian of the nation', publishing numerous tracts on moral and religious subjects, and helping to found the Religious Tract Society in 1799.

Francis Moylan (1735–1815)

One of the leaders of the Roman Catholic church in Ireland. Educated at Paris, Montpellier and Toulouse and briefly secretary to archbishop of

Paris. Parish priest in Cork from 1764. Bishop of Kerry 1775–87 and Cork 1787–1815. A strong pastoral reformer and opponent of Irish radicalism. Instrumental in establishing convents of nuns in his dioceses.

John Newton (1725–1807)

Former slave trader who became Evangelical Anglican clergyman. Initially refused Anglican orders for his Methodist sympathies, he became curate (to the non-resident vicar) of Olney in 1764. Published, with the poet William Cowper, *Olney Hymns* in 1779. Incumbent of St Mary Woolnoth in city of London from 1780. Strong supporter of campaign for abolition of slavery using his own experiences as evidence.

Thomas Lewis O'Beirne (1749–1823)

Former Roman Catholic who became an Anglican bishop. Educated for the Roman Catholic priesthood in France, he became an Anglican and entered Trinity College, Cambridge. After livings in England and Ireland he became bishop of Ossory 1795–8 and Meath 1798–1823. He was a strong reforming bishop in both dioceses.

Thomas Paine (1737–1809)

Radical writer. Child of a Quaker father and Anglican mother, having a varied career as a privateer, stay-maker, exciseman and schoolmaster. Published *Common Sense* (1776) in support of American independence and actively involved in the subsequent war on the republican side. Later present in France from the late 1780s, publishing *Rights of Man*, which strongly criticised Burke's account of the revolution there, in 1791–2. Awarded honorary French citizenship in 1792 but later denounced and imprisoned. Began to write *The Age of Reason* in 1793 but not completed until 1795. Also published another radical work, *Agrarian Justice*, in 1796. Retired to America in 1802 as adviser to Thomas Jefferson.

William Paley (1743–1805)

Influential mainstream Anglican theologian. Fellow of Christ's College, Cambridge from 1766. Published *The Principles of Moral Philosophy* (1785) and *Evidences of Christianity* (1794). Received from his friend Bishop Law of Carlisle various appointments in the diocese: vicar of

Dalston (1776), prebendary of Carlisle cathedral (1780), archdeacon (1782) and chancellor of the diocese (1785). A strong supporter of Sunday schools. Offered, but declined, mastership of Jesus College, Cambridge, in 1789. Published *Natural Theology* in 1802. A liberal in politics, he supported both prison reform and the abolition of the slave trade.

Spencer Perceval (1762–1812)

Evangelical politician. Called to the bar in 1786, he became deputy recorder of Northampton in 1790. Elected to Parliament in 1796. Solicitor-general 1801–2, attorney-general 1802–6, chancellor of the exchequer 1807–9 and First Lord of the Treasury 1809–12. Strong opponent of Catholic emancipation or increase in government grant to Maynooth seminary. Shot dead in the lobby of the House of Commons on 11 May 1812.

Thomas Percy (1729–1811)

Anglican clergyman and scholar. Rector of Easton Maudit and Wilby from 1756. Chaplain and secretary to Lord Northumberland from 1765. Published *Reliques of English Poetry* in the same year. Dean of Carlisle 1778–82 and Bishop of Dromore 1782–1811. An active diocesan bishop and promoter of pastoral reform.

William Pitt the Younger (1759–1806)

Son of William Pitt, first Earl of Chatham, a former prime minister. Elected MP for Appleby in 1780, making his mark immediately as an accomplished orator. Chancellor of the Exchequer 1782–3 and First Lord of the Treasury 1783–1801. Strong supporter of the relationship between church and state. Supported abolition of slave trade. Very hostile to French revolution and its aftermath. Resigned after refusal of George III to concede Catholic emancipation as the necessary price for the Act of Union. Briefly returned to office between 1804 and his death in 1806.

Beilby Porteus (1731–1809)

Distinguished Anglican clergyman, well known as an effective preacher in the 1760s and 1770s. Chaplain to Archbishop Secker from 1762 and rector of Lambeth from 1767. Bishop of Chester 1776–87 and London 1787–1809. An energetic diocesan who was a strong supporter of Sunday schools. Also supported the campaign against the slave trade and, though not himself an Evangelical, he was sympathetic to many Evangelical causes, especially the suppression of vice and other moral crusades.

Joseph Priestley (1733–1804)

Unitarian minister, theologian and natural philosopher. Educated at the dissenting academy in Daventry. Minister at Needham Market 1755–8 and Nantwich 1758–61. Tutor at Warrington Academy 1761–7 where he published extensively, culminating with *The History and Present State of Electricity* (1767). Minister of the Mill Hill chapel in Leeds 1767–73. Established *Theological Repository*, a journal of liberal theology, in 1769–71. In service of Lord Shelburne, a leading Whig politician, 1773–80. Published *Harmony of the Gospels* in Greek (1777) and English (1780) as well as large numbers of philosophical and scientific papers. Senior minister of the Birmingham New Meeting 1780–91 where he resumed publication of *Theological Repository*. Published *Lectures on History and General Policy* in 1788 and *General History of the Christian Church* in 1790. Priestley's strong support for the French revolution led to the destruction of his house and its contents in 1791. Minister in Hackney 1791–4. Emigrated to Pennsylvania in 1794.

William Robertson (1721–93)

Leading figure in the Moderate party within the Church of Scotland. Minister of Gladsmuir 1744–58 and became active within the General Assembly. Moved to Ministry of Lady Yester's Chapel in Edinburgh in 1758. Published a two volume *History of Scotland* in 1759. Minister of Old Greyfriars, Edinburgh, from 1761 and Principal of Edinburgh University from 1762. Elected Moderator of the General Assembly of the Church of Scotland in 1763. Published *History of America* in 1777. General supporter of government policy, including Catholic relief and war with America, in 1770s and 1780s. Helped to establish Royal Society of Edinburgh in 1782–3. Began new buildings for university, designed by Robert Adam, in 1789.

Daniel Rowland (1711–90)

Anglican clergyman and Methodist supporter. Curate of Llangeitho and Nantcwnlle 1734–63. Underwent conversion experience in 1735.

Met Howell Harris in 1737 and developed with him organisation of Methodist preaching in South Wales until they became estranged in 1750. Deprived of his curacy by the Bishop of St David's for refusing to abandon itinerant preaching tours and opened his own Methodist chapel at Llangeitho.

William Scott (1745–1836)

Ecclesiastical lawyer and politician. Camden Reader in Ancient History at Oxford from 1773. Called to the bar in 1780 and specialised in ecclesiastical law. Knighted in 1788. MP for Downton from 1790 and for Oxford University from 1801. Responsible for the 1803 legislation on pluralism and non-residence. Appointed judge of the high court of Admiralty and sworn of the Privy Council in 1798. Created Baron Stowell in 1821.

Thomas Secker (1693–1768)

Most influential Anglican clergyman of the eighteenth century and a committed reformer. The son of a nonconformist butcher, he was educated at a dissenting academy and later studied medicine in Paris and Leiden, graduating at the latter in 1721. Entered Exeter College, Oxford, in 1721 and ordained in 1722. Rector of St James, Piccadilly, 1733–50. Bishop of Bristol 1735–7 and Oxford 1737–58. Dean of St Paul's, London, 1750–8. Archbishop of Canterbury 1758–68. A distinguished preacher and excellent diocesan administrator. Also a frequent speaker in the House of Lords where he took a moderate Whig stance, though theologically a high churchman. As archbishop Secker was keen to promote links between the Church of England and foreign protestants, campaigned for the appointment of bishops for the American colonies and took a moderate line on Methodism.

Thomas Sherlock (1677–1761)

Influential high churchman and politician of Tory sympathies. Master of the Temple, succeeding his father in the office, 1705–53. Master of St Catherine's College, Cambridge, 1714–19. Dean of Chichester 1715–28. Bishop of Bangor 1728–34, Salisbury 1734–48 and London 1748–61. An effective bishop in his first two dioceses his period at London was dogged by ill health. Strong moral campaigner against drunkenness and immorality. Also published works against deism in the 1720s.

Charles Simeon (1759–1836)

Evangelical clergyman. Underwent conversion experience as Cambridge undergraduate in 1779. Fellow of King's College and vicar of Holy Trinity, Cambridge, from 1782. Strongly influenced Cambridge undergraduates to embrace Evangelicalism and organised classes for intending ordinands. Set up with others the Simeon Trust as a means of purchasing advowsons of livings so that Evangelicals could be presented to them. Co-founder of the Church Missionary Society, British and Foreign Bible Society, Colonial and Continental Church Society and Church Mission to the Jews.

Joanna Southcott (1750–1814)

Evangelical prophetess and writer. Daughter of Devon farmer. Began having visions in 1792. Published her religious experiences in a series of books and pamphlets, beginning with *The Strange Effects of Faith*, from 1801. Supported by some Devon and London clergy and moved to London in 1804. Claimed to be pregnant with 'Shiloh' in 1814 but autopsy after her death proved that the claim had been false.

Sarah Trimmer (1741–1810)

Evangelical Anglican writer and educationist. Wife of a wealthy brick and tile manufacturer in Brentford. Published *An Easy Introduction to the Knowledge of Nature, and Reading the Holy Scriptures* (1780) and *Sacred History* (1782–5). Established Sunday school at Brentford in 1786 and weekday school of industry for girls in 1787. Published various text books for use in Sunday schools and a guide to the establishment of such schools in *The Economy of Charity* in 1787. Founded and edited two periodicals, *The Family Magazine* (1788–9) and *The Guardian of Education* (1802–6). Popularised the use of pictorial material in books for children.

John Thomas Troy (1739–1823)

Leading Roman Catholic ecclesiastic in Ireland in late eighteenth and early nineteenth centuries. Joined Dominican order in 1755 and educated in Rome. Priest of San Clemente, Rome, 1772–6. Bishop of Ossory 1776–86 and Archbishop of Dublin 1786–1823. The leader of the reform movement in the Roman Catholic church, hostile to Irish radicalism and eager to secure Catholic emancipation through a programme of cooperation with the British government. Strong supporter of the Act of Union. Laid the foundation stone of the Roman Catholic pro-cathedral in Dublin in 1815.

Henry Venn (1725–97)

Evangelical clergyman. Though brought up as a high churchman, Venn was strongly attracted to Methodism whilst curate of East Horsley (1750–4) and Clapham (1754–9). Vicar of Huddersfield 1759–71 and Yelling 1771–97. Published *The Complete Duty of Man* in 1763.

John Venn (1759–1813)

Son of Henry Venn. Evangelical rector of Little Dunham 1783–92 and Clapham 1792–1813. Established clerical society at Little Dunham and in 1799 Society for Bettering the Condition and Improving the Comforts of the Poor. Co-founder of the Church Missionary Society. Strong campaigner on moral issues and against the slave trade.

William Wake (1657–1737)

Distinguished Anglican churchman. Chaplain to English embassy in Paris 1682–5 where he made contact with both Gallican Catholics and Huguenots and established his life-long interest in ecumenical projects. Rector of St James, Westminster, from 1695. Dean of Exeter 1701–5. Bishop of Lincoln 1705–16. Archbishop of Canterbury 1716–37. Sidelined by Whig government after 1719 and especially after appointment of Edmund Gibson as Bishop of London in 1724. Published *The State of the Church and Clergy of England* in 1703.

Robert Walpole (1676–1745)

Leading Whig politician. MP for Castle Rising from 1700 and King's Lynn from 1702. Secretary-at-War 1708–10. Imprisoned for alleged corruption in 1712. First Lord of the Treasury and Chancellor of the Exchequer in 1715–17. Opposed repeal of Occasional Conformity and Schism Acts in 1719. Returned to office as Paymaster-General in 1720 and became First Lord of the Treasury again, and first effective prime minister, in 1721. Formed ecclesiastical alliance with Bishop Gibson of London from 1724 to 1736. Resigned office in 1742 and created Earl of Oxford.

William Warburton (1698–1779)

Leading Whig churchman, publishing *The Alliance between Church and State* in 1736. Also a leading figure in eighteenth century literary circles being a close friend of both Alexander Pope and Samuel Richardson. Later published *The Divine Legation of Moses Demonstrated* (1738–41) and *A Rational Account of the Nature and End of the Lord's Supper* (1761). Dean of Bristol 1757–60 and Bishop of Gloucester 1760–79. Much criticised by Anglican high churchmen for his alleged erastianism.

Daniel Waterland (1683–1740)

Leading Anglican theologian and strong opponent of Samuel Clarke. Published *A Vindication of Christ's Divinity* (1719), *Critical History of the Athanasian Creed* (1723), *Scripture Vindicated* (1730–2) and *Review of the Doctrine of the Eucharist* (1737). This last was a reply to Bishop Hoadly's *Plain Account of the Nature and End of the Sacrament of the Lord's Supper* (1735) and was regarded as the leading orthodox exposition of Anglican doctrine on this topic for over a century after his death. Master of Magdalene College, Cambridge, from 1714, he refused offers of the bishopric of Llandaff in both 1738 and 1740.

Joshua Watson (1771–1855)

High church Anglican layman. A wine merchant by trade he retired from business in 1814 to devote himself to philanthropic work, including office as joint treasurer of the SPCK. Formed with Henry Norris, perpetual curate of South Hackney, and other Anglican high churchmen an informal church pressure group, known as the Hackney Phalanx, in the 1790s. Purchased with Norris the *British Critic* in 1811 to act as a mouthpiece for Anglican high churchmen.

Richard Watson (1737–1816)

Radical Anglican churchman and supporter of both ecclesiastical and political reform. Professor of Chemistry at Cambridge 1764–73 and elected Fellow of the Royal Society in 1769. Regius Professor of Divinity at Cambridge 1771–1816. Condemned government's American policy in 1770s. Bishop of Llandaff 1782–1816. Proposed ecclesiastical reform in 1780s but proposals considered too radical at the time. Early supporter of French Revolution but moderated his views after 1792. Despite being non-resident in his diocese Watson was an efficient administrator.

Isaac Watts (1674–1748)

Nonconformist minister in London from 1699 and writer of hymns. Published *Horae Lyricae* (1706–9), *Hymns and Spiritual Songs* (1707–9), *Divine Songs* (1715), and *Psalms of David* (1719). Also published three volumes of poetry and sermons: *Sermons on Various Subjects* (1721), *Reliquae Juveniles* (1734) and, posthumously, *Remnants of Time* (1753). Awarded doctorates in divinity by universities of Aberdeen and Edinburgh in 1728. Maintained close friendships with both Anglicans and dissenters and moderately sympathetic towards Methodism.

Charles Wesley (1707–88)

Anglican clergyman and Methodist leader. Ordained in 1735 but had conversion experience and became travelling evangelist in 1738, though obliged to give this up in 1756 because of ill health. Resident Methodist minister in Bristol 1756–71 and London 1771–88. Main contribution to Methodist movement was as a writer of hymns, of which he composed about 3,000.

John Wesley (1703–91)

Anglican clergyman and Methodist leader, elder brother of Charles. Established Holy Club at Oxford in 1729. Missionary in Georgia 1735–8. Underwent conversion experience shortly after Charles in 1738. Established Methodist societies in London and Bristol 1738–9. Itinerant preacher thereafter. Established Methodist Conference, to regulate work of circuits and societies, in 1744. Originally an opponent of the government's American policy but later changed his position. Opposed Catholic Relief Act of 1778 and supported Lord George Gordon's Protestant Association. Ordained first ministers for America and Scotland in 1784–5 but refused to do so for England. Early opponent of slave trade. Established *Arminian Magazine*, to counteract Calvinism of Evangelicals, in 1778. Published widely throughout his lifetime, notably *Appeals to Men of Reason and Religion* (1743–5), *Christian Library* (1749–55), *A Survey of the Works of God in Creation* (1775) and *History of England* (1776).

George Whitefield (1714–70)

Calvinistic Methodist leader. Strongly influenced by Charles and John Wesley and succeeded to leadership of Oxford Holy Club in 1736.

Ordained deacon in 1736 and served several curacies in London. Joined the Wesleys in Georgia in 1738. Ordained priest 1739 and made contact with Howell Harris. Preached in America in 1739–41. Minister of Calvinistic Methodist chapel in Moorfields, London, from 1742. Preached throughout England, Scotland and Wales following his return from America but returned there in 1744–8. Appointed on his return to England to a chaplaincy by the Countess of Huntingdon, who remained his patron for the next 20 years. Continued to undertake preaching tours in Britain and America.

William Wilberforce (1759–1833)

Evangelical politician and philanthropist. Elected MP for Hull in 1780. Strong supporter of Pitt's ministry though not in office. Had major conversion experience in 1785. Adopted leadership of campaign for abolition of slave trade in 1787. Became active member of Clapham Sect in 1792. Involved in establishment of Church Missionary Society (1799), the launch of the *Christian Observer* (1801) and the establishment of the British and Foreign Bible Society (1804). Achieved success of anti-slavery legislation in 1807. Supported, unusually for an Evangelical, Catholic emancipation, but retired from parliament, before it was secured, in 1825.

William Williams (1717–91)

Calvinistic Methodist leader and hymn-writer known as Pantycelyn. Ordained deacon in 1740 to serve curacies of Llanwrtyd and Llanddewi Abergwesyn. Accused of absenteeism as itinerant preacher and refused ordination to priesthood in 1743. Undertook extensive preaching tours in both North and South Wales from 1742. Published first collection of hymns in 1744 and further hymnals, all in Welsh, in 1751–4, 1757, 1762 and 1763–9. Also published devotional works in Welsh.

Thomas Wilson (1663–1755)

Anglican bishop and devotional writer. Chaplain to Earl of Derby 1692–8. Bishop of Sodor and Man 1698–1755. A reforming bishop who promoted education, catechising, parochial libraries and ecclesiastical discipline. Built several new churches in his diocese and repaired others. Published first known book in Manx, *The Principles of and Duties of Christianity* (English 1699, Manx 1707) and *Short and Plain Instruction for the Better Understanding of the Lord's Supper* (1734). Briefly imprisoned in 1722 in conflict with governor of Isle of Man over ecclesiastical discipline.

Churches and Chapels Retaining Substantially Unaltered Interiors

English shire counties

Bedfordshire:	Melchbourne (St Mary Magdalene) 1779
	Roxton (Independent Chapel) 1808
Cambridgeshire:	Wimpole Hall Chapel 1724
Cheshire:	Baddiley (St Michael) refitted 1811
	Saltersford (Jenkin Chapel) 1733
	Shotwick (St Michael) refitted 1812
Cumbria:	Ravenstonedale (St Oswald) 1738–44
Devon:	Loughwood (Baptist Chapel) early nineteenth-century fittings
	Molland (St Mary) refitted 1808
	Parracombe (St Petrock) mostly 1758
Dorset:	Bridport (Old Meeting, Unitarian) 1794
	Chalbury (All Saints) eighteenth-century fittings
	East Lulworth (St Mary, Roman Catholic) 1786–7
	Winterborne Tomson (St Andrew) eighteenth-century fittings
East Sussex:	Lewes (Jireh Chapel, Calvinist) 1805
Essex:	Audley End Chapel 1786
	Black Chapel refitted c.1800
Gloucestershire:	Didmarton (St Lawrence) early nineteenth-century fittings
	Little Washbourne (St Mary) eighteenth-century fittings

Oldbury-on-the-Hill (St Arild) early nineteenth-century fittings

Hampshire: Avington (St Mary) 1768–71
                Minstead (All Saints) refitted 1792

Hertfordshire: Stanstead Abbotts (St James) eighteenth-century fittings

Kent: Badlesmere (St Leonard) eighteenth-century fittings
                Fairfield (St Thomas) eighteenth-century fittings
                Stelling (St Mary) refitted 1792

Lancashire: Goodshaw (Baptist Chapel) c.1800
                Hoole (St Michael) late seventeenth- to early nineteenth-century fittings
                Pilling (St John Baptist) 1717–23, partly refitted 1812–13
                Slaidburn (St Andrew) late seventeenth- to early nineteenth-century fittings

Leicestershire: King's Norton (St John Baptist) 1757–75
                Lubenham (All Saints) refitted 1812
                Stapleford (St Mary Magdalene) 1783
                Withcote Chapel refitted 1744

Lincolnshire: Goltho (St George) eighteenth-century fittings
                Hannah (St Andrew) 1753–5
                Langton-by-Partney (St Peter and St Paul) c.1725
                Mareham-on-the-Hill (All Saints) refitted 1804
                Stragglethorpe (St Michael) eighteenth-century fittings
                Well (St Margaret) 1733

Norfolk: Bylaugh (St Mary) refitted 1809–10
                East Walton (St Mary) eighteenth-century fittings
                Reymerston (St Peter) late seventeenth- to early nineteenth-century fittings
                Warham St Mary (St Mary Magdalene) refitted c.1800

Northamptonshire: Ashby St Ledgers (St Leodigarius) eighteenth-century fittings
                East Carlton (St Peter) 1788
                Easton Neston (St Mary) eighteenth-century fittings

Northumberland: Chipchase Chapel eighteenth-century fittings

North Yorkshire: Aldfield (St Lawrence) 1783
                   Allerton Mauleverer (St Martin) 1745–6
                   Coxwold (St Michael) refitted 1774
                   Lead (St Mary) refitted 1784
                   Red House Chapel late seventeenth- to early
                   nineteenth-century fittings
                   Whitby (St Mary) late seventeenth- to early
                   nineteenth-century fittings

Nottinghamshire: Elston Chapel early nineteenth-century fittings
                   Winkburn (St John of Jerusalem) eighteenth-century
                   fittings

Oxfordshire: Besselsleigh (St Lawrence) eighteenth-century fittings
                   Chislehampton (St Katherine) 1762–3
                   Milton House Chapel (Roman Catholic) late
                   eighteenth-century fittings
                   Rycote (St Michael) eighteenth-century fittings
                   Shorthampton (All Saints) early nineteenth-century
                   fittings
                   Stonor (Holy Trinity, Roman Catholic) refitted
                   1796–1800
                   Waterperry (St Mary) eighteenth-century fittings
                   Wheatfield (St Andrew) 1745

Shropshire: Halston Chapel refitted c.1725
                   Leebotwood (St Mary) refitted 1776
                   Longnor (St Mary) refitted 1723

Somerset: Babington (St Margaret) 1748–50
                   Hardington (St Mary) early nineteenth-century
                   fittings
                   Holcombe (St Andrew) early nineteenth-century
                   fittings
                   Middle Lambrook (Independent Chapel) 1727–9

Staffordshire: Blore (St Bartholomew) eighteenth-century fittings
                   Elkstone (St John Baptist) 1786–8

Suffolk: Gislingham (St Mary) early nineteenth-century
                   fittings
                   Kedington (St Peter and St Paul) eighteenth-century
                   fittings

Ramsholt (All Saints) early nineteenth-century
fittings
Shelland (King Charles the Martyr) 1767
Walpole (Independent Chapel) early nineteenth-
century fittings

Warwickshire: Loxley (St Nicholas) eighteenth-century fittings
Stoneleigh Abbey Chapel early eighteenth-century
fittings

West Sussex: Chichester (Providence Chapel, Calvinist) 1809
Chichester (St John Evangelist) 1812–13
Greatham (Parish Church) early nineteenth-century
fittings
Stansted (St Paul) 1812–15

Wiltshire: Corsham (Monk's Chapel, Independent) early
eighteenth-century fittings
Derry Hill (Little Zoar Chapel, Baptist) 1814
Old Dilton (St Mary) eighteenth-century fittings

Worcestershire: Strensham (St John Baptist) eighteenth-century
fittings
Worcester (St Swithun) 1734–6

English unitary authorities

Bath and NE Somerset: Cameley (St James) late seventeenth- to early
nineteenth-century fittings
Bradford: Tong (St James) 1727–8
Bristol: New Room (Methodist) 1739–48
East Riding of Yorkshire: Marton (Holy Sacrament, Roman Catholic)
1789
Gateshead: Gibside Chapel 1812
Herefordshire: Clodock (St Clydog) eighteenth-century
fittings
Shobdon (St John Evangelist) 1752–6
Stoke Edith (St Mary) 1740–2
Isle of Man: Kirkbraddan (St Brendan) 1773
Kingston-upon-Hull: Charterhouse Chapel 1778–80
Liverpool: Toxteth Chapel (Unitarian) refitted 1774
London Borough of
Tower Hamlets: Stepney (St George, Lutheran) 1762–3

Milton Keynes:	Gayhurst (St Peter) 1728
Redcar and Cleveland:	Kirkleatham (Turner's Hospital Chapel) 1742
	Skelton-in-Cleveland (All Saints) 1785
Rutland:	Teigh (Holy Trinity) 1782
Trafford:	Hale Chapel (Unitarian) 1723
Wigan:	Chowbent Chapel (Unitarian) 1721–2
York:	Goodramgate (Holy Trinity) eighteenth-century fittings

Wales

Anglesey:	Llangwyllog (St Cwyllog) refitted 1769
Cardiff:	Museum of Welsh Life (Capel Penrhiw, Unitarian) 1777
Carmarthenshire:	Glanaman (Yr Hen Fethel, Independent) 1773
Denbighshire:	Llangar (All Saints) early eighteenth-century fittings
Gwynedd:	Llanfaglan (St Mary Magdalen) late eighteenth-century fittings
	Nanhoron (Capel Newydd, Independent) 1769
	Penllech (St Mary) early nineteenth-century fittings
Monmouthshire:	Llangyfiw (St David) early nineteenth-century fittings
Newport:	Nash (St Mary) refitted 1792
Pembrokeshire:	Bayvil (St Andrew) early nineteenth-century fittings
Powys:	Diserth (St Cewydd) eighteenth-century fittings
	Llandegley (Pales Meeting House, Society of Friends) eighteenth-century fittings
	Llandrindod Wells (Caebach Chapel, Independent) 1715
	Llanfihangel Helygen (St Michael) refitted 1812
	Maesyronnen (Independent Chapel) early nineteenth-century fittings
Vale of Glamorgan:	Llantwit Major (Bethesda'r Fro Chapel, Independent) 1806–7
	Michaelston-le-Pit (St Michael) early nineteenth-century fittings
Wrexham:	Worthenbury (St Deiniol) 1736–9

Scotland

Aberdeen:	St Nicholas West 1752–5
Aberdeenshire:	Bourtie (Parish Church) 1806
	Glenbuchat (St Peter) refitted 1792
East Lothian:	Spott (Parish Church) 1809
Fife:	Ceres (Parish Church) 1805–6
Highland:	Eriboll (Mission Church) 1804
	Golspie (St Andrew) 1736–7
Moray:	Spynie (Holy Trinity) early nineteenth-century fittings
	Tynet (St Ninian, Roman Catholic) 1787
Orkney:	South Ronaldsay (St Peter) refitted 1801
West Lothian	Torphichen (Parish Church) refitted 1803

Ireland

Antrim:	Dunmurry (Presbyterian Meeting) early nineteenth-century fittings
Armagh:	Archbishop's Palace Chapel 1781
Donegal:	Rathneeny (Presbyterian Meeting) early nineteenth-century fittings
Down:	Ardkeen (St Patrick, Roman Catholic) 1777
	Downpatrick (Presbyterian Meeting) 1787
	Hillsborough (St Malachy) 1772–4
	Rademon (Presbyterian Meeting) 1787–9
Dublin:	Rotunda Hospital Chapel 1757–62
Laois:	Timogue (St Mochua) early nineteenth-century fittings
Louth:	Ballymakenny (St Nicholas) 1785–93
Tyrone:	Ulster-American Folk Park (Mountjoy Presbyterian Meeting) c.1800
	Ulster-American Folk Park (Tullyallen Mass House, Roman Catholic) 1768
Wicklow:	Glenealy (St Gregory) 1791–2

Bibliography

Primary Sources

R.E.G. Cole (ed.), *Speculum Dioceseos Lincolniensis*, Lincoln Record Society 1913.

J. Fendley (ed.), *Bishop Benson's Survey of the Diocese of Gloucester 1735–1750*, Bristol and Gloucestershire Archaeological Society 2000.

W.F. Ford (ed.), *Chichester Diocesan Surveys 1686 and 1724*, Sussex Record Society 1994.

J. Gregory (ed.), *The Speculum of Archbishop Thomas Secker*, Church of England Record Society 1995.

W.J. Grisbrooke (ed.), *Anglican Liturgies of the Seventeenth and Eighteenth Centuries*, Alcuin Club 1958.

J.R. Guy (ed.), *The Diocese of Llandaff in 1763: The Primary Visitation of Bishop Ewer*, South Wales Record Society 1991.

E. Jay (ed.), *The Journal of John Wesley: A Selection*, Oxford 1987.

A.P. Jenkins (ed.), *The Correspondence of Bishop Secker*, Oxfordshire Record Society 1991.

H.A.L. Jukes (ed.), *Articles of Enquiry addressed to the Clergy of the Diocese of Oxford at the Primary Visitation of Dr Thomas Secker*, Oxfordshire Record Society 1957.

S.L. Ollard and P.C. Walker (eds), *Archbishop Herring's Visitation Returns*, Yorkshire Archaeological Society 1928–31.

M. Ransome (ed.), *The State of the Bishopric of Worcester 1782–1808*, Worcestershire Historical Society 1968.

M. Ransome (ed.), *Wiltshire Returns to the Bishop's Visitation Queries 1783*, Wiltshire Record Society 1972.

W.R. Ward (ed.), *Parson and Parish in Eighteenth Century Surrey*, Surrey Record Society 1994.

W.R. Ward (ed.), *Parson and Parish in Eighteenth Century Hampshire*, Hampshire Record Society 1995.

General Political and Social Histories

J. Black, *The English Press in the Eighteenth Century*, London 1987.

J. Black, *Eighteenth Century Britain 1688–1783*, Basingstoke 2001.

A.C. Chitnis, *The Scottish Enlightenment*, London 1976.

J.C.D. Clark, *English Society 1688–1832*, Cambridge 1985.

L. Colley, *Britons: Forging the Nation 1707–1837*, London 1994.

J. Davies, *A History of Wales*, London 1994.

H.T. Dickinson, *Liberty and Property: Political Ideology in Eighteenth-Century Britain*, London 1977.

H.T. Dickinson, *The Politics of the People in Eighteenth-Century Britain*, Basingstoke 1995.

E.J. Evans, *The Contentious Tithe*, London 1976.

B. Hilton, *A Mad, Bad, and Dangerous People? England 1783–1846*, Oxford 2006.

G. Holmes and D. Szechi, *The Age of Oligarchy: Pre-Industrial Britain 1722–1783*, London 1993.

A. Lacey, *The Cult of King Charles the Martyr*, Woodbridge 2003.

P. Langford, *A Polite and Commercial People: England 1727–1783*, Oxford 1989.

J.B. Owen, *The Eighteenth Century 1714–1815*, London 1974.

R. Porter, *English Society in the Eighteenth Century*, Harmondsworth 1982.

W. Prest, *Albion Ascendant: English History 1660–1815*, Oxford 1998.

J. Rule, *Albion's People: English Society 1714–1815*, London 1992.

R.B. Shoemaker, *Gender in English Society 1650–1850*, Harlow 1998.

T.C. Smout, *A History of the Scottish People 1560–1830*, London 1969.

W.A. Speck, *Stability and Strife: England 1714–1760*, London 1977.

General Religious Histories

W. Gibson and R.G. Ingram (eds), *Religious Identities in Britain, 1660–1832*, Aldershot 2005.

A.D. Gilbert, *Religion and Society in Industrial England: Church, Chapel and Social Change 1740–1914*, London 1976.

D. Hempton, *Religion and Political Culture in Britain and Ireland: from the Glorious Revolution to the Decline of Empire*, Cambridge 1996.

W.M. Jacob, *Lay People and Religion in the Early Eighteenth Century*, Cambridge 1996.

W.M. Jacob and W.N. Yates (eds), *Crown and Mitre: Religion and Society in Northern Europe since the Reformation*, Woodbridge 1993.

E.G. Rupp, *Religion in England 1688–1791*, Oxford 1986.

W.R. Ward, *Religion and Society in England 1790–1850*, London 1972.

S.J. White, *A History of Women in Christian Worship*, London 2003.

Religion in the English Regions

R.W. Ambler, *Churches, Chapels and the Parish Communities of Lincolnshire 1660–1900*, Lincoln 2000.

V. Barrie-Curien, *Clergé et Pastorale en Angleterre au XVIIIe Siècle: Le Diocèse de Londres*, Paris 1992.

J. Gregory, *Restoration, Reformation and Reform, 1660–1828: Archbishops of Canterbury and their Diocese*, Oxford 2000.

J. Gregory and J.S. Chamberlain (eds), *The National Church in Local Perspective: The Church of England and the Regions*, Woodbridge 2003.

D. McClatchey, *Oxfordshire Clergy 1777–1869*, Oxford 1960.

N. Orme (ed.), *Unity and Variety: A History of the Church in Devon and Cornwall*, Exeter 1991.

M. Smith, *Religion in Industrial Society: Oldham and Saddleworth 1740–1865*, Oxford 1994.

D.A. Spaeth, *The Church in an Age of Danger: Parsons and Parishioners 1660–1740*, Cambridge 2000.

P. Virgin, *The Church in an Age of Negligence: Ecclesiastical Structure and Problems of Church Reform 1700–1840*, Cambridge 1989.

A. Warne, *Church and Society in Eighteenth-Century Devon*, New York 1969.

N. Yates, *Church and Chapel in Portsmouth and South-East Hampshire 1660–1850*, Portsmouth 2003.

N. Yates, R. Hume and P. Hastings, *Religion and Society in Kent, 1640–1914*, Woodbridge 1994.

Religion in Scotland and Wales

D. Ansdell, *The People of the Great Faith: The Highland Church 1690–1900*, Stornoway 1998.

C.G. Brown, *Religion and Society in Scotland since 1707*, Edinburgh 1997.

J.H.S. Burleigh, *A Church History of Scotland*, London 1960.

A.L. Drummond and J. Bulloch, *The Scottish Church 1688–1843: The Age of the Moderates*, Edinburgh 1973.

G.N. Evans, *Religion and Politics in Mid-Eighteenth-Century Anglesey*, Cardiff 1953.

G. Jenkins, *Literature, Religion and Society in Wales 1660–1730*, Cardiff 1978.

D. Walker, *A History of the Church in Wales*, Penarth 1976.

G. Williams, W.M. Jacob, N. Yates and F. Knight, *The Welsh Church from the Reformation to Disestablishment, 1603–1920*, Cardiff 2007.

Religion in Ireland

D. Bowen, *The Protestant Crusade in Ireland 1800–1870*, Montreal 1978.

S.J. Connolly, *Priests and People in Pre-Famine Ireland*, new edn with new introduction, Dublin 2001.

S.J. Connolly, *Religion, Law and Power: The Making of Protestant Ireland 1660–1760*, Oxford 1992.

C.D.A. Leighton, *Catholicism in a Protestant Kingdom: A Study of the Irish Ancien Régime*, London 1994.

A.P.W. Malcolmson, *Archbishop Charles Agar: Churchmanship and Politics in Ireland, 1760–1810*, Dublin 2002.

P. O'Regan, *Archbishop William King of Dublin (1650–1729) and the Constitution in Church and State*, Dublin 2000.

N. Yates, *The Religious Condition of Ireland 1770–1850*, Oxford 2006.

Protestant Established Churches

A.R. Acheson, *A History of the Church of Ireland 1691–1996*, Blackrock 1997.

D.H. Akenson, *The Church of Ireland: Ecclesiastical Reform and Revolution, 1800–1885*, New Haven and London 1971.

G.F.A. Best, *Temporal Pillars*, Cambridge 1964.

F.R. Bolton, *The Caroline Tradition of the Church of Ireland*, London 1958.

S.J. Brown, *The National Churches of England, Ireland and Scotland 1801–46*, Oxford 2001.

E. Brynn, *The Church of Ireland in the Age of Catholic Emancipation*, New York and London 1982.

R.A. Burns, *The Diocesan Revival in the Church of England, c.1800–1870*, Oxford 1999.

W. Gibson, *Church, State and Society, 1760–1850*, Basingstoke 1994.

W. Gibson, *The Church of England 1688–1832: Unity and Accord*, London 2001.

W. Gibson, *Enlightenment Prelate: Benjamin Hoadly, 1676–1761*, Cambridge 2004.

F.C. Mather, *High Church Prophet: Bishop Samuel Horsley (1733–1806) and the Caroline Tradition in the Late Georgian Church*, Oxford 1992.

P.B. Nockles, *The Oxford Movement in Context: Anglican High Churchmanship 1760–1857*, Cambridge 1994.

J.P. Parry and S. Taylor (eds), *Parliament and the Church 1529–1960*, Edinburgh 2000.

N. Sykes, *William Wake, Archbishop of Canterbury, 1657–1737*, Cambridge 1957.

N. Sykes, *From Sheldon to Secker*, Cambridge 1959.

J. Walsh, C. Haydon and S. Taylor (eds), *The Church of England c.1689–c.1833: From Toleration to Tractarianism*, Cambridge 1993.

Protestant Dissenters

J.C. Beckett, *Protestant Dissent in Ireland 1687–1780*, London 1948.

J.E. Bradley, *Religion, Revolution and English Radicalism: Nonconformity in Eighteenth-Century Politics and Society*, Cambridge 1990.

B.L. Manning, *The Protestant Dissenting Deputies*, Cambridge 1952.

I.R. McBride, *Scripture Politics: Ulster Presbyterians and Irish Radicalism in the Late Eighteenth Century*, Oxford 1998.

R. Strong, *Episcopalianism in Nineteenth-Century Scotland: Religious Responses to a Modernising Society*, Oxford 2002.

M. Watts, *The Dissenters from the Reformation to the French Revolution*, Oxford 1978.

Roman Catholics

J. Bossy, *The English Catholic Community 1570–1850*, London 1975.

E. Duffy (ed.), *Challoner and His Church*, London 1981.

C. Haydon, *Anti-Catholicism in Eighteenth Century England, c.1714–1780: A Political and Social Study*, Manchester 1993.

B. Hemphill, *The Early Vicars Apostolic of England 1685–1750*, London 1954.

C. Johnson, *Developments in the Roman Catholic Church in Scotland 1789–1929*, Edinburgh 1983.

D. Keogh, *The French Disease: The Catholic Church and Irish Radicalism, 1790–1800*, Dublin 1993.

V.J. McNally, *Reform, Revolution and Reaction: Archbishop John Thomas Troy and the Catholic Church in Ireland 1787–1817*, Lanham 1995.

M. Mullett, *Catholics in Britain and Ireland, 1558–1829*, Basingstoke 1998.

I. Murphy, *The Diocese of Killaloe in the Eighteenth Century*, Blackrock 1991.

G. O'Brien and T. Dunne (eds), *Catholic Ireland in the Eighteenth Century: Collected Essays of Maureen Wall*, Dublin 1989.

Jacobites and Non-Jurors

G.V. Bennett, *The Tory Crisis in Church and State 1688–1730: The Career of Francis Atterbury, Bishop of Rochester*, Oxford 1975.

P.K. Monod, *Jacobitism and the English People, 1688–1788*, Cambridge 1989.

D. Szechi, *The Jacobites: Britain and Europe 1688–1788*, Manchester 1994.

Religious Thought

J.M. Creed and J.S.B. Smith, *Religious Thought in the Eighteenth Century*, Cambridge 1934.

J.P. Ferguson, *An Eighteenth-Century Heretic: Dr Samuel Clarke*, Kineton 1976.

U. Henriques, *Religious Toleration in England 1787–1833*, London 1961.

R. Hole, *Pulpits, Politics and Public Order in England 1760–1832*, Cambridge 1989.

R.A. Soloway, *Prelates and People: Ecclesiastical Social Thought in England, 1783–1852*, London 1969.

R.N. Stromberg, *Religious Liberalism in Eighteenth-Century England*, Oxford 1954.

Evangelicalism and Methodism

A. Armstrong, *The Church of England, the Methodists and Society 1700–1850*, London 1973.

F. Baker, *John Wesley and the Church of England*, London 1970.

D. Bebbington, *Evangelicalism in Modern Britain*, London 1989.

G.C.B. Davies, *The Early Cornish Evangelicals 1735–60*, London 1951.

R. Davies and G. Rupp (eds), *History of the Methodist Church in Great Britain, Volume I*, London 1965.

G.M. Ditchfield, *The Evangelical Revival*, London 1998.

E. Evans, *Daniel Rowland and the Great Evangelical Awakening in Wales*, Edinburgh 1985.

J.F.C. Harrison, *The Second Coming: Popular Millenarianism 1780–1850*, London 1979.

D. Hempton, *Methodism and Politics in British Society 1750–1850*, London 1984.

D. Hempton and M. Hill, *Evangelical Protestantism in Ulster Society 1740–1890*, London 1992.

M. Hennell, *John Venn and the Clapham Sect*, London 1958.

D.C. Jones, *'A Glorious Work in the World': Welsh Methodism and the International Evangelical Revival, 1735–1750*, Cardiff 2004.

J. MacInnes, *The Evangelical Movement in the Highlands of Scotland 1688 to 1800*, Aberdeen 1951.

C. Podmore, *The Moravian Church in England, 1728–1760*, Oxford 1998.

H.D. Rack, *Reasonable Enthusiast: John Wesley and the Rise of Methodism*, London 1989.

B. Semmel, *The Methodist Revolution*, London 1974.

C. Smyth, *Simeon and Church Order: A Study of the Origin of the Evangelical Revival at Cambridge in the Eighteenth Century*, Cambridge 1940.

A. Stott, *Hannah More: The First Victorian*, Oxford 2003.

G. Tudur, *Howell Harris: From Conversion to Separation*, Cardiff 2000.

W.R. Ward, *The Protestant Evangelical Awakening*, Cambridge 1992.

Charities and Education

W.K.L. Clarke, *A History of the SPCK*, London 1959.

M.G. Jones, *The Charity School Movement*, Cambridge 1938.

T.W. Laqueur, *Religion and Respectability: Sunday Schools and Working Class Culture*, New Haven and London 1976.

K. Milne, *The Irish Charter Schools, 1730–1830*, Dublin 1997.

Church Buildings and Worship

G.W.O. Addleshaw and F. Etchells, *The Architectural Setting of Anglican Worship*, London 1948.

B.F.L. Clarke, *The Building of the Eighteenth Century Church*, London 1963.

G. Hay, *The Architecture of Scottish Post-Reformation Churches*, Oxford 1957.

B. Little, *Catholic Churches since 1623*, London 1966.

N. Temperley, *The Music of the English Parish Church*, Cambridge 1979.

M. Whiffen, *Stuart and Georgian Churches*, London 1948.

N. Yates, *Buildings, Faith and Worship: The Liturgical Arrangement of Anglican Churches 1600–1900*, new edn, Oxford 2000.

Index

Aberdeen 122
Aberdeenshire 50
abolition of slavery 180
  bills 81–2
Act for the Better Preservation of
    Parochial Libraries (1708–9) 124
Act of Settlement (1701) 2, 16–17
Act of Union (1707) 2, 11, 12, 15, 17
Act of Union (1801) 47, 194
  support for 190–1
Addenbrooke's Hospital (Cambridge)
    113
Affirmation Act (1696) 61
Agar, Charles 149, 151, 160
Aliens Act 186
All Saints (Derby) 142
All Saints (Northampton) 111
Allen, Thomas 194
American colonies
  loss 3
American Revolution 182
Andersonian Institute 121
Angelsey 84, 93, 124, 145
Anglican clergy
  archdeacons 13
  attitudes toward the poor 110–11
  attitudes to dissenters 56–7
  career structure 165
  and church-state relationship 22–3
  clerical dress 140
  and *emigrés* priests 186
  episcopal incomes 132–3
  and Evangelicalism 78, 84
  and George III 26
  high churchmen 5, 6, 18–19, 27,
      56–7, 71, 78, 84, 178–9

improvement of livings 29–31
incomes 165
incomes and stipends 132–5, 172
Latitudinarians 5, 7, 23, 73–6
magistrates 105
marginalisation 18–19, 165, 178
patronage of livings 30–1
professionalisation 131
promotion of Sunday schools 123
scholarly writing 123
and Scottish Episcopalians 18
social background and education
    130–5
standards 165
visitations 168
and war with France 187–8
Anglican National Association for the
    Education of the Poor 121–2
Anglicans 183
  attitudes to dissenters 56–7
  church Sunday schools 122
  divisions among 180–1
  ecumenism 64–5
  Evangelicals 195
  high church 57
  low church 57
  orthodox 70–3
  relations with Roman Catholics 186
  and Welsh antiquarian movement
      123–4
Anne, Queen of England 19, 52
  and dissenters 56
  succession 2–3, 16–17
anti-Burghers 51, 89
anti-Catholicism 41–3, 192–4
anti-Christian propaganda 76–7

anti-Trinitarians 75–6
Antrim, Presbytery of 51
Appin 50
Arianism 7, 56, 58, 59, 75–6
Armagh diocese 149, 160
Armagh province 149, 150
Arminianism 73, 78
    in Wales 56
Articles of Religion 71, 75
Arundell of Wardour, Henry 39
Association for the Discountenancing of
        Vice 88, 173
Athanasian Creed 74–5
Athol, Duke of 11–12
Atterbury, Francis 22
    deprivation 23–4
    Jacobite sympathies 19–20
Atterbury plot 37
Avison, Charles 124

Bangor: diocese 13, 125, 144, 146, 147,
        161, 165
Bangorian controversy 19
Bantry Bay 189
Baptists 7, 52, 93
    and conformity 56
    discipline 60
    in England and Wales 14, 55, 57,
        59–61, 61
    and Evangelical Revival 78, 87
    meeting houses in England 55 table
    politcal pressure groups 53
    and poor relief 61–2
    revival 55
    Unitarianism 76
Barrington, Shute 123
Barrow, Isaac 131
Bath 42, 43, 44
    diocese 29
Bath Abbey 32
Bath and Wells diocese 168
Bathurst, Henry 192
Beckett, Dorothy 111
Bedfordshire 55, 182
Belfast Academical Institution 51
Benson, Martin 168
Beresford, George 149
Beresford, Lord John George 25, 149
Beresford, William Baron Decies 149

Berkeley, George 160
Berkshire 186
Berrington, Joseph 183
Bethesda proprietary chapel (Dublin) 88
Bevan, Bridget 96, 118
Beynon, Thomas 124, 146
Bible Christians 96
Bideford 63, 142
Birmingham 124, 125, 142
    sectarian violence 185
Black, Jeremey 1
Blasphemy Act (1697) 76
Bolingbroke, Viscount, *Idea of a Patriot
        King* (1749) 26
Book of Common Prayer (1662) 40, 49,
        57, 65, 75, 86, 90, 139, 141
    French translation 63
    state services 6
Book of Homilies 146
Borsay, Peter 142
Boston 59, 60, 125
Boswell, James 152
Boulter, Hugh 25
Bowdler, John 174
Bowdler, Thomas 108
Bowles, Thomas 145
Bradburn, Samuel 180
Bray, Thomas 78
Bristol 43, 44, 63, 124
    diocese 13, 29, 132, 168
    dissenters 54
Bristol Infirmary 113
British Isles
    Protestant confession 25–7
British and Foreign Bible Society 84,
        194
British Isles
    change of dynasty 2–3, 6
    ecclesiatical divisions 12
    ecclesiatical provinces 12
    elementary education 8
    established churches 27–32
    foreign Protestants 62–5
    government and ecclesiatical matters
        169–74
    historiography of eighteenth-century
        75–6, 82–3, 96–7, 104–5,
        108–10
    legal marriage 14, 40

British Isles (*continued*)
  monarchy 185–6, 195
    divine right 6, 26, 27
  political divisions 11–12
  Protestant confession 25–7
  religious dissent 177–81
  religious divisions 7
  religious freedom 1
  religious history
    historiography 1, 4–5, 8–9
    revisionism 4–5
  religious toleration 5, 26
    decline 194–5
  sectarian violence 41–3, 185
  theological tensions 5, 7–8
  Whig governments 165
    and church–state relationship 178
Brodrick, Charles 160–1, 191
Brooks, Thomasin 112
Brothers, Richard 84–5, 180
  *Revealed Knowledge of the Prophecies
    and Times, A* (1794) 84
  World's Doom, The (1795) 84
Brown, Callum 109
Buchan, Elspeth 84
Buchanites 84
Buckner, John 168
Bulkeley, William 112
Burgess, Thomas 92, 110, 123, 124,
    161–2, 165
Burghers 51
Burke, Edmund 27, 179
  Reflections on the Revoltuion in France
    (1790) 184
Burleigh, Principal 152
Burn, Richard 164
Burnet, Elizabeth, *Method of Prayer*
    (1709) 97
Burns, Arthur 168
Butterworth, Joseph 194

Caernarfonshire 93, 124
Caithness 87, 153
Calamy, Edward 56
Calvinism 59, 62, 78, 86
  in Ireland 51
Cambridge 81
Cambridge University 24
Cameronians 89

Canna 152
Cannon, John 5–6
Canterbury 43, 63, 110
Canterbury (diocese) 29, 132, 168
  church building and restoration
    143–4
  frequency of Sunday services and Holy
    Communion 141 *table*
  social and educational background of
    clergy 131–2 *table*
Canterbury (province) 12, 13
Cardiganshire 55, 124
Carlisle (diocese) 12, 29, 43
Carmarthen 55, 125
  academy 56
  eisteddfod 124
Carnarvon, Marchioness of, died 1768
    70
Caroline, Queen 24
Cashel (province) 150, 188
Cashel and Emly (diocese) 150, 160–1
Cashel cathedral 160
Castlereagh, Viscount 192
Castletown 125, 131
Catholic Emancipation (1829) 7
Catholic Relief Act (1778) 42–3, 47
Cazenove, Philip 64
Challoner, Richard 37–8, 40, 43
  Abridgement of Christian Doctrine
    (1770) 41
  Garden of the Soul (1741) 37, 39
Chalmers, Thomas 89
Chamber of Commerce (Dublin) 46
Channel Islands 11, 12, 13, 186
  structure of religion 12–14
Chapels Royal 13
chapels-of-ease 154
Charles Edward Stuart, Prince (the
    Young Pretender), later Charles III
    17, 49
Charles I, King of England 6
Charles II, King of England 6, 36
Charles, Thomas 93
  Welsh Methodists Vindicated, The
    (1802) 183
Cheshire 31, 55
Chester (diocese) 12, 13, 29, 132, 137
Chevenix Trench, Richard 149
Chichester diocese 136, 168

Chitnis, AC 73
Christ Church cathedral (Dublin) 150
Christian Brothers 48
church and state
  after prorogation of Convocation
      21–4
  Anglican state services 6
  historiography 5–6
  and political divisions 17, 25, 26
  relationship 5–7, 20–1, 177–9
  traditional models 27
Church Missionary Society 65, 81, 194
Church of England 25, 133
  and American loyalists 170
  Anglican–Lutheran initiatives 65
  Arianism 75–6
  Arminianism 73
  augmentation of benefices 171
  building and restoration of church
      buildings 142–4
  and Calvinism 72
  and Catholic emancipation 192
  and church–state relationship 23–4,
      27
  consecration of bishops abroad
      135–6, 180
  deacons 60
  deaneries 13
  design of church buildings 167–8
  developments 25
  diocesan administration 135–7
  dioceses 12–13
  disestablishment 27, 52–3, 178
  ecumenism 62–5
  episcopal visitations 135–6, 166–8
  episcopate and the French Revolution
      186–8
  equalisation of dioceses 29
  as established church 177–9
  and European Protestants 64–5
  and Evangelicalism 5, 83, 84, 93
  foreign missions 65
  frequency of Holy Communion
      137–41
  government involvement with 169–74
  high church revival 195
  housing 165
  improvement of livings 29–31
  Latitudinarians 5, 7, 23, 73–6

liturgical renewal 165–7
loss of support 185–6
and Lutheran churches 64–5
maintaining doctrinal orthodoxy
    93–5
missioning 84
and Moravian Church 78
music at services 141–2
and need for bishoprics abroad 135–6
non-residence 137–9, 166
  Act of 1529 171
  historiography of 138–9
ordination of clergy abroad 170
parishes 31–2, 165
pastoral care 139–40
pluralism 29–30, 137–9, 166
provision of organs 142
reformers 166–8
regularity of attendance 139
religious life in parishes 137–42
response to French Revolution
    184–5
rural deaneries 143, 168
  in Wales 164–5
schisms 90–1, 93, 94
shortage of churches 31, 173–4
social structure of congregations
    58 table
spiritual renewal 166
and tax reform 170–1
theology 71
theology of good works 125–6
and Tories 19–20, 25
visitations 134–5, 183
Church of England in Wales
  disestablishment 27
Church of Ireland 14, 25, 148–51, 189
  Arminianism 73
  benefices 148–9
  bishops 14–15
  church building and restoration
      150–1, 160–1
  converts to 46
  dioceses 14–15
  disestablishment 27
  episcopal bench 149
  episcopal visitations 150, 161
  Evangelicals 80, 88
  financial assistance to 159–60

Church of Ireland (*continued*)
  glebe houses 150–1, 160, 161
  parish numbers 150
  preparation of the clergy 160
  reform 160–1
  regularity of communion 150, 161
  restoration of rural deaneries 160
Church of Scotland 152–5, 168–9.
      See also General Assembly of the
      Church of Scotland
  abolition of episcopacy 12, 15, 16,
      48–9
  Associate Presbytery 79, 89
  attendance 152–3
  and Calvinism 72
  chapels-of-ease 154
  church building and restoration 154–5
  clerical income 173
  communion season 153–4
  criticisms of 152–3
  disestablishment 27
  divisions within 16
  ecclesiastical reform 168–9
  effectiveness 152
  Episcopalians 5, 18, 49
  Evangelicals 72, 79–80, 87, 152–3,
      169
  Gaelic services 153
  lay patronage 28–9
  lining out psalms 154
  Moderates 72–3, 94–5, 168–9
  permitted pluralism 153
  private patronage 15
  problems within 27–9
  schism and secession 169
  schisms 28–9
  shortage of accommodation 154
Church Union (Wales) 162
Civil Wars 3, 12, 59, 107
Claggett, Nicholas 146
Clapham Sect 80–1
Clark, Jonathan 1, 23, 26, 73, 177–9
Clarke, Alured 113
Clarke, Samuel 76
    Scripture Doctrine of the Trinity, The
      (1712) 74–5
Cleaver, William 161–2
Cleland, John, *Memoirs of a Woman of
    Pleasure* (Fanny Hill) 106, 108

Clogher diocese 148, 151
Clonfert and Killmacduagh diocese 148
Cloyne (diocese) 148, 161
  cathedral 160
Colley, Linda 1, 17–18, 26, 41
Collon church (Co Louth) 151
Commissioners for the Sale and
      Redemption of the Land Tax on
      Church and Corporation Estates
      171
Commissioners of the National Debt 170
Committee for the Relief of the Suffering
      of the Clergy and the Laity of
      France 186
Committee of Merchants (Dublin) 46
Committee of Public Instruction (France)
      113
Concordat (1802) 185–6
confessional religious states 1
  strength of concept 195
Confraternity of the Sacred Heart 48
Congleton 83
Congregation of *Propagande Fide* 45
Conventicle Act 91
conversion experience 59, 77–8, 89
Convocations of Canterbury and York
      prorogation 21–2, 30
Coram, Thomas 113
Cork 46, 150–1
Cork and Ross (diocese) 148–9, 151,
      161
  cathedral 48
Cornwall 80, 85, 182
Cornwallis, Frederick 163, 191–2
Court Yard (Southwark) 57
Courtenay, Henry Reginald 85
Couvert, Jacques 186
Crewe, Nathaniel 18
Croft, George 167
Culloden, Battle of (1746) 18
Cumberland 142, 186
Cutting, Mary 108

Dampier, Thomas 81
Danish church 64–5
Danish-Halle Mission (South India) 65
Daubeny, Charles 122, 167
  Guide to the Church (1798) 179
Davies, Edward 92

Davies, Thomas 92–3
Daviot 50
Deacon, Thomas
  Complete Collection of Devotions
    (1734) 18
deism 70
Derry (diocese) 149
Devon 55, 182
Devonshire, Dukes of 31
devotional literature 37, 39, 41, 97–8
  Welsh language 146
Dill, Samuel 88
dissenters
  and low-church Anglicans 57
  parliamentery pressure 24
  persecution 185
  polemics against 56, 57
  political pressure groups 53–4
  support for Whigs 53
Doddridge, Philip 62
Dorset 55, 186
Douglas 125, 131
Downpatrick cathedral 151
Downshire, Marquess of 151
Dr Williams's Library 55
Dromore (diocese) 160
Drummond, Robert 145
Dublin 46, 50, 150–1
Dublin (diocese) 148
Dundee 45, 121
Durham 124, 186
Durham (diocese) 12, 132

East Anglia 59, 133
Eaton, Daniel 195
ecclesiastical courts 107–9, 136
  power of excommunication 182
  Wales 146
ecclesiastical reform 5
  beginnings of movement 159
  church-inspired 9
  government involvement 9, 27–8
  historiography 165–6, 168–9
  mid nineteenth-century 4
  nineteenth-century 94
  and prorogation of Convocation 21
Edict of Fraternity 183
Edict of Nantes 6, 63
Edinburgh 42, 45, 121, 154

education 104, 113–23. *See also* social
    welfare
  among Irish Presbyterians 51
  charity schools 114–16, 117
  charter schools 118–19
  church provision 5, 8
  lay provision 116
  national initiatives 121–3
  role of women 96
  Roman Catholic provision 44
  Roman Catholic schools 41
  Scotland
    ambulatory schools 119–20
    education system 114
    educational provision 121
    industrial schools 120
    spinning schools 120
  and social control 185
  state involvement in provision 118
Edwin, Lady Charlotte 92
eisteddfodau (festivals of Welsh culture)
    124, 183
Elizabeth I, Queen of England 36
Ely (diocese) 29, 168
embassy chapels 40
emigrés
  in London 3
  Roman Catholic clergy 186, 192
Emly cathedral 160
England 11, 12
  charity schools 113–17
  ecclesiastical reform 165–9
  Evangelicalism 8
  Protestant dissenters
    toleration 26
  Protestant refugees 62–3
  Roman Catholics 17
  status of established church 177–9
  structure of religion 12–14
  Sunday schools 122, 123
England and Wales
  alliance between church and state
    23–4
  Baptists 14, 55, 57, 59–61, 61
  charity schools 114–15
  ecclesiastical administration 13–14
  ecclesiastical problems 29–32
  elementary education 115 *table*
  impact of theological liberalism 94–5

England and Wales (*continued*)
  increase of benefice incomes 173
  non-residency of the clergy 137–8 *table*
  parliamentary grants for churches 160
  Protestant dissenters 52–62
Enlightenment
  impact 77
Episcopal Church (Scotland) 50
episcopal visitations 135–6
erastianism 21, 74
Erskine, Ebenezer and Ralph 79
established church
  membership 13–14
established churches
  strengths and weaknesses 27–32
Europe 6
  established churches 6
  national systems of education 113–14
  religious establishments 27
Evangelical London Missionary Society
    194
Evangelical Revival 54, 59, 62, 70,
    77–86, 108–9, 195
  clerical conversions 79
  and educational initiatives in Scotland
    120–1
  impact 7–8
  link between European and British
    77–8
  millenarianism 84–6
  and missionary endeavours 84
  moral and social reform 81–3
  opposition to 83–4
  prophets 84
  role of women 95–6
  in Wales 147
Evangelical Society for Bettering the
    Condition of the Poor 110–11
Evangelicalism 70
Evangelicals 5, 173
  anti-Catholicism 192–4
  attitude toward the poor 110–11
  divisions among 88
  and *emigrés* priests 186
Evans, Dr John 55
Evans, Evan, *Specimens of the Poetry of
    the Ancient Welsh Bards* (1764)
    123
Evans, John and James 139–40

Evans, Mary 84
Evans, Theophilus, *Drych y Prif
    Oesoedd/Mirror of the First Ages*
    (1716) 123
Ewer, Bishop of Llandaff 135
Exeter 63, 185
Exeter (diocese) 135, 137–8, 143–4, 168
  cathedral 139

Family Magazine 95
Fanny Hill 106, 108
Faversham 63, 143
Feast of King Charles the Martyr 27
Feathers Tavern Petition (1772) 76
Fielding, Henry, *Enquiry into the Causes
    of the Late Increase of Robbers*
    (1751) 111
Fleetwood, William 23
Flintshire 147
Foley, John 134
Foundling Hospital (London) 113
Fox, Charles James 180
Foxe, John, *Book of Martyrs* (1563) 41
France 1
  ancien régime 1, 109
  attacks on religion 195
  education system 413
  emigrés priests 186
  and Roman Catholicism 6
  war with Britain 187–8
Francis Street Chapel (Dublin) 189
Frederick II of Prussia 113
Frederick William I of Prussia 113
French Hospital (Clerkenwell) 63
French Protestant School (Westminster)
    63
French Revolution 27, 43–4, 47, 109
  impact on Britain 3–4, 6, 182–8, 193
  reactions to 97, 179

Gaelic School Society 121
Gaidhealtachd 44
Gainsborough 59
  Monthly Meeting 61
Garrick, David 63
General Assembly of the Church of
    Scotland 15, 16, 28, 72–3, 87, 94,
    120, 154
  and ecclesiastical reform 168–9

General Baptists (Arminian) 59–60, 78
General Evangelical Society (Dublin) 88
George I 2, 7, 56, 71, 165, 178
　accession 16–17
　death 26
　and non-jurors 18
George II 2, 7, 56, 71, 165, 178
　death 26
　and non-jurors 18
George III 1, 47, 63, 130
　accession 2, 20
　achievements 3
　and Catholic emancipation 191–5
　death 26
　and Ireland 149, 151
　political agenda 178
　view of monarchy 25–6
Gibson, Edmund 20, 21–2, 25, 27, 65,
　　141
　episcopal appointments 23–4
　Pastoral Letter on Methodism 146
　reform initiatives 29
Gibson, William 134
Giffard, Bonaventure 37
Gilbert, Ann Taylor 98
Gilbert's Act (1782) 110
Gill, Jeremiah 59
Gillespie, Thomas 89
Girardin, Piers 64
Glasgow 42, 45, 121, 122
Glasites 89
glebe houses 150, 151, 160, 161
Glenmoriston 120
Gloria in Excelsis 75
Gloucester (diocese) 29, 94, 132, 168
　cathedral 124
Gloucestershire Quarter Sessions 134
Godwin, William 179–80
Gordon, Lord George 42
Gordon riots 43, 185
Gorsedd 124, 183
Gother, John, *Instructions and Devotions
　for Hearing Mass* (1705) 39
Griffiths, Sydney 96
Gunpowder Plot 6
Gurney family 61
Guy's Hospital (London) 112
Gwyneddigon 183
Gyllenborg, Count Carl 65

Haldane, Robert 89
Hampshire 186
Hampton Poyle 136
Handel, Georg Friederich, *Messiah* 113
Hanna, Samuel 88
Hanoverian dynasty 6, 25
Harcourt, Edward Venables Vernon 181
Hardwicke's Marriage Act (1753) 40,
　52, 136
Harris, Howell 79, 83–4, 89, 92, 96
　conversion experience 78
Harris' Lists of Covent Garden Ladies
　106
Harrowby, Lord 173
Hastings, Lady Elizabeth 97
Hastings, Paul 109–10
Haydon, Colin 43
Hayman, Henry 136
Headington 134
Hempton, David 193
Hengoed (Glam.) 57
Henley 136
Henry IX 17
Henry VII's Chapel 167
Hereford 41
Hereford (diocese) 13, 131, 136
　cathedral 124
heritors (landowners) 15, 28–9, 119,
　121, 154
Herring, Thomas 145
Herrnhut (Moravian community),
　conversion experience 77–8
Hervey, Frederick 149, 159
Hervey, James 79
Heythrop 135
Hibernian Missionary Society 88
Highland vicariate 45
Hildesley, Mark 125
Hill, George 73
Hilton, Boyd 82
Hinchcliffe, John 180
Hoadly, Benjamin 7, 17, 21, 23–4, 76
　doctrinal controversy 17–19
　*Plain Account of the Nature and End
　　of the Sacrifice of the Lord's
　　Supper, A* (1735) 74
Hoare family 61
Hogarth, William 63
Holdforth, Joseph 44

Holland Quarter Sessions (Lincs.) 134
Holman, Lady Anastasia 37
Holy Communion 60
Holy Spirit 94
Honourable Society of Cymmrodorion 123
Hopton, Susannah, *Devotions in the Ancient Way of Offices* (1709) 97
Horne, George 6, 27, 71, 123, 167
Horsley, Samuel 6, 27, 71, 110, 161–2, 180, 183, 185
    and French Revolution 186–7
    and non-residence 171–2
    reform initiatives 166–7, 170
    visitations 166–7, 187
Howard, Charles 11th Duke of Norfolk 44
Howard, John 118–19
Huddersfield 80
Huguenots 41
    contribution to British economy 62–3
Hull 43
Huntington, William 86
Huntley mission 46
Hussites 77–8
Hutchinson, Francis 72
Hutchinson, John 71

in commendam 133
Incorporated Society (Dublin) 118
Independents 7, 83, 93
    adoption of Unitarianism 76
    and Arminianism 56
    in England and Wales 14, 55, 57
    Evangelicals 87, 89
    gathered church 59
    hymnal 79
    in Lincolnshire 59
    meeting houses in England 55 *table*, 92
    political pressure groups 53
    and poor relief 61–2
    revival 55
Interregnum 3
Inverness 121–2
Ipswich 63
Ireland 4
    anti-Catholicism 46
    Catholic militancy 193
    church leadership 24–5
    clerical response to events in France 188–90
    concessions to Catholics and Presbyterians 159
    conquest and assimilation 11
    dissenters 26
    ecclesiastical reform 159–65
    educational provision 114, 118–19, 173
    established church 2, 177–9
    and Evangelicalism 8, 87–8, 94
    and Evangelicals 80
    and French expeditionary force 189–90
    impact of Methodism 89
    impact of theological liberalism 94–5
    Jacobism 17, 18
    Methodism 91
    parochial unions 191
    political instability 3, 188–91
    Protestant proselytising 194
    Protestants 14–15
    religious tensions 189
    religious toleration 24, 26
    Roman Catholics 17, 44, 159
    Scottish immigration 50
    sectarian violence 189, 190
    structure of religion 14–15
Irish Board of First Fruits 150–1
    and Church of Ireland 159–60
    parliamentary grant 173
Irish militia bills (1804) 181
Irish Presbyterians 159, 169
    clergy 51–2
    and Evangelicalism 88
    fragmentation 189
    political restrictions 50
    and rebellion of 1798 190
    response to French Revolution 188–9
    toleration 24
Irish Rebellion (1798) 51, 85, 180, 190
Isle of Man 12, 107
    assimilation 11
    communicant numbers 147
    libraries 125
    Methodism 91
    structure of religion 12–14

Jacob, William 107, 116, 145
Jacobins 180, 185

Jacobites 15, 134
  decline 42
  fear of 25
  in Ireland 24–5
  rebellion 1715 17, 18, 36
  rebellion 1745–6 15, 17, 18, 42, 45,
    49
  support for 17–18, 49
James I, King of Great Britain and Ireland
    11, 36
James II, King of Great Britain and
    Ireland
  succession 16–17
James III (son of James II) 2–3, 16–17,
    19
Jansenism 45
Jebb, John 160–1
Jews 40, 194–5
Johnson, Samuel 152
Jones, Dafydd 79
Jones, David 92
Jones, Griffith 96
  circulating schools 119–20
  Welch Piety 117–18
Jones, Mary 117–18
Jones, William 183–5
  Catholic Doctrine of a Trinity (1756)
    71
  Essay on the Church (1787) 71
  Scholar Armed, The (1780) 179

Kaye, Dean of Lincoln 122
Kent 110, 186
Keppel, Bishop of Exeter 180
Kerr, Daniel 121
Kilham, Alexander 91, 185
Killala (diocese) 148
Kilmore (diocese) 149
King, William 24–5
King's Lynn 125, 143
kirk sessions 15, 28, 109, 119, 121
  in Ireland 51–2
  and sexual licence 153
Knatchbull's Act (1722) 110
Knibworth (Leics) 62

Lacey, Andrew 6
Lancashire 31, 55
  Roman Catholics 38–9

Lancaster 39
Land, John 136
Laqueur, Thomas 122–3
Latitudinarians 5, 7, 23, 73–6
Law, William
  Christian Perfection (1726) 71
  Serious Call to a Devout and Holy Life
    (1729) 71
Lee, Ann 84
Leechman, William 72
Leeds, John 116
L'Église des Grecs (Soho) 63
libraries 123–5
  cathedral 125
  endowed and subscription 124–5
  in Wales 148
licensed chapels 14, 83
Lichfield cathedral 125
Lincoln 59
Lincoln (diocese) 13, 29, 168
Lincolnshire 122, 134
  dissenters 60
  Independents 59
  Presbyterians 59
Lindsay, Bishop of Kildare 161
Lismore 45
Lismore diocese 148
Little Plumpton 39
Liverpool 39, 43, 125, 142, 185
Liverpool, Lord 194
  and ecclesiastical reform 173–4
Llandaff (diocese) 92, 132, 144, 146,
    161
  cathedral 13
Llanddowror (Carms) 117
Llangammarch (Brecs) 123
Lochcarron 120, 152
Lock Hospital (London) 112
London 42–3
  diocese 20
  non-juring meetings 18
  places of worship 31
  Welsh antiquarian movement 123–4,
    183
London Abolition Society 81
London Churches Act (1711) 31
London (diocese) 132, 135, 137, 168
  frequency of Holy Communion 140
    table

London Hibernian Society 194
London Hospital (London) 112–13
London Society for Promoting
    Christianity Among the Jews 194
London Sunday School Society 122
London vicariate 37
Long Melford (Suff) 133
Lonsdale, 3rd Viscount 31
Louis XVI, King of France 183
love feast 89–90
Loyalist Associations 183
Lund, Bishop of Växjö 65

Macaulay, Zachary 80
Macdonald, Hugh 44
Mackenzie, Lachlan 87
Mackenzie, Sir Hector 87
Madan, Spencer 181
Maddox, Isaac 145
Magdalen College Chapel (Oxford) 167
Magdalen Hospital (London) 106
Maidstone 110, 124
Majendie, H.W. 161, 165
Manchester 31, 39, 43, 185
    non-juring meetings 18
Manchester Sunday Schools 122
Manners-Sutton, Charles, *Reasons for
    Declining to Become a Member
    of the British and Foreign Bible
    Society* (1810) 84
Markham, William 123
Marsh, Herbert 122
Martin, James 135
Marylebone 31
Maseres, Francis, *Moderate Reformer,
    The* (1791) 170
Maynooth 47
McClatchey, Diana 131, 133–4
McDowell, Benjamin 88
Meath diocese 149, 161
meeting houses
    destruction 185
    in England 55 *table*
    Methodist 183–4
Merioneth 93, 124
Methodism 62, 80, 86
    areas of strength 93
    Arminian 88–9, 89–92
    Calvinist 88–9, 92–3, 183

and Catholic emancipation 193–4
and conversion experience 89
divisions within 88–9
hymn singing 89
itinerant preaching 90, 92, 186
local impact 91–2
love feast 89
missions 87
New Connexion 86, 91
opposition to 83
organisation 89–90
and Protestant dissent 91
provision of Sunday schools 122
radicalism 180
rise 88–95
secessionists 185
separation from Church of England
    90–1
and Welsh antiquarian movement 123
Wesleyan 65, 80, 86, 90–1, 95–6, 98
Methodist Conference 91, 180, 194
Middlesex Hospital (London) 112
Middleton, Thomas 136
Midland vicariate 37
Milton House (near Oxford) 39
Mitchell, Thomas 80
Molony, John Baptist 42
monarchy 195
    divine right 6, 26, 27
    loss of support 185–6
Monmouthshire 55, 59, 124, 147
Moore, Archbishop of Canterbury 187
Moore, George 112
Moore, Henry 180
Moorfields Tabernacle 92
moral reform 81–3. *See also* social
    reform
    pornographic literature 106
    prostitution 106
    sexual licence
        concerns about 105–9
    and social control 105–9
Moravian Church (*Unitas Fratrum*)
    77–8, 83, 89
    missions 80, 87
More, Hannah 80–1, 95, 108, 183,
    185
More's Cheap Repository Tracts 81
Morganwg, Iolo 123–4, 183

Mortmain Bill (1735–6) 24, 53
Mother's Catechism, The (1758) 120
Moylan, Francis 47, 191
music
  church promotion of 123–4
  contribution of women 98
  festivals 124
  hymn-singing 60, 78–9, 86, 89
Myvyrian Archaiology (1801–07) 124

Napoleon, Emperor of France 3, 185
National Society for Education 162
new dissent 78, 180–1
New Licht Burghers 89
Newcastle 18, 42
Newton, John 82
Nicene Creed 75
Nockles, Peter 71–2
Nonconformists 53, 178
  occasional conformity 56
non-jurors 18–19
  ecumenism 64
  meetings 18
non-residence 137–9
  Act of 1529 171
  historiography of 138–9
Norfolk 31, 134
Normandy, Duchy of 12
North, Brownlow 181
Northamptonshire 59, 182
Northern Evangelical Society 186
Northern vicariate 37
Northumberland 186
  Presbyterians 55
Norwich 43, 63, 107, 124
  dissenters 54
Norwich (diocese) 29

O'Beirne, Thomas Lewis 160–1
occasional conformity 56
Occasional Conformity and Schism Acts
  (1718) 53
Octagon (Bath) 32
old dissent 93, 180–1
Old Licht Burghers 89
Old Whig 53
Orange Order 189
Ossory Clerical Association 88
Ossory (diocese) 160, 161

Oxford
  Jacobism 18
Oxford (diocese) 29, 131–2, 137–8
Oxford Movement 167
Oxford University 24, 167, 168
  and Evangelicals 83
Oxfordshire 133–4

Paine, Thomas
  Age of Reason (1794–5) 179
  Age of Reason (1816) 195
  Common Sense (1776) 179
  Rights of Man (1791–2) 179
Paley, William 123
Pantycelyn, William Williams 92
parishes 13, 165
  antiquated boundaries 31–2
  in Ireland 14
  lay patronage 137
  poor relief 104
  religious 137–42
  unions of 136
Particular Baptists (Calvinist) 55, 57,
  59–60
Partridge, Samuel 134
Patrician Brothers 48
Patripassionism 83
Patronage Act 73
Payne, William 42
Peace of Amiens 187–8
Penrose, John 80
Perceval, Spencer 83, 109, 172–3,
  193–4
Perigal, Francis 63
Perronet, Vincent 79, 91
Perth Academy 121
Perthshire 50
Peterborough (diocese) 29, 168
Petre, Benjamin 37, 38
philanthropy 104–5
Phillips, Henry 80
Phillips, Sir John 117
Picton Castle (Pembs) 117
Piers, Henry 91
pietism *see* Evangelicalism
Pin, Ellies du 64
Pitt, William 177, 191
  and Catholic emancipation 191–2
  and ecclesiastical reform 169–71

places of worship 31
  chapels-of-ease 154
  licensed chapels 14, 83
  meeting houses 55 *table,* 183–5
  meeting houses in England 55 *table*
  private chapels 83
  proprietary chapels 31–2
  qualified chapels 49
  Roman Catholic 39–40, 43, 45, 48
  Scottish Episcopalians 49
  unlicensed chapels 184
pluralism 5–7, 137–9
Plymouth 43, 63
political radicalism 3, 177–81
  attacks on 194
  church state relationship 179–80
political reform 3–4, 183
Pollock, Linda 97
Pomeroy, Joseph 85
poor relief 8, 104
  among Irish Presbyterians 51
  Independents and Baptists 61–2
  individual provision 111–12
  parochial charities 111–12
  Poor Law (1597) 109
  Poor Law (1601) 109
  statutory provision 109–10
  workhouses 110
Porteous, Beilby 108, 123, 168, 180, 183
Portree (Skye) 152
Portsmouth 43
Potter, John 24, 78
Presbyterianism 7, 25, 50
  adoption of Unitarianism 76
  and Arminianism 56
  decline in England 55
  in England and Wales 14, 55–6
  Evangelical 89
  and Evangleical revival 94
  Irish 14–15, 50–2
  in Lincolnshire 59
  meeting houses in England 55 *table*
  moderate 70–3
  politcal pressure groups 53
  and poor relief 61
  and rationalism 57–9
  in Scotland 2
presbyteries 28
Presbytery of Antrim 51

Presentation Sisters 48
Preston 39, 43
Pretyman-Tomline, George 123, 181,
      185–6
Priestley, Joseph 180, 185
Primitive Methodists 96
private chapels 83
Proclamation Society 108
proprietary chapels 31–2
Protestant Ascendancy 5–6, 148, 159
Protestant Association 42–3
Protestant dissenters 5
  disabilities 52–3
  in England and Wales 14, 52–62,
      56–7 *table*
  impact of theological liberalism 94–5
  social structure of congregations 58
      table
  strengthening 91
  toleration 21, 26, 52
  training of clergy 56
Protestant Dissenting Deputies 53–4
Protestant Union for the Support of the
      Protestant Religion and the Britsh
      Constitution 194
Pullen, Philip, *Hymns, or Spiritual Songs*
      (1807) 86
Puritanism 25, 57, 59, 106–7

Quaker Tithe Bill (1735–6) 24, 53,
      182
Quakers 24, 40, 61
  in England and Wales 55, 57
  meeting houses in England 55 *table*
  and payment of tithes 182
qualified chapels 49
Queen Anne's Bounty 150, 164, 172
  impact 30 *table*
Queen Charlotte's Hospital (London)
      112

radical Whigs 20–1, 26, 27
Radnorshire 124, 147
  Independents 55
  Particular Baptists 55
Ramsay, James 180
Randolph, John 179, 185
Raphoe diocese 148
Raphoe Statutes (1782) 48

rationalism 25, 57–9, 70
   and Church of England 23, 72–3, 94
   and Protestant universities 72–3
   and religion 7
Rattray, Thomas 49
Red House (Roundhay) 44
Redwood, John 75
Reformation 6, 12, 107, 181
Reformed Presbyterianism Church 89
regium donum 53
Relief Church 89
Relief Presbytery 28
religious settlement (1662) 7
Religious Tract and Book Society 194
Revocation of the Edict of Nantes (1685)
   6, 63
Reynolds, William 135–6
Riviere, Isaac 64
Robertson, William 72–3
Robinson, Richard 149
Rochester (diocese) 13, 29, 132
Romaine, William 79
Roman Catholic church 64, 189
   catechising children 41
   cathedrals 48
   in Ireland 44, 46
   and Irish rebellion 190
   liturgy 40, 45–6
   missioning 44
   numbers of priests 45
   places of worship 39–40, 43, 45, 48
   provision of schools 41, 44
   reform 46–8
   in Scotland 44–5
   structure 37–8
   training of priests 44–5, 47, 165
   vicars apostolic 37–8, 39, 40, 43
      increase in number 44
Roman Catholics 5, 183
   disabilities 2, 15, 36–7, 42
   emancipation 191
   in England and Wales 14, 36–44
   growth of community 43
   integration 41
   in Ireland 14–15, 26, 46–8
   and Irish rebellion 190
   numbers 38–9
   numbers of priests 38
   persecution 185

poverty of Irish 48
refugees 43–4
relations with Anglicans 186
relief from disabilities 42–3, 46–7
violence against 41–3
Romilly, Samuel 63–4
Rotunda Lying-in Hospital (Dublin)
   113
Rowland, Daniel 89, 92–3
   conversion experience 78
Rowland, Henry, *Mona Antiqua*
   Restaurata (1723) 123
Royal British (Lancastrian) Association
   121–2
Royal Chapel (Whitehall) 24
Royal Hospital (London) 112
royal peculiars 13
Rudé, George 43
Rule, John 116, 134
Rutland, Dukes of 31
Ryder, Henry 94

Salisbury (diocese) 29, 137
Sandimanians 28
Sargent, Anne 111
Saunders, Thomas 167
School of Venus 108
Scotland 4, 11, 12, 25
   ambulatory schools 119–20
   educational provision 114, 119–21,
      121
   episcopalian parishes 15–16
   established church 2, 177–9
   Evangelicalism 8, 86–7
   Gaelic language instruction 120
   industrial schools 120
   Irish immigration 45
   Jacobitism 17–18, 49
   Methodism 89, 90
   Protestant dissenters 26
   religious toleration 26
   Roman Catholics 17, 44–5
   sexual behaviour 153
   spinning schools 120
   structure of religion 15–16
   Sunday schools 122
   superstitious beliefs 153
   and theological liberalism 94–5
   universities 121

Scott, Sir William 172
Scottish Communion Office (1764) 49
Scottish Episcopalians 5, 48–50
Secession Church 28
Secker, Thomas 134–5, 141
    confirmation tours 136
    Instructions (1769) 131
    and need for bishoprics abroad
        135–6
    visitations 168
Second Reformation 193
Secret Society of Defenders 189
Selina, Countess of Huntingdon 79, 83,
        92, 95
    Connexion 86, 91
Serenius, Jacob 65
Shakespeare, William 108
Shaw, Robert 88
Sherlock, Thomas 20, 141–2
Shipley, Jonathan 177–8, 180
Shireburne, John 39
Shobdon (Herefs) 167–8
Shoemaker, Robert 106
Sidmouth, Lord 54
Simeon, Charles 80–1, 86
Skinner, John 50
Skye 50, 87, 120, 154
Smallbrooke, Richard 146
social reform 84, 183. *See also* moral
        reform
    campaign for public decency 108
    episcopal support 181
    reformation of manners 105–6
social welfare 104. *See also* education
    church provision 5, 8
    deserving poor 111
    promotion of culture and learning
        123–6
    provision of hospitals 112–13
Societies for the Reformation of Manners
        105–7
Society for Distributing Religious Tracts
        108
Society for Promoting Christian
        Knowledge 65, 84, 108, 114–15,
        119–21, 124–5, 131, 162, 186
    charity schools 117
    libraries 148
    Welsh language translations 146

Society for the Propagation of the Gospel
        124, 131, 135
Society for the Suppression of Vice
        108
Society of Ancient Britons 123
Society of Friends. *See* Quakers
Society of United Irishmen 188–90
Socinians. *See* Unitarians (Socinians)
Sodor and Man (diocese) 12–13, 131
'Sons of the Clergy' Society 124
Sophia, Electress of Hanover 16–17
Southcott, Joanna 84, 85–6, 180
Spaeth, Donald 9, 139, 181
St Andrew's (Canterbury) 143–4
St Asaph (diocese) 13, 125, 144, 146–7,
        161–2, 164–5
St Beuno's shrine (Clynnog Fawr)
        148
St David's College (Lampeter) 162
St David's (diocese) 13, 132, 144–7,
        161, 162, 165
St George's (Tiverton) 144
St George's (Windsor) 13
St Kew (Cornwall) 85
St Mary's (Bath) 32
St Nicholas (Newcastle upon Tyne)
        124–5
St Peter-in-Thanet 143
St Peter's (Drogheda) 151
Steele, Anne, *Poems on Subjects Chiefly
        Devotional* (1760) 98
Stephen, James 80
Stephens, Walter 88
Stock, Bishop of Waterford and Lismore
        161
Stockwood, William 136
Stokesley (Yorks) 41
Stoneyhurst (Lancs) 44
Stonor 40
Stonor, John Talbot 37, 40
Stourton, William, Lord 44
Stuart, Charles Edward, Prince (the
        Young Pretender), later Charles III
        49
Stuart dynasty 2–3, 12
Stuart, William 149
Suffolk 31
Sunday School Society 194
Sunday School Union 122

Sunday schools 114, 116, 117
    expansion of provision 185
    Irish Presbyterian 51
    Methodist 90
    movement 81, 121–3
    popularity 123
Surrey 186
Sutcliffe, Joseph, *Divine Mission of the
    People Called Methodists, The*
    (1814) 180
Swedish church 65
Sykes, Norman 4, 9, 21, 75–6, 104–5
Synod of Ulster 88, 189
    Evangelicals 80
    and Irish rebellion 190
    schism 51

Tain 121–2
Taylor, Jane
    Hymns for Infant Minds (1808) 98
    Original Hymns for Sunday Schools
        (1812) 98
Teignmouth, Lord 80
Terrick, Richard 168
Test and Corporation Acts
    repeal 7, 24, 30, 53–4, 56, 177, 184,
        192
Thirty-Nine Articles of Religion 52, 54,
    57
    and Scottish Episcopalians 49
Thomson, George 79
Thornton, Henry 80
Three Choirs Festival 124
Thurlyn, Dr 125
Tighe, Thomas 88
Tilson, John 136
Tindal, Matthew 76
    Christianity as Old as the Creation
        (1730) 75
tithes 181–2
Toleration Act (1689) 7, 52, 183
Tone, Wolfe 189
Tongue 87, 153
Tories
    church and state 17
    and Church of England 73
    declining influence 19
    marginalisation by C of E 25
    rehabilitation 26–7

relationship between church and state
    6
religious toleration 7
theory of kingship 20
Tottenham Court Chapel 92
touch-pieces 17
Townshend, Thomas, 1st Viscount 125
Trench, Bishop of Elphin 94
Trimmer, Sarah 185
    Oeconomy of Charity (1787) 95
    Servant's Friend, The (1787) 95
Trimnell, Charles 23
Trinity 7
Trinity Act (1813) 195
Troy, John Thomas 47, 188, 190
Tuam and Ardagh (diocese) 149
Tuam (province) 150
Tufton, Thomas, 6th Earl of Thanet 30
Tullyallan mass house 48
Turner, Isaac 60

Ulster 50
Ulster American Folk Park (near Omagh)
    48
Ulster Evangelical Society 88
Unitarians (Socinians) 7, 55, 56, 58–9,
    59, 76–7, 94, 185
United Church of England and Ireland
    2
United Kingdom. *See also* British Isles
    change of dynasty 6
    formation 2
United States: Methodism 90
unlicensed chapels 184
Urquhart, Jean 87
Ursuline Sisters 48

Van Mildert, William 179
Venn, Henry 79, 80
Venn, John 80–1, 86, 111
Virgin, Peter 9, 138–9
    historiography 165–6
Vivian, Thomas 80
voluntaryism 104
Vowler, James 80

Wade, John 44
Wake, William 20, 24, 75
    ecumenism 64

Wales 2, 4, 12
  antiquarian movement 123–4
  bishops in 144–5
  Calvinistic Methodism 92–4, 145,
    147, 183
  charity schools 117–18
  church building and restoration
    147
  clerical incomes 146–7
  communicant numbers 147
  conquest and assimilation 11
  critics of Methodism 92
  cultural contribution of the clergy
    123–4
  difficulties of communication 144
  druidic tradition 123
  ecclesiastical courts 146
  ecclesiastical reform 161–5
  education 96, 117–20
  education of the clergy 146
  episcopal visitations 145, 161–3
  Evangelicalism 8
  libraries 148
  nonconformity 56
  non-residence 162–3
  pluralism 146, 162–3
  Protestant dissenters
    toleration 26
  and Queen Anne's Bounty 164
  reaction to French Revolution 183
  reformers 161–4
  revival in state of parishes 147
  Roman Catholics 17
  rural deans 164–5
  ruridecanal conferences 162
  secessions from established church
    145
  South 59
  status of established church 177–9
  structure of religion 12–14
  Sunday schools 122
  survival of superstitions 148
  Welsh-speaking clergy 144–6
  Wesleyan societies 92
Walker, Mydhope 80
Walker, Samuel 80, 86
Walmesley, Charles 39, 41
Walpole, Sir Robert 20, 23–5, 53,
  125

Warburton, William 26, 71, 179–80
  Alliance Between Church and State
    (1736) 22–3
  church–state alliance 27
Ward, WW 135
Wardley family 84
Wardour Castle 39
Warne, Arthur 108
Warren, John 161, 183
Waterford 46
Waterford and Lismore (diocese) 48,
  148, 149
Waterland, Daniel, Review of the
  Doctrine of the Eucharist as laid
  down in Scripture and Antiquity
  (1737) 74
Watson, Richard of Llandaff 92, 123,
  145, 161, 170, 178, 181, 183, 187
  reform initiatives 162–4
Weld, Thomas 39–40
Wells (diocese) 29
Wells-next-the-Sea (Norf) 96
Welsh Circulating Schools 96
Welsh langue
  decline in use 147
Wesley, Charles 78–9, 98
Wesley, John 79, 89–93, 98
  conversion experience 78
Wesley, Susannah 98
Wesleyan Methodism 86, 98
  missioning 80
  separation from Church of England
    90–1
  women preachers 95–6
Western vicariate 37
Westminster Abbey 13, 167
Westminster Confession 16, 51, 58,
  72
Westminster Hospital (London) 112
Westminster Lying-in Hospital (London)
  112
Whigs
  alliance with crown 2
  and Church of Scotland 73
  and church–state alliance 26, 52–3
  dominance 20–5
  radical 26
  relationship between church and state
    6

Whigs (*continued*)
    religious toleration 7, 56
    and restrictions on dissenters 52–3
    toleration of dissenters 21
Whiston, William 75, 76
White, Susan 96
Whitefield, George 89, 92
    conversion experience 78
Wilberforce, William 80, 81–2, 108,
        169–70, 180
William III, King of Great Britain and
        Ireland 16, 36
Williams, John Henry, *Piety, Charity and
        Loyalty* (1793) 187–8
Wilson, Thomas 78, 107, 131, 181
Winchester 13, 124, 132, 186
Winchester (diocese) 113
witchcraft 105
Witham, George 37

women: role in churches and society
        95–8
Woodward, Bishop of Cloyne 148
Woolston, Thomas 76
    Six Discourses on Miracles (1727–30)
        75
Worcester 29
Worcester (diocese) 168
    cathedral 124
Wordsworth, Christopher 84

Yates, Isaac 60
Yates, Richard, *Church in Danger, The*
        173–4
York (diocese) 132
York (province) 12–13
Yorke, Bishop of Ely 168

Zinzendorf, Count von 77–8